Creating
Musical Theatre

Creating Musical Theatre

Conversations with Broadway Directors and Choreographers

LYN CRAMER

B L O O M S B U R Y

LONDON · NEW DELHI · NEW YORK · SYDNEY

Bloomsbury Methuen Drama
An imprint of Bloomsbury Publishing Plc

50 Bedford Square   1385 Broadway
London   New York
WC1B 3DP   NY 10018
UK   USA

www.bloomsbury.com

First published 2013

© Lyn Cramer, 2013

British Library Cataloguing-in-Publication Data
A catalogue record for this book is available from the British Library.

ISBN: HB: 978-1-4081-8543-8
PB: 978-1-4081-8532-2
ePub: 978-1-4081-8459-2
ePDF: 978-1-4081-8475-2

Library of Congress Cataloging-in-Publication Data
A catalog record for this book is available from the Library of Congress.

Typeset by Newgen Imaging Systems Pvt Ltd, Chennai, India
Printed and bound in Great Britain

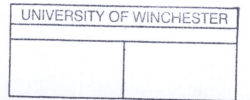

CONTENTS

To Fran Bizar,
whose generosity and kindness made this book possible

FOREWORD

I was 18 years old when I walked into Lyn Cramer's Level 1 Tap class at Oklahoma City University. I was as green, sheltered, and self-protected as the embryonic underbelly of a tapping tadpole. Lyn Cramer, however, was like a powerful, sexy, and VERY LOUD giant, perhaps in a cinematic/dreamlike production of *Into the Woods*, seemingly ready to pounce on my fairytale dreams. Instead, she lit fire. She burned, and she breathed life into my little fallap-ball-change body.

My first big role in college was playing "Hope Harcourt" in a production of *Anything Goes*. Lyn choreographed and told me I was going to be engaging in a pas de deux a la Ginger Rogers and Fred Astaire. This was only days after watching an episode of Seinfeld in my dorm room where George Costanza was trying to engage in a ménage a trois. I remember calling my father to ask him what these phrases meant and causing him great concern about what exactly I was learning at college, especially when I wasn't even enrolled in French class yet.

All this to say, I was stepping into a foreign land, and without the leadership of one fearlessly creative teacher named Lyn Cramer, I might have fallen on my face. Thanks to Lyn, I found myself standing on my feet in New York City upon graduation and staring straight into the eyes of Jerry Mitchell as he assessed my abilities as the proverbial "singer who moves well."

I had no idea how much "dancing" it would take to be on Broadway. Gone are the days of singers standing in the back. During that first big job (the national tour of *Jekyll & Hyde*), I started to understand what it meant to be an actor with my whole body. Jerry Mitchell's take on the show (as he reconceived it from the Broadway version) added numbers and transitions that incorporated more dance, and he helped each of us find our individual stories. He called me Becky Thatcher because I was so "green" and, therefore, insisted I "smoke" a cigarette through entire numbers to add some edge.

My next show was Sondheim's *Follies* on Broadway, marking my first of four educational experiences with Kathleen Marshall. Kathleen always wears many hats: director, choreographer, and even dramaturg. Not only in *Follies,* but also in *The Pajama Game, Bells Are Ringing,* and *Nice Work If You Can Get It,* Kathleen arrived on the first day of rehearsals with an entire world already assembled in her hands. All she had left to do was lay it out before us so we could become citizens. Everything from clothing, behavior, and politics of the period would come alive in artwork, vintage photos, and video.

Kathleen has always pushed me to dance a little, and as much as it scares me, her insistence has resulted in some of the most exciting stage moments of my career. "There Once Was a Man" with Harry Connick, Jr, "Mu Cha Cha" with Jeffrey Schecter (aka Shecky), "Just in Time" with Will Chase, and, most recently, "S'Wonderful" with Matthew Broderick. The last resulted in a 2012 Fred Astaire Nomination.

Let me assure readers that all this "dancing" never included long extensions with fan kicks or layouts. It was all character driven, simple, and fantastically fun. It was formed out of the choreographer's ability to find my capabilities and build on those. For instance, when I worked with Christopher Gattelli in *South Pacific,* he suggested I go into a soft shoe with a mop during "Wonderful Guy," but when my attempts to bring an inanimate object to life didn't result in the desired "Donald O'Connor" effect, he changed course and suggested Emile De Becque's HAT be my partner instead. I could hold it, love it, and substitute it for something in my heart. This made me want to dance. Christopher knew that and built a whole number around it. He allowed me to be part of the process.

When I started my career, Casey Nicholaw was already a mainstay on the Broadway stage. He was well-known among my peers for being an all-around amazing guy. When he later directed me in a few readings, I found him to be just that. No airs. No power trips. There is a familiarity with Casey that makes me comfortable, and his humor and humility make his success all the more celebratory.

I am also grateful to have worked often with Rob Ashford on numerous workshops and especially the Kennedy Center Honors. Watching him put together entire numbers for national television with everyone from Beyonce to Carol Channing is monumental, and his athletic and daring choreography on Broadway is often mind-blowing. All these artists, in fact, share that gift of taking technical dancing and making it exciting, sexy, and relevant to the story. So it's fitting that so many have now collaborated to fill this wonderful book.

What Lyn Cramer has so brilliantly done here is to gather these artists together, open a window to their process, and give us all a chance to be better prepared. These interviews read like pop-culture-true-Hollywood (ahem! Broadway) stories that you can't put down for fear of missing something, but they absorb like a college textbook, giving more useful information and links to the working world than some four-year programs.

My experiences with these director/choreographers have been priceless. Some I have yet to work with, but they have all influenced me in some way. It has taken me 14 years in New York City plus 4 previous years of college to benefit from them, but here in one skill-fully crafted book of candid, amusing, and personal interviews, a hungry artist can fill up on lessons and ideas and go behind the scenes. Then, by the grace of Lyn Cramer, they can enter this daunting world of dance and theatre a little less green than I did.

Merde,
Kelli O'Hara

PREFACE

How do today's great visionaries of the Broadway stage begin the creative process? How does a dancer become a choreographer or a director? What makes up their preproduction process? What do they look for in an auditioning dancer, actor, or singer? These questions have been asked by writers seeking to reveal the nuts and bolts of the creative process for musical theatre artists in years past. Now it is time to have a direct dialogue with this generation's creative thinkers of the Broadway stage. The artists answer these questions and more.

Each interview with these directors and choreographers in this book is different, yet the objectives are the same: to transcribe their thoughts and creative processes along with their rise in the world of musical theatre. For the researcher, this book will be an insight into on how these artists work. For the musical theatre performer, this text will serve as an insight into exactly what these artists are looking for in both the audition process and the rehearsal environment. To the aspiring director or choreographer, this book will serve as an inspiration detailing each artist's pursuit of his or her dream and the path to success. For the reader, this volume will give an insider's perspective on the creative world.

These personalities demonstrate the striking differences and surprising similarities in the way they work. Their stories demonstrate how luck is made by work ethic and reputation. Many artists have crossed over into film and television and several work in opera and ballet. Each facet of the artist's career is explored and the reader will take satisfaction in the fact that each and every one of these talented people is working till today. Several are just beginning, while others are established award winners. Many have been the backbone of the theatrical community for years. All of these visionaries offer their personal journey from dancer to choreographer and director-choreographer. All are fascinating and worthy of our curiosity and interest. We hope you enjoy their journeys.

ACKNOWLEDGMENTS

I would like to thank the following individuals who contributed their time and talent to make this book a reality: Zach Connor, Angelo Moio, Rena Cook, Nick Demos, Tom Spector, Shawn Churchman, Kristen Beth Williams, Ben Feldman, Jordon Beckerman, Peter Filichia, Max Weitzenhoffer, Kristen Chenoweth, Victoria Clark, Lara Teeter, Jeff McCarthy, Judy McClane, David Andrews Rogers, Curtis Holbrook, Brian Marcum, Dontee Kiehn, Nikole Vallins, Paul Christman, Mary Margaret Holt, Greg Kunesh, Joel Ferrell, Wendy Mutz, Shea Sullivan, Clayton Cornelius, Danielle McKenzie, Michael Baron, Rich Taylor, Amy Luce, Jenny Hogan, Scott Bishop, Ginger Tidwell, Nathan Lehmann, Derek Hersey, Pamela Raith, Alison Jenkins, Stephen Sposito, Nick Stimler, Jenny Ridout, and everyone at Bloomsbury Methuen Publishing, as well as all the University of Oklahoma alumni from the Weitzenhoffer School of Musical Theatre for their assistance in the videotaping of each interview. Special thanks go to Kelli O'Hara and Mary Aldridge.

Interviews

CHAPTER ONE

Rob Ashford

Rob Ashford grew up in Beckley, West Virginia, and aimed initially for a career in law. At the behest of a law professor at Washington and Lee University in Virginia, Rob became active in the theatre department hoping to improve his verbal skills in the courtroom. This, in turn, led Rob to study dance at Point Park University in Pittsburgh. Like many young dancers, he honed his performance skills in industrials and summer theatres such as the MUNY in St. Louis and Pittsburgh Civic Light Opera.

After graduation, he migrated to New York City, sharing an apartment with his dear friend and fellow choreographer, Kathleen Marshall. He got his start on Broadway in the Lincoln Center revival of *Anything Goes*. *The Most Happy Fella, My Favorite Year, Crazy for You,* and *Victor/Victoria* followed. Rob served as both a swing and dance captain developing his future interest as both a choreographer and a director. His choreographic career started when Rob Marshall (Kathleen's brother) sent him to Buenos Aires to restage *Kiss of the Spider Woman*. Subsequently, he assisted Pat Birch and Kathleen Marshall, and choreographed several productions at City Center Encores. Rob won a Tony Award for his Broadway choreographic debut, *Thoroughly Modern Millie*. Since then, every Broadway show he has choreographed has received a Tony nomination. He has worked in virtually every medium as both a director and a choreographer. Ashford is on the executive board of SDC, the Stage Directors and Choreographers Society, the Board of Trustees for the Joyce Theatre, and an Associate Director at the Donmar Warehouse in London, working extensively in the West End.

CRAMER: Welcome, Rob. Thank you for taking the time out of your hectic schedule to be here. You're in the middle of tech week for *How to Succeed in Business Without Really Trying* on Broadway.

ASHFORD: It's my pleasure. Thanks for asking me. And, that's right; we're working on all things technical right now just down the street.

CRAMER: Let's talk about your odd start in this business. You were born in Florida and raised in West Virginia. Originally, you were going to be a lawyer.

ASHFORD: I *was* going to be a lawyer—yes. I attended Washington and Lee University in their prelaw program, and had never danced a step in my life.

CRAMER: When did you catch the theatre bug?

ASHFORD: The first week I was at Washington and Lee, my advisor informed me that if I wanted to be a trial lawyer, I should either major in English or theatre. I'd been involved in high school drama, so I majored in theatre. It's a small school and department, so we were involved in everything. Once you start—once that bug bites—it's hard to do anything else.

CRAMER: You subsequently transferred to Point Park University in Pittsburgh?

ASHFORD: Yes. After two years at W&L, I transferred to Point Park to start dance training.

CRAMER: When you were in school, what form of dance did you study?

ASHFORD: I was lucky. Two years at W&L enabled me to complete most of my academics, so I could really focus on dance when I got to Point Park. I took every kind of class. I participated in ballet, tap, jazz, Dunham technique (a form of modern dance), and partnering. We had all that variety, so it was a great training ground. Also, Pittsburgh itself has quite a sizable theatrical community, so I was able to dance in industrials, summer stock at Pittsburgh Civic Light Opera, as well as other venues. I ran the gamut from dancing in a ballet company to dancing in the musical *Guys and Dolls*.

CRAMER: So, when you made the move to New York, you felt like you had a lot of experience under your belt.

ASHFORD: That's right.

CRAMER: Your first show in NYC was the revival of *Anything Goes.*

ASHFORD: That was my Broadway debut.

CRAMER: After *Anything Goes* you danced in *Most Happy Fella, Crazy for You, My Favorite Year, Victor/Victoria,* and a show you proved to have a long history with—*Parade.* You assisted choreographer, Pat Birch, on *Parade.*

ASHFORD: I did. I was also the dance captain and swing.

CRAMER: You have been a dance captain and swing for most of the shows in which you were cast.

ASHFORD: Yes, that's right. I was even the assistant dance captain on *Anything Goes.*

CRAMER: Alright, so bearing that in mind, tell readers what you think is a critical trait for a good choreographer.

ASHFORD: Being a choreographer is about being able to sit out in the house and see everything at once. It's about having some kind of an overall vision, as opposed to a vision of detail. The dance captain must see every detail. I think that was a big part of my training in becoming a choreographer. That's the job; seeing the big picture as well as the details. A good choreographer knows exactly where to place focus, where you want the audience to look at a certain time.

CRAMER: Was this visual skill something that you possessed and recognized even before you came to New York?

ASHFORD: I don't know. I guess I've always been kind of a visual person, as far as that goes. But I have to say, I believe it really began when I started dancing and was selected to be a dance captain and swing. At the time I started assisting Kathleen Marshall regularly. I learned so much from her, and from her brother Rob Marshall, who I also assisted.

CRAMER: Rob asked you to go to Buenos Aires in his stead. Is that correct?

ASHFORD: Yes. I was the dance captain for the national tour of *Kiss of the Spider Woman*. The show was being produced in Buenos Aires and Rob couldn't go, so he asked me to go in his place to stage the choreography. It was a thrilling and amazing city. The cast as well as the people of Buenos Aires were equally amazing. What a wonderful opportunity! That was my first time being on the other side of the table, and I didn't have any worries about creating the work. Rob had created the work. All I had to do was teach it and figure out how to communicate and get the ideas across. When I say "communicate," I'm not referring to the spoken language. I speak a little Spanish and had an interpreter, so it was all fine. What I mean is that I had to communicate the bigger ideas in the show. It was a unique and fabulous challenge. It's a great show. Director Hal Prince and Rob did such a good job with it. I love the show so much, so it was thrilling because I got to exercise the part of my creative self that I've hadn't really exercised before—communication skills and teaching in a new language. I never had to worry every night, with thoughts like "Oh, my god! What's everybody going to do tomorrow? What are the steps going to be?"

CRAMER: And also the worry of, "What if it's not good?"

ASHFORD: That's right! I knew it was good because Rob Marshall did it, so I already had that guarantee.

CRAMER: What a great training tool for you.

ASHFORD: It was. Then, I got to do the same thing again in Tokyo with the show, and that was another opportunity in a different language and culture. It really was those two opportunities that got me interested in being on the other side of the table.

CRAMER: So, after those two projects you began assisting Kathleen Marshall.

ASHFORD: We moved to New York together, so we were already great friends. From the beginning she included me in the meetings with designers, producers, all casting meetings, and working with the dance arranger. I got a firsthand look at how it's all done. Not only that, but how to collaborate, and how you choose your battles and fight for the things that are important to you. It's tough, some things you win and some things you don't. You know how compromise works so you can still keep your vision. Kathleen taught me all of that. It was thrilling, especially on a big show like *Kiss Me Kate* because there was a lot of attention placed on her vision. Her choreographic work was so integral to the show that we took a research trip to Verona, Italy, to authenticate the extensive creative work.

CRAMER: Your first job as a choreographer was the Broadway hit *Thoroughly Modern Millie*. You won the Tony for your effort. How did that project come to you?

ASHFORD: It all started with Hal Prince, who was the director of *Kiss of the Spider Woman*. He came to Argentina so I got to spend time with him. He is a remarkable man—a genius, as we all know—and such a good mentor and teacher. When I said, "I think I'd like to be a choreographer," he's the one who said, "Put some of your work together and show me your voice." He was so supportive. So, I got a group of my dancer friends together—many from the cast of *Victor/Victoria* that I was in. As luck would have it, one of my friends had a partner who was the company manager for the Martha Graham Dance Company. He secured one of the company studios to use for one week, free of charge, and I put together two pieces. One was a large piece with 20 dancers, about 12 minutes. The other was small—three women and one man. Hal came and brought his casting director and other people from his office, and a few producers. Honestly, saying that I wanted to be a choreographer, writing it in my journal, and telling people—that was one thing. Actually taking that step and putting yourself out there like that? That was the toughest thing, especially in a forum like that; with people whose opinions you respect to such a high degree. So, that was a really, really hard step; it was an important step. I don't know what would have happened had I not taken it.

CRAMER: So, it was quite a pivotal moment.

ASHFORD: Even though I got no job out of it, it *was* a pivotal moment. You know what I mean?

CRAMER: Yes. It was crucial for your development as an artist. How did this segue into *Millie*?

ASHFORD: I heard that *Millie's* producers were looking for a choreographer, and that they were interviewing some people, so I spoke to Hal and asked if he would recommend me. Hal wrote a letter to Michael Mayer, the director, and told him that I had been the dance captain on *Kiss of the Spider Woman* and that it wouldn't hurt to take a look at me. So, I met with Michael Mayer and he told me that they had a choreographer for *Millie*, but he was doing a play at the Vineyard Theatre in Manhattan and it has a little bit of movement in it, a little choreography. He asked me to work with him on that project and I said, "Okay, great, I would love to!" Then, during the very end of our work on the play at the Vineyard, Michael came to me one day and said that the choreographer they were going to use in *Millie* had to be replaced, so he asked me to prepare something. In other words, he wanted me to audition. There were about five choreographers putting together pieces to audition for *Millie*. The criteria was two pieces: one piece from the show itself, using music from the show, and the second piece was your own choice. The only other requirements concerned size: one must be large and the other small.

CRAMER: You certainly knew what you were doing. That is exactly how you prepared for Hal Prince and the other producers who saw the showcase of your earlier work.

ASHFORD: When the audition came around, I was assisting Kathleen on *Saturday Night* at Second Stage Theatre in Manhattan. We were in the middle of tech and Michael said I needed to be ready by the following week. I knew I didn't have time to put together a large ensemble number. So, I choreographed a version of the famous elevator dance from *Millie*, using music from the show, and presented that to Michael and the producers. An hour later, Michael called and told me I had to do the big number. I said, "Michael, there's just not time." He said, "No, no, no, you *have* to do the big number." So I said "Okay, I'll do it somehow." Kathleen generously released me from tech so that I could get it done because she knew how incredibly important it was. Once again, I gathered a group of dancers and we put a speakeasy number together. So the story is, Millie goes to the speakeasy and figures out how to get in by watching other people. Once inside, she sees the most handsome guy in the place and spends the whole evening trying to get his attention. Then, when they actually meet, they sit at a table and he ends up being a bore. Of course, she ends up drinking and drinking and drinking, then starts dancing—leading the pack, and everyone dances with her. So it was just a very basic idea, but we did it and they really liked it. Michael called that night and told me I got the job.

CRAMER: Cliché as it might sound, the rest is history. You received a Tony Award for the show, and for every Broadway show you've choreographed since then.

ASHFORD: I have.

CRAMER: Every single one.

ASHFORD: I have. Yes.

CRAMER: Your trajectory has been somewhat traditional. I always ask this question about climbing the creative ladder. You were a dancer, a dance captain, a swing, an assistant or associate, then a choreographer in your own right. What was it about the creative process that made you decide to become a director? Did Michael Grandage decide for you?

ASHFORD: Well, he certainly helped.

CRAMER: We should let our readers know that Michael Grandage is the Artistic Director of the Donmar Warehouse Theatre of London, one of the most prestigious theatres in the West End.

ASHFORD: I first worked with him on *Guys and Dolls*. He did a production in London that starred Ewan McGregor and Jane Krakowski. Michael asked me to choreograph, making it our first collaboration together, and it went very well. He's brilliant, and I learned so much from him. If everything I learned choreographically is the result of working with Kathleen, then I've learned the other half from Michael. He taught me how to look theatrically at the big picture, the design, the concept, and the truth. Of course, you learn from everybody that you're fortunate enough to work with. I've been so lucky. While we were working on *Evita*, he said to me, "You know you're a director who's choreographing, right?" And I said, "Well, okay, I buy that. If that's what you say, thank you for that." Then he said, "If you were going to direct a musical—your first musical—and you were going to direct it at the Donmar, what would it be?" And I said, "*Parade*."

CRAMER: Without a moment's hesitation.

ASHFORD: Without a moment's hesitation.

CRAMER: Your experience working with Pat Birch on *Parade* here in the states must have really been something for your answer to be so immediate. She is a gifted choreographer. You were dance captain of that show, right?

ASHFORD: Yes, and I love the show so much. You know, I'm a Southern boy and it had such an element of that spirit. It's an extraordinary story, and the score, by Jason Robert Brown, is simply gorgeous. To be a part of that show from the workshop all the way to the Lincoln Center production was just thrilling. But I never felt it got the attention it deserved. It is an important piece of musical theatre. Michael listened to the show, not knowing it, but after listening to it, he loved it. He invited me to come and direct my first musical at the Donmar.

CRAMER: You have also directed plays. How did your directorial debut come about?

ASHFORD: After the London production, I said to Michael, "My God, how can I thank you? I don't know how to thank you enough." He said, "You can thank me by doing your first play at the Donmar as well."

CRAMER: You directed *Streetcar Named Desire*. We should tell our readers that your relationship with the Donmar has resulted in your appointment as Associate Artistic Director. What do you think is the most important characteristic a director has to possess to have a successful process?

ASHFORD: Wow! Well, obviously, you do need to have a vision of some sort. You need to keep everyone firing on their own cylinders within your vision. That's it. You have to keep everyone doing what they were hired for—what they do well—inside the framework of your vision, as opposed to trying to make them do what you want.

CRAMER: Comparing your early career with the present, do you feel like you can pick and choose your projects?

ASHFORD: Yes. I'm very fortunate in the way that I get many opportunities now. I am able to say no to certain things if they don't interest me. There's a finite amount of time, and you really want certain projects. You don't want to work just for work's sake; you want to work because you want to keep pushing yourself, to keep growing and keep creating things that move people and push your own boundaries.

CRAMER: You have a longstanding relationship with the La Jolla Playhouse in San Diego, California. Several of your shows have had out-of-town runs there before coming to Broadway. Can you address this process?

ASHFORD: You almost always have to go out of town with a new musical. Producers almost never let you go out of town with a revival. They will claim it's basically an extra million dollars added to your budget to produce out of town. So, I've done all new shows at La Jolla. We did *Millie* and *Cry Baby* there, and I'm going back to do *Finding Neverland*. The old notion of out-of-town tryouts is quite different from today's process. Today, you workshop new shows in regional theatres like La Jolla. The great thing about regionals is that you are under the theatre facility's umbrella. In other words, regional theatres have a subscription base, or a built-in audience and a machine to assist in all aspects of project development in the early stages of producing a musical. It has a template, if you will. I just did a new musical called *Leap of Faith* at the Ahmanson Theatre in California. They took us in and helped us get the show up, and supported us with their staff, their buildings, and their artistic eye as well. The theory used to be you'd go out of town so no one knew what you were doing, and by the time you got to New York, you had worked out all the problems with the show. Needless to say, that doesn't exist anymore. Now, after your first preview in Poughkeepsie or anywhere, United States, you're on the internet and you're reviewed by intermission. Regional theatre is still the best place to develop a show. I particularly think new musicals need that development.

CRAMER: How does the aforementioned process differ from a workshop?

ASHFORD: Workshops are a different thing. I'm not much of a workshop fan. When you are in the process, you end up with workshop solutions to big show problems. You are using ladders for trees, wearing sweatshirts and jeans for costumes, and you end up falling in love with the simplicity and cleverness of it all. The problems with a full stage production are seldom solved, if even addressed. Here's the other difficulty about workshops: you only get four weeks to stage an entire show; you never get time to actually work on the show. The whole point of a workshop is to fine-tune the material, but it takes the entire four weeks just to get the show up on its feet.

CRAMER: Do you believe a reading of a new work is a worth-while process?

ASHFORD: I think readings are great and I really prefer staged readings. Normally, the cast sits at music stands and takes the stage when their character has a scene. It is so helpful to hear the material out loud and see how the show flows. I am a big fan of readings.

CRAMER: What is your process with scenic, lighting, costume designers, production assistants, and other members of your creative team?

ASHFORD: I think my process is pretty normal. You know the show's happening. You choose your designers and you sit down with them and talk about your vision, as well as what you don't want. They bring some ideas to the table, you bring ideas, and eventually it all gels. What is really important is starting early, very early. I'd say the sooner, the better.

CRAMER: Do you have a group of performers that you find you're working with more and more, repeatedly, if you will?

ASHFORD: Yes, I do. There are people that you like; you have a short hand with them. I do love working with new people, how-ever. Sometimes the show needs a specific energy, or as a director or choreographer, you see something in someone new that you like and their intent or approach could be good for a particular show. Many times I mix it up using both types of performers when it suits the project.

CRAMER: As you create, do you sketch, draw, visualize, or do you verbalize ideas?

ASHFORD: I do it all. I tear out a lot of pictures out of magazines, books, and other printed media—visual things. I don't watch a lot of old movies because I don't like to get images and steps and things imprinted in my head, because then I feel like I can't shake those images. So, I try to stay away from that a bit. When I start working on a show, I keep all those torn out pictures right inside the script, and every time I'm at a production meeting or creative meeting, I just put them on the table and the pile seems to grow. Everyone sits around talking about the show, no one's talking about the pictures per se, but there they are, and it starts binding the show together, somehow.

CRAMER: When you work in preproduction, you have an assistant or a set of assistants. Do you find you use the same people repeatedly?

ASHFORD: Yes. I think it's essential. I mean, the only way I can succeed is with a familiar group of creative people. For example, David Chase does the dance arrangements for all my shows and he's brilliant. He's currently my musical director for *How to Succeed*, as well as my dance arranger. He's terrific and smart and not just a musical collaborator, but a collaborator in every sense of the word. I think that's what I love about the whole team; everybody collaborates on every aspect of the show. I was lucky enough to have my assistant choreographer from London get his green card and move here. So, once again, I have someone on *How to Succeed* that I have a short hand with. We have the same tastes and I trust him completely. I can stay in one room directing, and because he is a choreographer in his own right, he can handle the entire second room. He has such respect for performers, and he's so great with people and so patient. He's very analytical too, and can help people figure out things that they can't on their own. An example of this is pushing singers to dance past their natural capabilities—a thing I often do. These are important traits in an associate or an assistant choreographer.

CRAMER: Since you discussed your approach to singers who dance, may I ask you to comment on the Vocal Minority in *Promises, Promises*? Those four roles are normally singing roles only. Yet, you had them dancing a great deal, correct?

ASHFORD: Yes. They all danced. We worked really hard to find singers that could dance, but when you have associates like I just mentioned working with these performers, we can get much more out of them that anyone expects. I also have a terrific associate director who is great in every department. He's really good at dealing with designers and keeping everything on track in each creative department so I can focus more on the actors in the rehearsal room. Don't get me wrong, he's great in the rehearsal room too, but what's so wonderful about a great assistant director is that he can take care of it all and keep things flowing.

CRAMER: Do you have to bring in additional dancers when you're working out numbers in preproduction?

ASHFORD: I do, and I call them "The Team." I recently hired a young dancer, a kid–22 years old. He is simply amazing to me. He was our assistant dance captain in *Leap of Faith,* out of town, and is presently cast in *How to Succeed.* He comes from a different time and place, and seemingly endless with his own astonishing ideas and steps, not to mention a brilliant dancer. So, adding him into "The Team" has been just a tremendous lift, especially in choreography. The entire creative team works together in that way.

CRAMER: It sounds as though you encourage your creative team to offer substantial input.

ASHFORD: Well, of course. I have to because you can't do it alone. Why would you even want to pretend you do or want to? There's one more member of "The Team"—our dance captain. She was the dance captain on *Promises,* and now, *How to Succeed.* It's great having someone that stays with the show who was a part of the creation effort. She has the respect of the company as well, because she was in the room and helped create it, so she knows. We have this kind of joke on "The Team" that they are so good, I say, "I'm just a figurehead." I just wave and they figure everything out, and they usually make it better than I even dreamed it could be. It's great because I can sit back and keep my eye on the big picture almost all the time, and "The Team" handles all the rest of it.

CRAMER: Do you differentiate in your own mind between staging and choreography, and do you approach your actors and your dancers differently?

ASHFORD: I don't. I think it's all motivated by character, whether you're dancing or staging or moving; it's all dancing to me.

CRAMER: If I walk into an audition, what's the first thing you're going to look for?

ASHFORD: Well, I'm going to look for *you* in you. Let me explain. I don't want you to come into the audition and "put on" a character. I don't want to see any extra "stuff." I don't want to see anybody that isn't you. I just want to see you turned up about 20 points. If you're going to be too laid back in the short amount of time allotted to your audition, I'm not going to get it. So, dial yourself up a little bit so the real you pops through.

CRAMER: Do you think you can see true acting chops when performers dance? Can you see the actor in the dancer?

ASHFORD: Absolutely. We look for that all the time. It's crucial. There are some amazing dancers that are technically incredible, but because there's nothing "there," we can't use them.

CRAMER: With show budgets now, everybody's got to sing, dance, and act with real capability. Can you get the cast you need, keeping your eye on the budget?

ASHFORD: Absolutely. Though it would be great to use the same people time and again, occasionally, you'll employ a policy whereby you hire half the dancers you've worked with before, and half new. You do this because the ones you've worked with before know you, and they give you a sense of comfort. They're calm and without an eagerness to please. On the other hand, you've got this burst of energy with new dancers, that not only lifts the room, but inspires you.

CRAMER: Do you read music, or do you feel that it's necessary for direction and choreography?

ASHFORD: I do read music. I played the piano growing up, so I read quite well. I don't think it's completely essential, but I do think it is incredibly helpful. For example, I've choreographed four or five shows at City Center Encores! You get their score and dance arrangements, and you have to edit them down, so you need to be able to tell the difference between the verse, the chorus, the bridge, and where the melody sits. In other words, it's helpful to have a basic knowledge of music and structure.

CRAMER: So, you have to seriously shrink the dance music on all Encores! productions, right?

ASHFORD: You do, because in one week, you don't have time to choreograph a whole score. I choreographed one called *Bloomer Girl* that Agnes De Mille did originally. The last half hour of the show was a Civil War ballet. We probably did about half of it, about 15–18 minutes worth; 20–25 minutes of a ballet in one week is crazy. You can't possibly do that.

CRAMER: The shows you have done include *Tenderloin, Bloomer Girl, Pardon My English,* and *Connecticut Yankee.* Explain to our readers why these titles were chosen.

ASHFORD: That's the mission of Encores! You rework old shows that are usually quite dated but have amazing scores.

CRAMER: Do you prefer working on a revival, or a new show? Which process takes more time?

ASHFORD: That's a great question. A new show definitely takes more time; there's no question about it. Quite often, I'm brought in at the show's inception, so you are talking about the complete development of a project, even auditioning the writers. It takes a long time, coordinating schedules and getting through the first reading, so it is a time-consuming process over a long period of time. I think a new work is like doing two shows. You have to do the out-of-town production, which takes a certain amount of time, and then you have to make changes and iron out details on the show. Then show two begins when you bring it to New York. With a revival, you don't do an out-of-town, so you just do the one in New York. You don't get the advantage of having an out-of-town production, but then again you're not really working with brand new material. With the new musical, no one knows what it is yet, and the audience is open to whatever you do. In a revival, everyone has these ideas of what it should be. There are adamant fans of the show, and they either have fond memories of what it was, or they just have a sense of it. I wrestle the constant feeling that you have to win them over. So, it's tricky. I try not to think about that; as a team we treat it as a new piece. When I agreed to direct and choreograph *Promises,* I can't tell you how many people were anxious about my treatment of Michael Bennet's iconic number, "Turkey Lurkey." I truly didn't understand what all the fuss was about and it's all because of YouTube and all the accessibility to view the original number on video. It's a very real but different kind of pressure. Do you pay homage to the original or do you totally reinvent the number? It's a very tricky thing. Revivals are always going to put the creative team into a comparative situation with the past; that's just part of the package.

CRAMER: Can you discuss the different rehearsal periods for the Broadway shows you have done, and what effect that time length had on opening night?

ASHFORD: We definitely had more time on *Shrek* than most shows; we had a longer rehearsal period and a longer tech period. If memory serves, we previewed six weeks on *Cry Baby*. It was a long time and wasn't that helpful. I think there's a finite amount of time you can be in that state of "we're ready-we're not ready." Nowadays, the producers are nipping and tucking everywhere to save money where they can. We're doing *How to Succeed* in four weeks. That's a short amount of time.

CRAMER: With your extensive career in London, please compare ensemble auditions here, versus ensemble auditions in London.

ASHFORD: They're so different. Here, everyone's very eager to give you their heart, to perform for you, give you their soul, and not be extremely precise in the choreography. In London, every-one is more cerebral, so before they'll perform the choreography, they literally want to know where every hand is. They ask ques-tions about everything: feet, direction, style, focus, the works. I have to pull a performance out of them. It's a real effort. They are so wrapped up in technique. In New York, it's just the opposite. Dancers could care less. They just want to get the gist, and let go and dance from their heart. I have to reinforce specifics like "that's a single pirouette, and the leg is straight here and not so high," etc. They want to do it their own way because they want to dance *for* you. There's a real difference.

CRAMER: It's my understanding that the number of auditioning dancers is smaller in London. Can you contrast that with audi-tions here in the states where numbers are huge and competition is dramatic?

ASHFORD: London has equally great talent; we just have a lot more of it to choose from here in the states. So, let's say that here we would have 25 outstanding, front row, A-list male dancers, and London might have 10 in comparison. If you're lucky enough to cast them and they remain available, then you're in great shape because you have the men you need. If not, you have a problem. Running out of great dancing men here is not an issue. England is a small island, less to choose from. We're this huge country with a constant influx of dancers pursuing their careers.

CRAMER: Who do you think was the biggest creative influence in your life with whom you are not directly associated?

ASHFORD: I would say Jerome Robbins because of his story telling and his economy in doing it. He is not a person who will sit inside a dance forever and show off. If he could tell the story, if he could get you from A to B with two steps, he would do that. If you can do it with one look, movement, or gesture, then we move on. But some creative people don't understand economy, and I try—I always *try* to exercise economy. Here's an example. We do our preview cuts in tech, because after we run the entire show in the studio, we always see where the fat is in all the numbers. We go ahead and start trimming that out right away in tech. We don't even wait for previews. Any fat is a disservice to the number. We try to keep the number moving and not stand on something so long because you like that, or it feels good, or the dancers look good doing it. That's just what Jerome did, and I think that's his brilliance.

CRAMER: You've talked a great deal about the people who have helped you in your career, starting with Rob and Kathleen Marshall and continuing with Hal Prince and Michael Grandage. Please share your thoughts on other creative people in your life, and how they influenced your approach to directing and choreographing.

ASHFORD: I choreographed for Scott Ellis, Michael Mayer, and Mark Brokaw. All of those directors gave me really important information, knowledge, and humanity. All of the directors I have ever worked for included me. The lines between a director and a choreographer should be blurred. They should overlap. Those directors allowed me to have substantial input far beyond dance numbers. My input was always welcomed just as it was when I assisted Kathleen.

CRAMER: When you integrate your research into your work, is it a practical application or is it something that simply enhances your own creativity?

ASHFORD: I do just enough to show the audience that our approach to the period is authentic—no more, no less. When I choreographed *Thoroughly Modern Millie*, my goal was to do the show without one Charleston. I was adamant that we couldn't just do Charlestons over and over because it's the 1920s. Well, I confess, we did do a Charleston in the opening, but it was totally bastardized in very slow motion. I don't think audiences want to see historical dance. I think people want to see something fresh and new, and I would never let historical authenticity dominate creativity and originality. I think audiences want our contemporary energy.

CRAMER: Do you believe you have a signature style? For example, has anyone ever said, "Oh, that looks like Rob's work?"

ASHFORD: Some people say that. Some people say, "I knew that was you. I could tell it was you," and I don't think one way or the other about it. You try to reinvent yourself every time, or try to bring originality to the material, but sometimes a certain step that happens or a certain pattern happens and it just feels like "you." Obviously it's going to happen the more you work as a director and choreographer, but that can be great if you figure out a way to keep it fresh. A great example of this is evident in one of my new assistant choreographers who is working with me now. I can do my step or my "thing," and then he does his version of it, which is the same intent, yet completely different and better with a more contemporary energy. Now, I don't mean contemporary dance, I just mean a kind of "now" energy. The way a 22-year-old dancer approaches a dramatic beat is going to be different than I would.

CRAMER: Let's talk about your transition into film. Your first gig as a film choreographer was on the movie, *Beyond the Sea,* the story of Bobby Darin starring Kevin Spacey. Is it my understanding that you were on a road trip when you got a phone call from Kevin Spacey?

ASHFORD: True. I was going to visit relatives in Boston for Christmas. I listened to my voicemails and it was like this, "Hey Rob. Kevin Spacey. Give me a call. I really want to talk to you." I was completely shocked. I'd never met Kevin. It was about a year after *Millie,* and Rob Marshall's film, *Chicago,* was about to be released. Rob Marshall and I had the same agent at the time, and our agent had a new assistant. Of course, I thought I had it all figured out. The ditzy reception guy had given Kevin my number and information, thinking it was Rob Marshall's. As it turns out, that was not the case. Kevin had seen *Millie,* and he wanted me to do *Beyond the Sea*, a movie he was going to star in, direct, and produce.

CRAMER: Was it on-the-job training?

ASHFORD: I was literally learning on the job.

CRAMER: As a great example of learning on the job, please share your charming *Moulin Rouge* story.

ASHFORD: I find it very amusing that everyone assumes that since you're a Tony-winning choreographer, you know what you're doing on your first film job. The movie people from *Beyond the Sea* called, and asked how many couples I needed for the dance in the tea garden. They had given me a list of available dancers, and I told them I'd look it over and get back to them. The film *Moulin Rouge* had just come out. The film's director and choreographer was Baz Luhrman. He and I had worked together on the Academy Awards, and I love and admire his work. I watched the "Tango of Roxanne" in *Moulin Rouge* and thought, "Ok, that's 20 couples. That looks outstanding to me. I need 20 couples for the tea garden."

CRAMER: You share an Emmy with Baz Luhrmann for your work on the Oscars. Tell us what you learned on that project.

ASHFORD: When you're working with, and in the presence of a real genius, you become a sponge. He is so visual and passionate, and someone who is a truly significant artist. We had a month really, putting that number together, and it was glorious. Those types of projects are quite difficult and high pressure, but mainly, I had fun. Along with 200 drummers and 40 dancers, we had Hugh Jackman and Beyonce, Zac Efron, Vanessa Hudgens, Amanda Seyfried, and Dominic Cooper because the film *Mamma Mia* had just come out. So, we prepped here in New York with Hugh for one week, and then an additional week with 12 New York dancers that were going to Los Angeles. Once there, we picked up the other 28 dancers. We taught and folded them into it. The concept never changed. The content changed constantly, because Baz's brain never stops. I would literally come into rehearsal the next morning and he'd state, "We're not going to do the Dream Girls section; we're going to do the following." It would be something brand new out of his head. I would get a call at midnight with changes for the next day because he'd already been to the studio to figure it out and edit it. He'd send me the edit and I would call the dancers to meet me at eight because we had to change the choreography yet again. But it was thrilling, you know? It's a great challenge, and again, everybody had fun. I had my core group from New York; my dancers I knew were going to be there for me, and then I had 28 new dancers from LA that I didn't know at all. So it was very much like working on Broadway, but with larger numbers. You become a traffic expert.

CRAMER: The Oscar telecast was not your first television event. You have done several tributes that have been filmed for the small screen.

ASHFORD: Yes. I have been at the helm of Kennedy Center tributes to Barbra Streisand, Jerry Herman, and Andrew Lloyd Webber.

CRAMER: So, you weren't completely blind going into your prep work for *Beyond the Sea*. You filmed in Berlin?

ASHFORD: I must say that filming a staged production is not truly preparing you for shooting dance on film. It is a different process all together. So I was a bit blind as the *Moulin* Rouge story attests. That said, yes, we worked for three months in the Berlin winter.

CRAMER: In winter? But you had many outdoor sequences dressed for a much milder season. Didn't the dancers freeze?

ASHFORD: We did freeze. It was cold. It's just remarkable what dancers endure. Beyond the chaos that ensued at times, it was a fun shoot. Originally, there was to be so much more dancing in the movie. So many numbers we had prepped, we didn't get to shoot. There were some issues. We were doing the shoot in Berlin for many reasons. East Berlin is so preserved from the 1960s. It was like nothing had changed. We could go to houses, clubs, government buildings, studios, etc., and have this great advantage. Also, we got some sort of tax credit if we used a certain number of Germans and other Europeans, and the smallest number of Americans. That made it advantageous. We got over there, we were mid-production, and there was some snafu with tax laws, and suddenly we weren't getting half the break we thought we were. So we were over budget. We had to pull a couple of the numbers we hadn't filmed yet, because they were the most expensive.

CRAMER: Were you at all surprised that Kevin Spacey's really a pretty good dancer?

ASHFORD: He said, "I don't dance." He does. But I've never seen anybody like that, someone so gifted, but also, work so hard. He would be in makeup at 4 in the morning, and then he would work a whole day directing and acting, as well as viewing dailies, and then he would come to me and my assistant in the studio at 11 at night. We would dance for an hour or two, literally to the point where he could not stand up. I'd say, "Kevin, we're done for the day. We're done," and he'd say, "No, one more time, I've got to figure that out. I've got to get it right."

CRAMER: Inspirational.

ASHFORD: That's how that man worked. I learned so much from the entire shoot, filming close-ups, long shots, editing, shooting indoors, outdoors, camera focus, continuity, cut-aways, you name it. I also learned a great deal from Kevin and his miraculous work ethic. I wouldn't trade that experience for the world. I am ready for my next film, thanks to the entire process. Luckily, I do have some film projects in the works.

CRAMER: I know you've got a lot of projects coming up—an *Evita* revival with Ricky Martin and *Finding Neverland*—based on the film and several others. Is there an unusual project that you would really like to pursue?

ASHFORD: There are so many things in my mind that I'd like to do. We started work on this reimagining of *Brigadoon*. It's all music.

CRAMER: No book to speak of.

ASHFORD: Very little book. All singing and dancing. Quite different. I'm terribly excited about the project. It's got to be the right time and the right place, so it's tricky. I want to do an opera and work on a large scale. Based on my experience, I feel I understand how to move people around the stage, and I understand the epic nature of an opera. There are some great film projects just around the corner. Much of it is finding the time to work on each project, to be honest.

CRAMER: Can you give any advice to students about perseverance, something about getting here to NYC, being here, and sticking with it? Because based on your own experience and your longevity, you should have some pearls of wisdom.

ASHFORD: Yes, of course. I think that you have to remember that you're on your own journey, and you can't be influenced by the journeys of your friends. For example, some people will come to New York and be lucky like me and get a Broadway show in two months, and some people won't. If that happens to your best friend, that doesn't mean that you're not right for this business; it just means that you weren't right for that show. You know what my philosophy was when I came here? I auditioned for absolutely everything, even if it was a show I didn't want to do, because I thought it would lead me to something else. Let's take *Anything Goes,* for example. The way I got *Anything Goes* is because Michael Smuin, the choreographer, remembered me, and really liked me from another audition for a show he choreographed that I didn't even get! But because of that audition, I got a Broadway show simply because Michael remembered me, and really liked my work. It's all that time you put in. You have to think of it all as an investment in your future. You have to persevere. You have to stay in touch with the business; you have to stay in touch with the people that are in it. You must network. I used to wander around the Broadway theatre district and visualize my name on the marquees. You do have to want it, but the other thing is, you need to have your own full life. If it's so lopsided, out of balance, and all there is centers around the theatre, then that's a huge percentage of negativity in your life if you're not getting work. And also, the other thing about having a full life is that it will only help your art when you get there. Sometimes, rather than taking the fifth ballet class because Broadway hasn't happened, take four and go to the museum. Take three and go to the museum and go to a movie. Go see a play, and don't just say, "I don't have the money to see a play." Find the money to see a play. That'll inspire you in a different way as well. You don't have to just go see musicals. I'll say the same thing for actors; go see a musical. Step out of the box. You just have to persevere. You have to have a dream and go for it.

CRAMER: Well, thank you so much for doing this, and I wish you the best of luck with all your future endeavors.

ASHFORD: You're most welcome.

CHAPTER TWO

Andy Blankenbuehler

Andy Blankenbuehler developed a love of the arts from a very young age. His sisters both danced and his dad loved the stage. Andy's parents were big supporters of the arts and it made sense for Andy to start dancing at the "ripe old" age of three, excelling as a tap dancer. He was always involved in sports throughout his school years, but when he became a sophomore in high school, all that changed. He was cast in *Godspell* and the theatre bug took hold.

Andy had designs on a college major in architecture, but that quickly morphed into a dance major and even that didn't last long. After training for a year at Southern Methodist University, he was cast by Disney to perform in Tokyo. And Andy never looked back. He moved to New York City just after his stint with Disney. After an extensive touring career with Andrew Lloyd Webber's *Music of the Night, Fosse, Camelot, Guys and Dolls,* and *West Side Story,* Andy hoofed his way through footwork-heavy Broadway musicals like *Guys and Dolls, Steel Pier, Saturday Night Fever, Contact, Fosse, Big,* and *Man of La Mancha.*

As a choreographer, Blankenbuehler claims to have become an architect anyway. He builds dances instead of buildings and creates storyboards instead of building plans. Andy has won the Tony Award, Drama Desk, Outer Critics, and Lucille Lortel Award for his choreography on *In the Heights,* his third Broadway effort. *In the Heights* follows his work on the revival of *The Apple Tree,* and *9 to 5.* In 2012, Andy directed and choreographed the critically acclaimed *Bring It On!* and choreographed the revival of *Annie.*

Blankenbuehler has created choreography for City Center Encores!, crafted the world premiere of Frank Wildhorn's *Waiting for the Moon,* staged concert work for Bette Midler and Elton John, created commercials, and choreographed for regional theatres around the country. Andy's work was also seen on *So You Think You Can Dance, The Sopranos,* and in the West End production of *Desperately Seeking Susan.*

In addition to these, Andy is still a teacher. He holds classes at Broadway Dance Center in New York City on a regular basis and is a member teacher for New York Dance Alliance, an organization that conducts dance conventions and workshops across the country for students of all ages and levels.

CRAMER: Andy, you were born in Cincinnati and started dancing at three because your sisters were both dancers. I understand your parents were big supporters of the arts, so they encouraged you. But you also participated in sports until you were cast in *Godspell* in high school. I read that it was a life-changing experience. Can you share that with us?

BLANKENBUEHLER: Yes. I did a lot of community theatre because my father did. I liked it enough. I danced my whole life and I liked that enough, too. I was always the only boy, so it was socially awkward sometimes. I was a really good tap dancer, so I at least felt accomplishment in that discipline. I was cast in my first show in high school when I was a sophomore. We did *Godspell*, and it really changed my life. For the first time, I felt like I fit in, and the theatre department at my high school was really good. So, all of a sudden, everything just got elevated, and I felt that my accomplishments were accepted, valued, and an integral part of the process. More than anything else, it was social. I felt great connections with people. It felt a bit like a high school retreat. So, after that, I knew bit by bit that I wanted to choose it as a career.

CRAMER: Did you move to New York pretty quickly after high school?

BLANKENBUEHLER: Yes, but the plan was to attend college for architecture, and I got accepted. When I graduated, I foolishly thought, "I can go study architecture for six years, then be a dancer with a back-up plan." Right. Put dance on hold. Then reality hit me. "What am I thinking? That's not even possible. I had to have a new 'dance' plan." I was introduced to Southern Methodist University in Dallas. It was after all the application deadlines. The school brought me down there. I visited on a Tuesday, and was enrolled on Wednesday.

CRAMER: SMU has one of the strongest ballet and modern programs in the nation.

BLANKENBUEHLER: True. They took really good care of me in my first year. The technique classes were great for me because I had danced my whole life, but had really bad technique. Being in that environment, dancing with other men, was a huge help and a great influence. But I'm an impatient person, and after my first year, I took a job at Disney World for the summer. During my second year in school, Disney asked me to go to Tokyo Disneyland for a year. I lived there and moved to New York City right after that job. I was 20.

CRAMER: Your Broadway debut was *Guys and Dolls*. You did the national tour first, and then came to Broadway. Many of your contemporaries in the choreographic and directing field now were your cohorts on stage in the revival in 1992. Who comes to mind?

BLANKENBUEHLER: It was an amazing show, and it came on the heels of Chris Chadman dancing with Bob Fosse, and passing on the essence of the way Fosse worked, not his vocabulary necessarily but his determination and intellectual way he constructed his choreography. Many people, who worked on that show with me, had just come off *Jerome Robbins Broadway*. There wasn't a really deep, heavy, thick dance show after the Robbins piece. When *Guys and Dolls* came along, Chadman developed this big, masculine piece of choreography, and we all jumped onboard. Every male dancer in the city wanted to do it. We opened the first tour: me, Sergio Trujillo, Chris Gattelli, Jerome Vivona, Darren Lee, and John Crutchman, all of whom became choreographers and directors.

CRAMER: That's quite a testament to that unique time in New York City.

BLANKENBUEHLER: Chris Chadman was so inspiring to me. He was a real taskmaster and tough on everyone, but I was very lucky because I had a very similar body type to him. I felt like whatever he choreographed worked on my body. Consequently, he was very nice to me. He moved me to the front, gave me solos, and took really good care of me. I ended up in the show for two and a half years.

CRAMER: So, you did *Big, Steel Pier,* and *Contact* all for Stroman. This was followed by *Fosse,* where I first saw you and heard you sing *Mr. Bojangles*.

BLANKENBUEHLER: Yes. That was really big too, because I had done several Broadway shows and had a lot of great jobs, but all of a sudden, when I got to *Fosse*, I was seen as a soloist. Mind you, I never had any desire to get out of the chorus. All I ever wanted to do was dance. But I wanted to be recognized, as everybody does. I wanted to know that my contribution was a valuable building block to the show. All of a sudden I was in a feature capacity in the show. I knew my performance was moving people, and that was really big for me emotionally. It also gave me a bit of a name, not a star but people knew who I was.

CRAMER: I knew you from the show, and then I recognized you on the faculty list for New York Dance Alliance.

BLANKENBUEHLER: That was a turning point for me because I was just about to start choreographing. When I did, even though people weren't ready to give me a Broadway show to choreograph, at least they were looking at me. That was really important, because when I started putting my work out there in the late 1990s, I was very open in saying, "Listen, I'm going to give you something that might crash and burn, but I'm going to show you what I eventually want to accomplish. I'm not going to be gray right now and choreograph a cookie-cutter piece. I'm going to show you, idealistically, what I want to accomplish, and you might find it's not ready yet." That's actually what happened. I wasn't looked at seriously until 2002 or 2003.

CRAMER: What happened between *Fosse* and the Frank Wildhorn show, *Waiting for the Moon?*

BLANKENBUEHLER: A great deal. After *Fosse*, I went over to *Saturday Night Fever*, which was tons of fun and where I met my wife. Then I did *Contact*, and my final show on Broadway was *Man of La Mancha*. Those last few years, I was juggling two careers at once. I would teach and choreograph all day long, and then perform in my Broadway show at night. Once or twice a year, I would take a leave of absence and go to Goodspeed or Paper Mill Playhouse and choreograph a show. So, I was starting to get my work out there. The very first thing I ever presented was in 1997. It was part of a choreography concert called *The Gypsy Project*. That was the first time people saw my choreography, so that was important to me. Then I did *DanceBreak*, which was the union's showcase of "up and coming" choreographers. My piece was a story ballet set to music from *Parade*. It stood out from others in the showcase because I really took a chance with my approach. I went out on a limb and stayed away from anything in a traditional sense. It paid off because that's where I met Jeffrey Seller and Kevin McCollum.

CRAMER: For our readers, these gentlemen produced *In the Heights*. You choreographed that Broadway hit, and won the Tony Award for your work.

BLANKENBUEHLER: They said to me, "You do the kind of work we want to do, let's stay in touch." We knew we saw eye to eye even though we had nothing to work on yet. Through *DanceBreak*, I started getting jobs at PaperMill and Goodspeed, as I mentioned earlier. Then the realization hit me that I could not do both if I wanted to excel as a choreographer. Ultimately, I was going to have to choose.

CRAMER: Did you have a sense that choreography would be a natural segue after a professional dance career?

BLANKENBUEHLER: I'm sure I did. Literally, I choreographed my entire childhood. I choreographed the musicals my junior and senior year of high school. All through the early 1990s I was choreographing benefits, music videos, and other projects constantly. I was always choreographing on the side.

CRAMER: I heard you were injured during *Guys and Dolls*. Did that sway you at all?

BLANKENBUEHLER: Well, it was a couple of things. I got hurt when I joined the Broadway company and was out for about 18 months. During all the physical therapy and taking floor barre, I was going crazy. All I wanted to do was dance. I would listen to music all day long, music from the 1940s and 1950s. All of a sudden, it was like the matrix; I could see the numbers. In my head, I could see the colors, and what the music was telling me. So, I felt like my creative instinct was truly blossoming. Even though I went back to performing after that, I knew choreography was my destination. Then I had a string of frustrating projects, and all I wanted to do was figure out why they didn't "catch." The architect major wanted to figure out the math problem. Why is the backrow coughing? Why is that pick-up not grabbing people? Why does that music not feel like the character? I didn't know the answers when I was younger. But I couldn't leave performing, so I was willing to gamble. Many of my friends, like Rob Ashford and Kathleen Marshall, were assisting other people, so I wondered if that's the direction I should go. But, I didn't want to stop dancing. I felt like it was a full-time career to assist somebody. So, I made the very firm decision that I was going to continue dancing full time and choreograph on my own. That meant I had many lessons to learn that my friends did not, because they were assistants.

CRAMER: Did you ever serve as dance captain?

BLANKENBUEHLER: That's not me.

CRAMER: That's of interest to me because yours is not a traditional path. Many choreographers were dance captains and assistants.

BLANKENBUEHLER: Right. Plus, there's a selfishness that I have, that wouldn't allow me to do that. I want to do my gig; I don't want to do anybody else's gig. I had total contentment in performing. I wasn't even totally content choreographing my sidelines projects. I hadn't done a project yet that said, "Oh, my God! My life is coming true because I'm choreographing this." That didn't happen until *In the Heights*.

CRAMER: What about the Encores! projects, *The Apple Tree* and *The Wiz*?

BLANKENBUEHLER: Encores! should have put me in the hospital—no, literally. When I did *The Apple Tree* at Encores!, it was probably the most stressful situation I've ever been in, because there was no time. The expectations are so high because you're right on Broadway's door. I was working for the director and the musical director for the first time, and it was very stressful. I realized in that show that preparation was the key for me. I could not wing it. I could not make it up on the spot. I had no desire to abbreviate the process. I *can*; I have the talent to, but I have no desire to do it. It makes me miserable. I know that my work is 60 percent of what it should be when I work under those situations. It is hugely compromised. I've never been more unhappy with my work. Also, as a beginning choreographer, I was establishing a relationship with a brand new director that I had never worked with, so that's always hard.

CRAMER: Have you ever auditioned for a job?

BLANKENBUEHLER: I did a presentation for the Andrew Lippa musical called *The Little Princess*.

CRAMER: When you say presentation, it's an audition format where you present a number to the creative team, correct?

BLANKENBUEHLER: Correct. I interviewed with the producer, the director, and with Andrew. I was invited to present two numbers. Interestingly enough, it was the week of my wedding, so, pressed for time, I took a gamble and picked two numbers. Of course, they asked for two *different* numbers. So, I choreographed four numbers—15 minutes of dance—with dancers working for free. I paid my own studio expenses. I have to say, I was really proud of my work and I got the job. I left *Man of La Mancha*, and the next year I choreographed *The Little Princess*. It was out in California. The show didn't make it to Broadway, and I was really disappointed. I thought that show was going to be my entrée to Broadway. Then right out of that I choreographed *Waiting for the Moon*, the Frank Wildhorn musical, and *The Apple Tree*. They happened the same month.

CRAMER: Would you say you're a visual choreographer, you see images before you create steps?

BLANKENBUEHLER: Yes. I have the ability, as lots of choreographers do, to see it far away. I can see it as a movie before I've choreographed a step. So, I know what it wants to be. I know the temperatures, the movements, and the energy, even though I don't know what the steps are yet. Many choreographers can't predict things like that. I have to figure the entire show out, mathematically, and that's a big part of my process. I have to pound it out on my own. *Waiting for the Moon* was a big deal for me because the director gave me free rein, and I choreographed huge dances. The show featured six full-length dance sequences: one that lasted over 10 minutes. It was all transferred to my choreography reel, and even though the show didn't move to Broadway, it got me noticed.

CRAMER: It got you a Barrymore nomination.

BLANKENBUEHLER: I choreographed one of the things I'm most proud of in that show, which went on to my reel and became a good calling card for me. In the number, F. Scott Fitzgerald was writing *The Great Gatsby*, and it was a song, but it needed to be transition music. I think that is where I started doing transitions and people would say "Andy Blankenbeuhler does transitions." Anyway, we needed to get him from the conclusion of his book-writing to his book-signing party. But, there was no connective tissue. So, I took his song "I Want Some" from the first act, and his song, "I've Got Things to Say," combined, and reorchestrated them. We had a track that moved onstage, so we put him at his typewriter stage right, and the whole number did nothing but move his typewriter to stage left. When it got to stage left, he was at a party, and there were five tap dancers around him as he was typing. Right then, I started to understand how I wanted to move people. I always feel like there's speed and there's motors that are emotional gear. For example, your brain is thinking a thousand thoughts: "I've got to do this. I've got to do that. Oh, what if I did this?" All of a sudden, it's like fingers snapping fast. That is what you hear, which is not unlike a typewriter, which is not unlike taps. I have to figure out what the motor is. I think of the words "motor" and "engine" a great deal. It all defines the speed of the number or the groove it sits in. What makes a number like "Cool" from *West Side Story* absolutely the right tempo? It grinds and shifts just like you want it to. Everything I am trying to create has to fold into the orchestration. We have to establish a vocabulary. So, when I did *Waiting for the Moon*, I realized that there was a great deal more for me to do when creating transitional dance. I had no desire to be a concert choreographer, but when I create transitions on the musical theatre stage, there's an overlap. With no spoken narrative and no singing, just orchestration, I continue to tell a story. There is a gorgeous transition in *In the Heights,* and people have said to me that it is one of their favorite moments in the show. It's what we called the "break-up transition." The character of Navi just lost his girl, and I don't want the audience to leave that moment. That moment's not over; it wants to resonate. If I'm going to the next moment, why not let their break-up continue right into it? So I had all the dancers starting the transition as pairs. Everything went into slow motion, and then one by one, a girl would walk out of a guy's arms and everybody would keep walking singly. By the end of the transition, everybody was single. It continues the emotional arc of the narrative without words or lyrics, and that became more and more interesting for me to do.

CRAMER: I want to ask you about choreographic approach. You talk about through-line versus texturing. Would you explain what you mean by that?

BLANKENBUEHLER: I view a lot of choreography as impressionist painting. So, when you see such a painting, your eye is forced to go to the focal point, and that's what happens in musical staging and choreography. Your eye should be forced to go to a focal point. If it's not, there's usually a problem. Sometimes you don't want to know where to look because that mayhem makes the focus resonate. In general, you want to have a focal point. What's around the focal point tells the audience how to feel about the focal point, and that's what the artist says in an impressionist painting. That's what I view as texture. Focus is the narrative line. So, let's say the guy takes the girl, kisses her goodnight, and she goes into the door. It's an amazing first date, so he's about to sing "Singing in the Rain" or something. That's direct. That's through-line and that's what you want to see. However, the world around that scene can tell you how he's feeling. I'll make something up. Let's say that the world around the couple are dancers in the park like *Band Wagon's,* "Dancing in the Dark." None of the girls are touching the ground. The whole stage is filled with girls just floating, and the guys are hovering underneath them. You know how the lovers feel. The lovers are not touching the ground. If I've done my job well, I'm not looking at the other dancers. I'm only looking at the focal point, the couple, or the man about to sing. However, my brain is taking in the feeling around them, and that's what I call texture.

CRAMER: You were able to choreograph *Apple Tree* at City Center Encores! and then it moved to Broadway. *In the Heights* started off-Broadway and also moved. When you have the opportunity to improve your work, does it change dramatically?

BLANKENBUEHLER: *Apple Tree* is not such a good example because I did improve it a great deal on my side. We had so much more time to improve it when we were in rehearsals for Broadway compared to prepping for Encores! *In the Heights* was the life-altering experience so they are not comparative. I'll tell you, this is the bittersweet lesson that I learned. We all can't do the job that we want to do; not unlike the project I'm working on right now, entitled *The People in the Picture.* I'm only really content and happy when I'm working on a piece that at its core must dance. My current project does not.

CRAMER: In other words, dance must be the most important component?

BLANKENBUEHLER: That's the bottom line. I do not want to do shows that are not about dance. So as I become a director-choreographer, the dance isn't becoming less important and the directing becoming important, quite the contrary. I'm only going to direct shows where dance takes the lead.

CRAMER: *Bring It On!* just opened at the Alliance Theatre in Atlanta in January, and is moving to Los Angeles, then touring, and finally Broadway bound. You directed and choreographed the show. Will you continue to work in both capacities?

BLANKENBUEHLER: Yes and no. People love to declare, "Oh, you're going to be a director-choreographer," and I say, "Yes, but I'm not really ready yet." I would like to continue learning, so I'm going to be going to work on the revival of *Annie* with director James Lapine. It's a big dance show, but it's not about dancing. It's about raw emotion and visceral enough to be communicated through dance. Next, I'm choreographing a brand new *Peter Pan* and I am quite sure it's going to be extraordinary. The music embraces a hip-hop and rock style. It possesses the energy of a kid, or young adult, with characteristics of courage, inspiration, and determination. All those things demand dance. Those are the projects I seek. When the music plays, I'm going to do my best as a choreographer to translate the lyrics. When you close your eyes and listen to an orchestration, the music should deliver the whole emotional world because of what you're hearing. If it doesn't, there's a problem. I think the difficulty in musical theatre lies in overchoreographing or underchoreographing a show.

CRAMER: Meaning?

BLANKENBUEHLER: The music department and the dance department aren't at the same level. For example, if the music is less important on an emotional level, I don't care how good my choreography is; it's not going to convey meaning. If the music is simplistic, my choreography can only go so far. What's demanded is that the music is true, and that's exactly what Lin-Manuel Miranda does when he writes.

CRAMER: For our readers, Lin-Manuel Miranda is the composer of *In the Heights* and *Bring It On!*

BLANKENBUEHLER: I don't understand how he does it, but no matter what he writes, it dances. His music has soul and life to it, and I'd have to be an idiot not to choreograph to every note. One of the reasons the show works is because the music and dance departments are on the same level. One effectively cannot exist without the other.

CRAMER: When you teach your choreography for *In the Heights,* you teach using the lyrics, scatting (ba ba do bop), and through visualizing movement, such as "you're down into the earth on this section." When I watched the video clips of this instruction, it was easy to understand exactly what you wanted. Our readers should know that you are still actively teaching in the classroom. You are a guest teacher on national convention circuits and at Broadway Dance Center in New York City. My question is, do you teach the same way, whether in class, or on a show?

BLANKENBUEHLER: Dancers get frustrated when they don't know what they're doing, so I always count everything. I can say to a student, "The foot's on the end of four," but that's just math. That's not important. What's important is why it's there. I taught an audition all day yesterday, and there were dancers claiming they didn't understand, so I had to count, one and a two and three and a four. But then it's really important for them to understand how they're doing it, so, I have to say the lyric or hum it musically. That's why I scat a lot. What I've learned in the past couple years is that I tend to choreograph from a rhythmic place, not necessarily a text place. So, it only works really well if the rhythmic world already matches the text world. I'm not going to disregard the text; I still have to communicate that, but what moves me is rhythm. When I'm teaching I always say to students, musicality isn't about counting music; it's the energy that matches the rhythm and meets the accent. Remember, I was a kid watching *Fantasia.* I'm coming from that world, so I see colors in music. I visualize the old stereo system where you would watch the sound waves on the receiver. That's how I see the rhythm and the movement. I see that peak, and then I know the valley's not important. So, when I decide to hit something with an accent, it's the syncopation on either side that makes it interesting.

CRAMER: In keeping with your comments on rhythm, you've often said pauses are important in choreography. Can you elaborate?

BLANKENBUEHLER: I learned this from Chris Chadman, Bob Fosse, and Jerome Robbins. You have to create pauses so the audience can take in the picture. Our responsibility in that pause, or in that picture, is to make the meaning clear. Take "Cool" from *West Side Story*. Robbins has created pauses that declare the Jets want to kill themselves, or they are frustrated, or they are cool. If the performance matches what Robbins is giving you choreographically, the audience gets it. All of a sudden, their eye catches it long enough to understand because they've experienced it. That's what I'm talking about with the pauses. You've got to hit the accent, and, in that one instant, the audience loves it. Then you move on.

CRAMER: What do you mean when you say, "Good dancing takes tremendous intellect?"

BLANKENBUEHLER: Everybody needs to know why something is happening. I'm not talking about motivation. What I'm talking about is; I'm facing sideways. Why are you facing sideways? If I'm facing forward, the audience is going to look at my face. If I'm facing sideways, they're absorbing my body language and looking past me to the lead character, who's standing right there. But if I all of a sudden start doing the step facing front, I'm telling you, 5 percent of the audience is going to look at my face and not the storyline. Those things go in one ear and out the other with many people, whether they are performers, stage managers, or dance captains.

CRAMER: Do you have different assistants for different projects?

BLANKENBUEHLER: Yes. I use different people because I do such different shows.

CRAMER: How do you select them and how do you use them?

BLANKENBUEHLER: I have a great dancer, Rachel, who has done ten shows with me, including *9 to 5*. She's very smart and organized. She's a great dance captain, a great people person, and a choreographer in her own right. She does it all. I met Rachel through another assistant who had to pass on something and she recommended Rachel. Then there are other shows where I need somebody to make the choice that I'm not going to make. Rachel and I often make the same choice. For *In the Heights*, Joey Dowling, who's a very successful teacher and choreographer, was my assistant. I used to teach with her, and so that's how we started to work together. Presently, my full-time assistant is Stephanie Klemons. She was the dance captain on Broadway for *In the Heights*. These people will make crazy choices from right field or left field, and I'll be in a completely different place, but I like what they're doing, so we meet in the middle and find the step. I give them an enormous amount of responsibility.

CRAMER: I'd like to talk about your research process. I understand that you took six months of salsa and hip-hop on your own preparing for *In the Heights*. Using that as a jumping off point, can you discuss your research process?

BLANKENBUEHLER: If the material is good and I know the story, I joke about it, but I can see the matrix. When I listened to the demo for the first time of *In the Heights*, I was in the car. I was coming back from the dentist, and my interview with the producers was the next week. I heard the song for the first time and got goose bumps, teary-eyed, and knew what the dance was. I knew what the story was going to be. I knew what was going to happen in the steps. I didn't know any of the steps, but I felt it; I really understood it. So, I knew it was meant to be. I listened to the music constantly: on the treadmill, in the subway, in the dance studio, for hours a day. I would listen until I had every nuance memorized. It becomes a joke with the musical department because those demos were improvisations.

CRAMER: You were listening to a demo recorded by arbitrary musicians that would ultimately change.

BLANKENBUEHLER: Right. Well, I'll make a really cool moment literally happen off of this musician playing (click, click) on a woodblock. Then I waltz into rehearsal and I say, "Where's the woodblock?" The common reply is, "What the hell are you talking about?" I need that woodblock, because I build off that blueprint that smart people compose.

CRAMER: I want to make this clear. You were working on *In the Heights,* primarily with demos.

BLANKENBUEHLER: Yes, but this is important to say. In the old-school approach, everything was always on the piano. I cannot work with that. So, in a new musical, if it's written on piano, my choreography is going to be bad. But Lin doesn't play the piano. He writes everything on Garage Band. So, from the beginning, it was orchestrated. There were drums, additional percussion, trumpets, and singers. That's why *In the Heights* was so good. So, for months, all I did was imagine what it could be. I had never done salsa or hip-hop. I grew up rhythmic, dancing tap and swing. It's not dissimilar. I started taking everyone's classes and watching whose work I liked. The hip-hop that looked like pantomime was really interesting to me. Several teachers out there had work that was so chiseled and sharp, like Lin's score. When I watched it, I could see storylines. So, I decided that's how I wanted to choreograph. I started imitating everybody I loved. I tried to make hip-hop dance a bit abstract, deconstructing it, so I could apply it to the way people would simply walk down the street. I would only use Latino dance in a social setting like the club or the carnival number. Latino and salsa dance would never be turned into story language like hip-hop. I surrounded myself with very smart people. I studied many videos, attended competitions, and I learned enough salsa to provide a slow building process to form a number. With the hip-hop, I decided I needed to be able to do it, actually dance the style. So, once I could see the number in my head, I would start to choreograph it on my own. Sometimes my work would look like a tap step, and sometimes it would look like a Jack Cole step. Then I would bring these fierce hip-hop dancers into the room, and I would say, "How can this be better? How can this look like a real hip-hop step?" We would take my steps and convert them. I just needed help.

CRAMER: How much preproduction time do you spend working alone, versus having help in the room from assistants or additional dancers?

BLANKENBUEHLER: I spend 70 percent of preproduction totally alone. Half of that time I sit in a chair listening to the music, writing charts. I draw a map of the stage so I can see where people might be. I just listen and write notes. Then I get in the studio. I'm by myself, and start to work up vocabulary ideas.

CRAMER: Do you record anything?

BLANKENBUEHLER: I record everything in the room, because I spend hours and hours in there. Even if I don't have steps yet, I find what the dance wants to be. I find my general ideas. That's another 25 percent of my process. Then I bring in my assistant, and I help them understand the roadmap. Next, we immediately bring dancers in the room. I bring in people who, again, maybe aren't going to do the show, but are going to make an outlandish choice. I bring in one particular female concert dancer, a Julliard graduate and former competition kid, who always makes a choice no one can accomplish because no one dances like her. Still, she makes such an aggressive choice; it helps us find a middle ground. With *Bring It On!*, I brought this African dancer in. He was in the studio with us daily. It was the same situation.

CRAMER: So, you're really prepared on day one of rehearsal.

BLANKENBUEHLER: When I did *In the Heights*, I had about 6 hours of choreography on video. I could pull up steps and interchange anything I wanted. I like those two counts of that version, these two counts of this version. The decisions I make on the spot are things like: I'm going to make you turn sideways and you're going to do it in half time.

CRAMER: Do you approach actors and dancers differently when you are teaching movement?

BLANKENBUEHLER: This is where I went wrong ten years ago. Movement for the actor is not jazz squares and step-touch. That's not the way to go. When you're creating musical staging, it means you have to have conceptual ideas. That's what I've learned. Musical staging can be about step-together, step-together, but trust me; I'm not going to sleep at night. I'm going to be miserable if I put that on a stage. I must find bigger ideas, like going into slow motion. That's a quintessential part of *In the Heights*. When the whole cast says the world is turning, the cast is walking in slow motion. It's not hard to walk in slow motion. You have to hit it well and you have to be good at it, but it's not a dance step. Dance has to have a vocabulary, and musical staging must have an idea or concept.

CRAMER: Do you read music?

BLANKENBUEHLER: Yes.

CRAMER: Do you find that it is a necessary skill for a choreographer?

BLANKENBUEHLER: No. It used to be more necessary. If I was doing *Bells Are Ringing* in summer stock, sure I'd need it. That's different. Now we're bringing shows up from scratch. I know every note in *Bring It On!* inside and out. I've never looked at a piece of sheet music.

CRAMER: Is it fair to say that you would prefer to work on something new, from the ground up, as opposed to a revival?

BLANKENBUEHLER: Well, it depends on what it is. I'm not at all opposed to doing a revival, but here's often the problem. If there is no liberty to continually improve the show, the creative process stopped with the original creators. So, I can try to improve it, but it doesn't always happen. That's why I was unhappy with *The Apple Tree*. I didn't have the flexibility to make instinctual changes. There are many smart, creative people out there who think differently and want a fresh approach. I'm not saying I must reinvent the wheel. I'm not saying throw away the brilliant work of the original team, but let's face it. Audiences have different sensibilities now.

CRAMER: What kind of environment do you create in the rehearsal room?

BLANKENBUEHLER: You have to be completely prepared. From day one, if I know a thousand things I have to communicate to the cast, the room follows my lead. If I ask my cast's opinion on something like, "On that lift, how do you think it would be best executed?" then the room is mayhem, and performers' spirits go down. Here's a great example. Chris Chadman, the choreographer we spoke of earlier, walked into the room on *Guys and Dolls* and said, "This is the way you're going to do it, this is where you go, this is when you go, and this is how you get there."

CRAMER: Don't you think dancers appreciate that?

BLANKENBUEHLER: Dancers *do* appreciate that. And if it doesn't work, then I say, "You know what? Let's try it this way. I was wrong about that. What is your instinct?" We can open it up. Then we can say, let's try these six different versions because I've given you a blueprint that's already detailed. You can give them all those things that help them find the performance. If you're just wishy-washy about everything, the morale of the show goes down fast, and that's a big deal. It's a really big deal when performers don't have footholds, because they can't commit. What we do for a living is hard, and it's hard to commit emotionally and physically. If there's anything making you question, then you can't give yourself to it and the workplace gets dark and frustrating. I don't want to be part of that. I was joking around with people on the show that I always have this little Susan Stroman on my shoulder. I got my Equity card with Rob Marshall, and then I did several shows for Stroman. They're two of the best, not only with final product, but with treating people well. In those three shows I did for her, I heard her slightly raise her voice once, and she didn't yell at anybody. She just demanded that the room concentrate. I thought, "How can you do all these Broadway shows, and be totally calm?" People respect her. She comes in prepared. She's very genuine. She takes care of everybody around her. So trust me, I have this little "Stro" on my shoulder, and whenever I'm snippy or having any moment of sarcasm, she's there whispering to me, "I can't believe you did that."

CRAMER: Who are your biggest influences, since we're talking about mentors?

BLANKENBUEHLER: Jerome Robbins.

CRAMER: I know you're a big Gene Kelly fan.

BLANKENBUEHLER: I am both a Gene Kelly and Fred Astaire fan, Gene more than Fred.

CRAMER: Who else besides Robbins influenced your life or career?

BLANKENBUEHLER: Michael Jackson. He was a colossal influence in my life. I had the bug to the point where I was thinking about dance 18 hours a day when *Smooth Criminal* came out. The blackout ending of Act One of *In the Heights* was influenced by that music video. There's a number in *Bring It On!* that's inspired by Michael's *The Jam* video. Michael Jackson was huge to me. *The Way You Make Me Feel,* that video changed my life as a teenage dancer, as did *White Nights.* I admired Baryshnikov, of course, but I wanted to work with Gregory Hines. I was more of a song-and-dance guy than I was a concert dancer. Baryshnikov came to the show and used the word "amazing" to describe *In the Heights*; I couldn't speak for a day. He saw it three times. Gregory Hines called me at home once when I was a teenager, just a random thing. I was in a competition that he promoted. I sent his public relations assistant a picture of Gregory and me together. He autographed it, sent it back, and called me at home. He was filming a movie in my hometown. He just calls me out of the blue on a Tuesday night, asked how I was doing. It's like things like that, when somebody touches you, that fuels you for the next five years. That's precisely the reason why I do try to give back.

CRAMER: You are still out there teaching young dancers. You must enjoy it.

BLANKENBUEHLER: It's not like I'm this altruistic person who's out there, but I do love teaching. Because, A, selfishly, it helps me articulate my own process, and B, because I know it makes a big difference. I remember being a teenager, feeling gawky, and having that teacher come in front of me, and it was completely cool. Those moments really stay with you even if you're not going to be a professional dancer. So, it makes a big difference to me to continue to teach.

CRAMER: How much of your dance background do you see in your work? Has it evolved a great deal over time?

BLANKENBUEHLER: Yes, it's greatly evolved. The emotional component I put behind all movement was always consistent.

CRAMER: Even as a young person.

BLANKENBUEHLER: Yes. I didn't know what to do with it, but it was always there. Stylistically things are very different. As a performer, in my mid- to late-twenties, I lived in the 1950s, that "Jack Cole" place. I got to perform that style a lot with *Fosse* and *West Side Story* and those kinds of shows. I'd like to choreograph that style more often, but nobody writes that kind of music anymore. So, hip-hop is a natural extension of that, but I'm reaching my personal end of that style, because I'm not a hip-hop choreographer.

CRAMER: I understand you are a writer and want to develop the stories you've written?

BLANKENBUEHLER: I have already written a story set in Paris in 1928, and I'm working on it with a British pop artist. I think it's going to be a really exciting project, and already on its way. Stylistically, it's much like *Spring Awakening* where it doesn't matter what you do, so, I'm going to take hip-hop and African, and just throw it all in. As long as the emotional story is true, the means by which you get there can be whatever you want.

CRAMER: I'd like to ask you about casting. When dancers come into a room, what draws your focus to a dancer?

BLANKENBUEHLER: I always felt like presence is the most important thing, and it's not stage presence. It's connection. In the room, it's knowing that something's vital to that person; they want to do it, to be a part of it. Onstage the person is an open book, an open screen, somebody like Kristin Chenoweth. You look at them; they're there, present. You want to be that person's friend, or that person's girl, or guy. For me, technique has to be solid. I'm not saying it's secondary. You *have* to *have* it. The person has to be a good dancer. I'm not going to say that a dancer has to kick their head or dance like Baryshnikov. I take pieces and I push them around to suit the dancer. I assume they are going to be talented, but I have to find the *right* person. Believe me, dancers come in the room and there's nothing going on. There's no sense of excitement about learning. There's no intuitive attack. There's just not any glow. I need to see somebody. I said it yesterday in a *Bring It On!* audition. In 90 percent of the dances I do, my interest is standing on the edge of a cliff. That's what musical theatre is. If something's worth singing and dancing about, you're about to take a chance. You're about to find something. You don't know what it is. So they have to come to the table with that presence all the time, and dancers don't. Now, most young dancers come to the table like they're learning steps in a dance studio. Once a show is in rehearsal, I never talk about performance. I never give performance notes in all these Broadway shows I've done. I could never say "smile." What I do say is things like, "This step is all through your eyebrows, this step is down into the earth." I don't care what they do with it. Just take the idea and run with it, because if I see a step just for the sake of the step, without purpose, the dancers have killed the movement. After seeing someone a few times, I like to give them chances. If they're not so good at hip-hop, but I like them, I want them to be able to show me their strengths. I am always of this mindset: don't ask me to do one thing. Ask me to do ten things. And after I'm exhausted, if I'm not right for you, we part ways and it's absolutely fine, because I showed you my best. It's also what the casting director deserves to see. So I dance, and I dance, and I dance, and I do more combinations, and then I do one more. I want to see the way dancers take corrections. I want to see the way they laugh. I want to see the way they react when people are getting tired. I was just in tech and a male dancer was having a bad day; he snapped at me and rolled his eyes. I'm never going to hire that person again. It's not because he was mean to me. It's because when things got ugly in the trenches, he went with it. Musical theatre is hard enough. We just can't do that. I want somebody who's going to bleed, go crazy, have fun, do all those things. So it's really about livelihood. It's about attack and passion for me.

CRAMER: Once they're hired, is there something dancers need to know before they walk into the rehearsal room?

BLANKENBUEHLER: I expect people to take chances. I expect people to take what I give them and go further with it. What I teach is the beginning of where we need to go, and the frustration that I find is when people take it like they're doing manual labor, like it's just a job. There's nothing I hate more than people acting like it's just a job. This is going to sound ridiculously dramatic, but to me, it's life and death. Let me tell you, my wife's a heart surgeon, so I understand the concept. There are shows that audiences enjoy, good shows that don't leave the theatre with them. It doesn't change their life. But there were crying audience members at *In the Heights*. There were people who had cathartic moments and apologized to their families and loved their children better. It's our job to affect people, not just entertain them.

CRAMER: Do you have rehearsal pet peeves?

BLANKENBUEHLER: Yes. I cannot stand it when people wear gym shoes in rehearsal. It drives me crazy. If your gig is to be dancing in the ghetto, people didn't wear gym shoes in the Jewish ghetto in 1940. It drives me crazy when people wear socks. That's a bad contemporary dance habit. There's not a show where you can dance in socks.

CRAMER: Do you prefer that your dancers always dance full out in rehearsals?

BLANKENBUEHLER: Chris Chadman made us dance full out all the time in *Guys and Dolls*. Many choreographers prefer it. I let people mark if I know they're sure of what they're doing. If they can't show me they know what they're doing, I'm going to demand they dance it full out, I need to see it. It drives me crazy when they don't do that on their own. If I didn't have it, I worked until I did. Then, if I had it, I could show you in marking that I knew what I was doing. That should be a personal sense of integrity. If I have to instill that in someone, I don't want to work with that person again.

CRAMER: Here is one of your many terrific quotes: "Having a good voice got me many great dance opportunities."

BLANKENBUEHLER: In Broadway shows you have to sing. Yesterday, I saw a dancer at my auditions who was on *So You Think You Can Dance.*

CRAMER: Oh, I should tell our readers that you were a guest choreographer on that television show.

BLANKENBUEHLER: So, this guy is a great dancer, so much personality, tremendous technique, great passion, but he's not the strongest singer. I can't put him in the show because there's so much understudy responsibility. In musical theatre today, the chorus is much smaller. In a traditional chorus, like *Guys and Dolls,* I could put him in the show, because you have six male dancers, I could afford one who was not a singer, because the others were. So, I sang well enough to get in shows and to have featured parts. It enabled me to work with the people I wanted to work with, and it was a huge step forward.

CRAMER: What do you think is your single most rewarding theatrical experience to date?

BLANKENBUEHLER: I guess it would have to be accepting the Tony award. The most exhilarating performance moment I ever had was the number in *Fosse* called "From This Moment On," which Bob Fosse did in the film *Kiss Me, Kate*: 55 seconds long, Mary Ann Lamb and I danced the Bob Fosse, Carol Haney duet.

CRAMER: Did you do Bob's famous slide entrance?

BLANKENBUEHLER: I did it all, yes. It was opening night out of town, and it was the best moment I ever had dancing. Literally, there was one moment, a quick pivot, and then it jumps out to second position and balances. I was so far forward. I was on the edge of the cliff, totally stuck. I was not going to fall. I remember that so specifically, and I think if it was five seconds longer I probably would have collapsed, because I gave everything I had. That was the most exhilarating performance moment I have ever experienced. With *In the Heights,* there have been so many stunning moments of sitting in the house and thinking, "How could I ever feel this fulfilled not dancing?" but it was joyous. Not the least of which was the last night I saw the show because I couldn't attend closing. I'll probably start crying now. So, a month before closing, I sat house right with my son, who was born during the first production of the show. He sat on my lap and we watched the entire show, leaning over the edge of the box, mesmerized. He's really smart.

CRAMER: How old is he?

BLANKENBUEHLER: Four. He'd say, "Daddy, the guy in the green is really good." So, that was a stunning moment.

CRAMER: When you became a choreographer, you gave up dance as a performance art to a significant degree, I would imagine. How does that affect your choreography?

BLANKENBUEHLER: I'm not in good dance shape right now, and it's affecting my choreography because I don't have as many options. If I hear a piece of music, I'm not exploring all of the options, because I'm stuck in a cookie-cutter place. So, I do have a daily routine. I go to the gym every day for an hour, and then when I'm choreographing—which isn't all the time because I do so much book work—I go to my studio and do a full warm-up. Then I start playing around. I keep my studio really hot so that I stay warm. I like to call it Bikram dance. In the summer, I'm trying to get back a little bit. Every time I would work on a new hip-hop project, I would go to Los Angeles for a week and take a hip-hop class to get some music in me. So, like this, in the next two months, I'm going to try to get my body going a little bit more. There's not enough time in the day to be good at what I'm good at, and stay in that kind of shape. All my dancer friends are going to take dance class at 3:00 in the afternoon. I can't take a dance class at 3:00 in the afternoon. I have 9 hours of work every day of my life, in front of a computer. I don't know how I can take that dance class, but it's a weird thing because I'm a choreographer. I feel like I have to be in the trenches. If I'm going to teach a movement, I want to know what it feels like, and I don't want my dancers to get hurt. I enjoy my good track record. There haven't been a lot of chronic injuries in my shows.

CRAMER: What one piece of advice or maybe words of wisdom would you give performers that are headed to New York to start a stage career?

BLANKENBUEHLER: I think you have to be very open-minded. You have to see lots of different things. You have to try lots of different things. Going down one avenue is never going to work. There's no career in it. You have to take tap class so you have rhythm, and parlay that into hip-hop class, so you have some funk about you. Even if you're going to be a contemporary dancer, everybody's got to do a little bit of everything. It's the well-rounded person who is worth watching and, if that person doesn't have life to me, I don't care. I don't care if it's tap. I don't care if it's Broadway dance. I don't care if it's contemporary. If I can't see real life in that person, it's not interesting to me. So, I think people need to live real lives, they need a relationship; they have to have a five-floor walk-up so they know how it feels to survive. All those things really come in to your dancing, but it's hard. So, if you want it, you have to have a tremendous amount of passion, and know that you've just got to kick your ass to do it. It's much harder than you ever thought it would be. That's the vicious thing about our career. The lows are really low, and the highs are really high. Our roller coaster ride is substantially more dynamic than that of the average person.

CRAMER: I think our readers could use a little choreographic advice. Do you think a dancer knows early whether they've got tendencies toward choreography?

BLANKENBUEHLER: Yes. Dancers can't fake it. Many people are 35 years old, and think they're going to try to choreograph now—well, don't. It's not going to work. If you weren't sleeping it, if you weren't dancing in your living room, if it wasn't in your thought process already, forget it. That's not to say you can't make money choreographing. There are different kinds of choreographers. There are choreographers who replicate, who say, "This is a Charleston. But then there are choreographers who say, "I'm going to take the Charleston and make it look like a drunken man walking down the street." That's a different thing. I think people know inside, and I think if you do feel something inside, that doesn't mean you have to pursue it immediately. Just keep feeding it. It's okay to analyze and criticize. It's okay to go see that really bad show so you can understand why it's bad. Then go see that really good show so you can be inspired by it. I wrote Bill T. Jones a fan letter after I saw *Fela!*, because I had no idea what the hell I saw. I loved it. I loved the show, and it was completely depressing at the same time. It's so thickly rich in choreographic vocabulary from hundreds of years ago, and you can't fake that. So, I want to say something with substance, but do I have hundreds of years of experience in a form? It was really impressive to me. The day before, I had just rewatched the Jerome Robbins' PBS special: totally inspiring, totally depressing. But at least I understand that. I understand *West Side Story*. I'm not going to say I can choreograph like that, but I understand that thought process. I did not understand *Fela!*, in terms of how he made it. But I wrote him this fan letter like a googly-eyed kid that said, "Thank you for inspiring me and I hope I can touch something like that one day." You have to have those things to admire.

CRAMER: Yes, and aspire to, in your own way.

BLANKENBUEHLER: At all ages. Or quit. Go to the woods and sit alone.

CRAMER: I want to wish you the best of luck with future projects. Thank you so much for your inspiring comments.

BLANKENBUEHLER: Thank you.

CHAPTER THREE

Jeff Calhoun

Jeff Calhoun spent his youth as a football player and tap dancer in Pennsylvania, just north of Pittsburgh. In the late 1970s, he began his professional dance career in the ensemble of the Kenley Players in Ohio, a summer stock theatre created by John Kenley. It was there that he met and understudied his mentor and friend, Tommy Tune. This liaison helped to shape Jeff's career as a director and choreographer.

Calhoun made his Broadway debut as a dancer in *Seven Brides for Seven Brothers*, and took over the lead role in *My One and Only*, opposite Twiggy. Jeff's collaboration with Tune on *The Will Rogers Follies* resulted in the 1991 Tony for Best Choreography. The revival of *Grease!* came next, followed by *Annie Get Your Gun, Bells Are Ringing, Brooklyn the Musical*, and *Grey Gardens*.

He has also danced, directed, and choreographed off-Broadway, and for film and television.

Jeff has had an extensive career in Los Angeles, highlighted by his long relationship as a director and choreographer with Deaf West Theatre. His first production for them was the world premier of *Oliver!* His award-winning production of *Big River* premiered the following season, and was subsequently produced at Roundabout Theatre Company's American Airlines Theatre, reaping a 2004 Tony Award for Excellence in Theatre. *Pippin* followed and included new material from composer Stephen Schwartz. In addition, he directed the first American Sign Language Musical, *Sleeping Beauty Wakes.*

Calhoun is an Associate Artist at the Ford Theatre in Washington, DC. At the time of this interview, Jeff's new musical, *Bonnie and Clyde,* with collaborators Frank Wildhorn, Don Black, and Ivan Menchell, as well as *Newsies* were scheduled to open on Broadway in the spring of 2012.

CRAMER: Welcome, Jeff. I'm so delighted that you've taken time out of your busy schedule to chat about your career and artistic process. Thank you.

CALHOUN: It's my pleasure. I remember college. I wish they had something like this when I went.

CRAMER: So, to begin, you grew up in Pennsylvania, and were a football player and tap dancer. What a combination!

CALHOUN: Well, yes. If you lived in Pennsylvania, especially near Pittsburgh, football was your life. We had season tickets for the Steelers, and were there almost every Sunday. When I was in school, I had to leave football rehearsal, as I liked to call it, early on Wednesday afternoons because that's when my tap dance classes were held. That was a very long walk off the football field, I can assure you. I watched the Carol Burnett Show religiously in the 1970s, just wanting to be an Ernie Flatt dancer. He set all the production numbers on her show. Just recently, I was lucky enough to be asked to direct and choreograph the National Tour of 9 to 5. I agreed to do it because I knew I wanted to celebrate the 1970s, and pay homage to the Ernie Flatt dancers. With those influences as my inspiration, coupled with my experiences working for John Kenley in the summers, I had a wonderful start. John was an extraordinary man who basically created summer stock. He took huge stars from MGM as their contracts were dissolving, and he brought them to Ohio. So, these stars you watched in movies and on TV, he put them onstage and exposed them to live theatre. It's quite remarkable. He brought live theatre to small towns in Ohio, like Columbus, Dayton, and Athens, among others.

CRAMER: How did you get your first job with John Kenley?

CALHOUN: He needed a tap dancer for *Anything Goes*. So, my mom drove me to the audition, and I tap danced for Mr. Kenley. He said, "Okay." It was the greatest summer of my life. Ann Miller was starring in *Anything Goes,* and I got to dance with her. I was in the ensemble of that show, as well as *The Merry Widow.* Tommy Tune was starring in *Walking Happy,* and he needed an understudy. I was the tallest ensemble member, so by default, I got it. At 16, I was going to go on for Tommy Tune. I don't know if it was our sensibility, but we became best friends. Then, the next two seasons I went back. In addition to Tommy, almost every person that has influenced my life, I met when I was 16, 17, and 18 years old dancing in the chorus of the Kenley Players.

CRAMER: Prior to your Broadway debut, you were in the National Tour of *The Best Little Whorehouse in Texas.* Is that correct?

CALHOUN: Yes, Tommy asked me to do the show. My Broadway debut was in *Seven Brides for Seven Brothers.* But my big break came when I replaced Tommy in *My One and Only.* I only did the role for two weeks. Tommy left town to direct the national tour of *Nine.* As a performer, those two shows were it. I'm a realist. As much as I'm a dreamer, I'm a realist. I knew I wouldn't star in a Broadway show again. So, I closed the door on performing, going out on that rush of starring in a Broadway show. I went to California to begin my directing and choreography career. I got hired to re-create the Broadway version of *My One and Only* for theatres everywhere. Of course, I had to adapt it for each theatre. That's really the beginning of my directing career.

CRAMER: You must have learned so much at each venue.

CALHOUN: Well, that's how it works. You can't learn to direct until you direct. I showed producers that I knew the piece very well, and I just tweaked it for the cast I currently had, and then molded it to the venue. So, that's really where you cut your teeth, and you start learning what you're made of. As fate would have it, the AIDS epidemic was at its peak, and I was asked to direct the first AIDS benefit west of the Mississippi. That was a very big deal. We got the entire original cast of *A Chorus Line,* complete with the original costumes, the original *Dream Girls* cast, as well as *Tommy.* It was star-studded, and I took advantage of every favor owed to me at the ripe age of 25. It was such a success that I started receiving calls to do other benefits. I feel a bit guilty that I was learning and capitalizing on such a terrible tragedy, but that's actually how I got many jobs as a director, and made many contacts.

CRAMER: How and when did Tommy ask you to work with him on *Will Rogers Follies?*

CALHOUN: Well, Tommy participated in just about every benefit I ever did. He saw many productions I directed over the course of six or seven years, and finally said to me, "You know, I think you're ready, and I have something you should hear. Betty Comden and Adolph Green wrote it and Cy Coleman composed the music."

He handed me this little demo, and he said, "We think we're going to call it *The Will Rogers Follies.*" Of course, that meant nothing to me. He said, "I'm going to be very busy collaborating with the writers for this project, so the choreography is your job." He also reminded me that he usually wins Tony Awards, but no pressure.

CRAMER: Sure, but the show won the 1991 Tony Award for Best Choreography! The show is done all the time, Jeff, everywhere. It is very popular with audiences, even now. When most people think of the show, they think of the number "Favorite Son," that has Will Rogers and the line of chorus girls sitting on benches, doing that rousing and complex choreography that requires an inordinate amount of coordination. That number is done all the time, even out of the show's context, because of its patriotic style.

CALHOUN: True, it's done a lot, but my favorite memory or homage to my work was at a restaurant here in New York, called *Sam's.* On Friday nights, the waiters would take the chairs and line them against the wall. I would say there were 20 of them. They would put on the music and re-create the choreography, lip-syncing and loving it. It would make me cry because I was so honored. Then schools all over the country were renting costumes in red, white, and blue, and doing the number. That's the first time I understood the power of television. I presume dancers and choreographers watched it on the Tony Awards, and taped it. Back then we had those huge VHS machines, no YouTube. Kids everywhere knew my choreography. I was floored. Of course, now, I understand the power of a Broadway show, and how that showcases what you do. People know you from your work. They may not have known my name then. They knew Tommy Tune's name, but it didn't matter. For a long time I would get very teary-eyed and emotional when I would see dancers performing my work.

CRAMER: You have a long relationship with Deaf West Theatre in Los Angeles. You have directed *Oliver!, Pippin,* and *Big River* for them. Will you talk about how that developed?

CALHOUN: It was a life-changing experience. You know, you pray to have those kinds of experiences in the theatre, because that's why we're doing it. What other reason than to create memories for people, to relive emotions, and to touch people? It's been so long, but this is what I think happened. I got a phone call from a friend,

Phil O'Brien, who played Will Rogers for me at Sacramento Music Circus. He said, "Listen, I have a strange request. I'm working for this theatre company and we're looking for a director. There are only two prerequisites. One: the show has to be a musical, and two: half the cast must be deaf." At the time I really thought it was a practical joke, but he was dead serious. And you know what? I told him I had to think about it, and hung up. I talked to all my friends, and said, "This is what my career has come to? I'm being asked to direct musicals with deaf actors?" Now, I'm embarrassed by that statement because it feels so arrogant. But at the time, I had *Grease!* playing on Broadway. It was in its third or fourth year. To be completely honest, I was disillusioned with Broadway and my career as a Broadway director. It wasn't the dream or fantasy you thought it would be when you were a kid. You don't get to do any show you want. You have to fall in love with the shows you're offered unless you are developing your own project. While your project is in development, you have to work, so you fall in love with *Grease!* Anyway, I was disillusioned with New York theatre. I remember reading Bob Fosse's book that stated, "All you need is a black box with shafts of light and an imagination." So I kept saying that to everyone. My friends reminded me of how unique the opportunity was. I thought, "That's absolutely right. Why am I complaining? How dare I." So, I called Phil back and said, "Okay, as scared as I am, I will take your 500 dollars." I was paid that amount to go to North Hollywood for two months and direct *Oliver!* That was the very first show I did for them. It was the hardest thing I've ever had to do, the most fun I've ever had, and probably the most fulfilled as an artist that I've ever been. It was such a lesson learned, and it changed everything. It opened up the sandbox to me again. It reminded me what it's like to be an artist without the limitation of doing commercial theatre. There's so much pressure to deliver a Broadway show, and so much money on the line, that I think artistically you re-create what you know works. You do it out of fear, so there aren't many fresh ideas because you're pulling out old tricks that are tried and true. So, guess what? I wasn't able to pull out any old tricks because, to my knowledge, no one had ever tried to do a musical with deaf actors. In trying to figure that out, and solving those challenges, it seemed like this new art form was born. It was such an inspiration to me to be part of that, and to watch it happen. I felt like an artist again.

CRAMER: I saw *Big River,* and many times, a role was played by both a speaking actor and a deaf actor, while other roles were handled differently. Can you clarify that process for me?

CALHOUN: Yes. It was always different, no common rule. There were about four ways it could go. To use *Big River* as an example, Puck was the deaf actor, and he played the role of Puck singularly. However, Mark Twain, who was our narrator, voiced for Puck. Another way we handled characters—the one you're referring to—was the role of Pap. Pap existed with two actors: one hearing, one deaf. You didn't have Pap if you didn't have both of those. The third way had another deaf actor playing a role, and someone in the ensemble voiced for him. Last, you had a hearing actor who was playing the role himself, who had to learn sign language. So, the whole show was signed and voiced every second of the show, but the rules kept changing. No one ever got bored.

CRAMER: We spoke of *Grease!* earlier, but that wasn't actually your Broadway debut as a director.

CALHOUN: No. My debut as a director was earlier that season with *Tommy Tune Tonight,* a concert that I directed and choreographed. But *Grease!* was my first book musical, and I've learned a lot since then.

CRAMER: And you were directing and choreographing. Is that correct?

CALHOUN: Yes, but I had Jerry Mitchell, and he really helped a lot, because as a director you have your hands full. He is a great friend and wonderful assistant. Jerry and I not only danced together in the movie *The Best Little Whorehouse in Texas*, he was a featured ensemble member of *The Will Rogers Follies.*

CRAMER: Do you have different assistants on various projects, and how do you select them?

CALHOUN: Yes. It's like casting. People just come into your life at the right time. I am a believer that the universe provides if you're open to it. It just makes sense. I knew Jerry already. Michael Bennett mentored Jerry, just as Tommy mentored me. We had very parallel experiences. Then Michael passed away, so Jerry was a bit at odds. That's why *Will Rogers* was a life vest for him, and the start of our creative liaison. When it came time to do *Grease!,* I asked him if he would be my associate, knowing all the while he was qualified to do it himself. Then after that, I collaborated on a show called *Busker Alley* with Tommy, and again, Jerry was my associate. So, I like to use the same people at different times. Then Jerry started his own career. The world said, "Jerry, it's time," and he had his own opportunity.

CRAMER: *Busker Alley* never made it to Broadway because Tommy broke his foot.

CALHOUN: A week before we were set to come to Broadway. We had the theatre, had it painted, and even had our marquee up. Yes, that was a hard break. But, that's a book all in itself.

CRAMER: *Grease!* catapulted you to Broadway Director-Choreographer status. Did you entertain the idea of working solely as a choreographer again?

CALHOUN: When I finished *Grease!*, I just thought, "Oh, my god! The phone's going to ring, and I'm going to direct Broadway shows, two a year." Well, it doesn't really work that way, certainly not for me. I didn't think I was arrogant, but looking back, I was. I didn't pick up the phone and try to get my next job. I sat back and waited for the phone to ring, and then realized, "God, why isn't the phone ringing?" Lucky for me, Graciela Daniele asked me to co-choreograph the revival of *Annie Get Your Gun.* I'm thinking, "I'm a director, but you know what? It's Graciela Daniele, and her mentor was Bob Fosse. I have so much to learn." Luckily, I accepted, and she's become one of my best friends in the world. So, you get over yourself in a way, and you realize it's not necessarily just about billing. If you're an artist, it's about working with other artists and creative people that are smarter and more experienced than you are. I was grateful for that opportunity. Then I choreographed *Bells Are Ringing.* That was a turning point. I remember seeing the show and thinking, "I don't think I can do this anymore unless I am able to realize my vision as the director." But never say never, because Michael Greif asked me to do the musical staging for *Grey Gardens.* Then I thought, "You know, I said I would never do this again, but here's the director of *Rent* asking me to work with him." I knew after reading the prologue. I called Michael, and said, "Thank you. I will be so honored to be a part of this."

CRAMER: It won three Tony's.

CALHOUN: That it did. I just wanted to be involved with something I knew in my heart was going to be good. I'm glad I'm older and wiser now, and don't have the arrogance of youth to know I'm never going to say never again. I would do anything to be involved with certain artists. I would be a fly on the wall for certain people. I am still so in awe of some directors. I'd be willing to make coffee just to observe their process.

CRAMER: I have to ask you about being a choreographic consultant on *Taboo* because I've never seen the term "Choreographic Consultant" used. What is that exactly?

CALHOUN: Well, first of all, it's a lot of money. When a new musical is in trouble, it's always the choreographer or the lighting designer who is elected scapegoat. I have to be honest with you; the choreography was not the problem in *Taboo*. The artist who choreographed the show is talented and is responsible for some of the strongest things in the show. That's all I can tell you. I didn't know what my billing was going to be, but I went in and I tried to do my best. My theory is, and this is difficult to say, that ultimately the show did not work because Rosie O'Donnell was an inexperienced producer. She had a lot of great people around her, but she didn't want to use anyone's ideas other than her own. So, she hired a talented creative team, but the job was to execute *her* ideas. What did I learn? For each job, you have to know why you're taking it. If you're doing a job for money, know why you're doing it, and don't look for it to fulfill your artistic void. If you're doing a piece of art, don't expect to make a lot of money. It may not be commercial. If you're doing it just to work with someone, reap the benefits of that person's knowledge. Don't expect it to deliver in every area. Know at the outset why you're doing a job, and don't lose sight of that. Then you won't be disappointed. It's an important lesson to learn, and I try to do that now.

CRAMER: In keeping with "life lessons" in the world of musical theatre, discuss your Tony for *Big River*. I'll remind our readers that it was not a "regular" Tony Award. *Big River* received a Tony Honor for Excellence, a unique award.

CALHOUN: I don't know why or how we got it, but it's really quite an honor. I was thinking at the time, "I'm really proud of *Big River*. Wouldn't it be fun to be nominated for Best Musical?"

Then, the nominations came out, and we were omitted. The show didn't receive the kind of recognition a nomination brings. So, you can run one of two ways. You can be angry, or you can decide it's about the work and not the award. To be really candid, I wanted to be able to go up on stage and thank my parents and my teachers. That's really the motivation for a nomination or a win, the exposure it gives you. You get to thank people who made it happen. Quite frankly, that might be the best moment in the world as an artist. I wouldn't know. I haven't had it yet. That's the only reason to receive an award. Other than that, it's about the work.

CRAMER: You're an Associate Artist at the Ford Theater in Washington. Tell me how that differs from working on Broadway.

CALHOUN: I have a great relationship with the Ford Theatre's Director, Paul Tetreault. He produced one of the three productions of *Big River*. We had the Broadway production, the tour, and finally the Ford Theater production. He wanted it at the same time the tour was out on the road. So, we created a separate company, and my associate director really helped put that together. Ultimately, we produced *Shenandoah* together at my suggestion. It was very successful, so we were off and running. It's a venue that allows me to examine a project in development or production elsewhere, and bring it to the attention of the Ford Theatre. I also have the opportunity to bring new ideas to the table and discuss projects I am interested in pursuing. It's quite an honor to be a part of such a prestigious theatre.

CRAMER: You directed and choreographed the national tour of *9 to 5* in 2010. Seeing as how you stake claim to the 1970s dance style, as you mentioned in the beginning of our interview, how fast did you say yes?

CALHOUN: Let me tell you how disappointed I was when, several years ago, I heard they were doing *9 to 5,* and I didn't get the job. There aren't a lot of jobs like that. I have to be honest, I was so jealous! From performing in *Whorehouse,* the movie, with Dolly Parton, to possibly directing her show. Now, that would be perfect. But I didn't get the job, and I thought, "That's the end of that." Then, I get a call inviting me to direct and choreograph the tour. The producers wanted to go in a new direction, and decided to hire a new creative team. It took me about a second and a half to say, "Yes, I'll do it!" The producers assumed I would want to read it first. I said, "No, tell Dolly I'll do it." Of course, I had to meet with Dolly and get her "blessing." I took a photograph that we had taken together during the *Whorehouse* shoot. As soon as I showed it to Dolly, she said, "Oh, yeah, you've got the job!" She thought it was divine intervention. So, the process of *9 to 5* was one of the best times I ever had. When I directed *9 to 5*, I had three days off. I went to Sarasota, Florida, to do the second incarnation of *Bonnie & Clyde*. That turned out to be our out-of-town "try-out" for Broadway.

CRAMER: You had already done a reading in New York, as well as a full production?

CALHOUN: Yes, I really believe in readings and in workshops. They are so important in the development of a new work. After the reading in New York, the show premiered at the La Jolla Playhouse in California. This was a full year before the Sarasota production. Boy, we did learn a lot. We were in great shape for a new musical, but it was still "a new musical." I mean, you have to get it right. The only show that I've been involved with that was a huge success without an out-of-town production was *Will Rogers Follies*. We developed it in New York City at the Palace Theatre. It was so expensive we couldn't afford a production in Philly, Boston, or Chicago. We did it all right there in front of everyone. Let me tell you, that show was bad until it wasn't. I'd walk home from the theatre every night, and during previews I overheard one couple say, "I know that Tommy Tune is really something. They say he can fix anything, but I don't think he's going to be able to fix this one." This was my big break, and I was just crushed. I'd have tears in my eyes, thinking, "Is it my fault? What can we do?" And then, like anything, there's no substitute for time. So with that said, yes, we learned a lot with *Bonnie & Clyde* in La Jolla, and then we were fortunate enough to have another opportunity the next year to go to Asolo Repertory Theatre in Sarasota. I got to work in two great theatres with great associate artists Michael Edwards and Christopher Ashley. That really helped. Those theatres and associates helped shape the show. After Sarasota, I would say the show was 70 percent ready.

CRAMER: Do you think of this show as your big return to Broadway?

CALHOUN: Well, I hate to say return because that implies you've been gone, but I do, I suppose. Again, I don't really care if we are on Broadway, or in Chicago, or Florida, because it's simply about doing good work. When I was young, I thought Broadway was the "be all, end all" period. You weren't successful if you weren't working on Broadway. It took me until late in life to realize that when you don't have review constraints or the pressure of having to deliver something successful to the masses, you can do really interesting, and much deeper work. So, I love the regional theatre process. Now, ideally, you start there, and you move on to Broadway. I think *Bonnie & Clyde* has a very good chance of being something truly special. I'm still looking for that show that's going to outlive me. When I move on, high schools and community theatres are going to be doing *Bonnie & Clyde*. That's my unfulfilled dream.

CRAMER: Let's talk about the process of choreography and direction in preproduction. You have established earlier that you like to use some of the same assistants frequently. How do you work with an assistant to develop the choreography for a show whether new or a revival?

CALHOUN: First of all, I find, as a man, I like to have a female assistant. If you're doing any partnering, it's just practical. But I also like to have more than one person. It's good to have an odd number. If you're looking in the mirror and you want to step out of it, I like to have myself and two others in the early phase before you bring in the skeleton crew.

CRAMER: Meaning?

CALHOUN: Additional dancers that you need for the bigger sections of choreography, and to create your stage picture. But actually, I sit with my assistants and review the script and score. We just listen and talk, listen and talk. Examples include "Why is this number here, and who's performing it? What is the purpose? What has to be accomplished by the end of the number?" Once we define that, we understand the point of view. You have to have a reason behind it, or you shouldn't do the number. The reason can even be simplistic. We need 2 minutes of entertainment here to create a certain energy before the next scene. So, now you know what you need, and that will inform you as to what the steps will be. Usually a musical number is to forward the story to some degree. Once you know the story you want to tell and which character is performing it, you get on your feet and begin to move like the character, uncovering his quirks and his limitations. Hopefully, out of that comes a pallet of unique choreography that's indigenous to that character's moment in time. The big mistake I see onstage is generic choreography. Perhaps the time period has been captured a bit, but it just looks like everything you've seen before.

CRAMER: Do you do an extensive amount of research before you start a show?

CALHOUN: Yes. I want to read and view everything I can to understand the truth of the period. Then I like to know the rules so I can break them, make it my own, and put it in my own "words."

CRAMER: So, your research informs your work more than it has practical application?

CALHOUN: Yes.

CRAMER: Other than assistants, do you find you hire or work with the same people many times?

CALHOUN: I'm now at the point where I want to have a good time when I'm working. I hire people I want to go out and have a drink and talk with after rehearsal because I become obsessed about the project. When I'm doing a show, it's almost all I think about 24 hours a day. Even in the grocery store, I'm seeing colors, composition, and shapes. I'm a visualist. I admit I need material that's already really good. I'm an editor. I'm a good editor, but I'm not a writer, and I make no bones about that. So I'm only as good as the material that I have. I think I'm very good at taking from the page and turning it into something good for the stage. I think I create in a three-dimensional way. I do that pretty well, and I learned from the best—Tommy Tune.

CRAMER: How do you work with an arranger?

CALHOUN: It's a bit back and forth. If you find a step sequence or something you like and it looks good on you, or your dancers, then the arranger scores it. You might love a riff he's playing, and then you ride his wave, coming up with movement that compliments his musical idea. I think it's a good give-and-take for me.

CRAMER: Do your assistants write your work? Do you chart or graph? Do you use pennies?

CALHOUN: I love to use pennies or dimes, but then I found this color gadget of doughnuts. I did most of *Will Rogers Follies* with this gem. There were enough color doughnuts to represent all the girls. I also like to storyboard. They're terrible, but I have so many books of everything. I was lucky to have Patti D'Beck as my assistant on more shows than anybody else.

CRAMER: She wrote it all out for you.

CALHOUN: She did. If I made it up, I wasn't going to forget it. Then, as I started to direct more, my notation skills went by the wayside, and so she did all the notation. But I haven't done pure dance choreography in a long time.

CRAMER: Perhaps your associates are creating steps now, but you're still looking at the big picture and putting the entire package together.

CALHOUN: I think the director's job is to order the number, yes. You see what has to happen. You're responsible for telling the story visually. That's what your job is. I learned that from Tommy, too. Even though I choreographed every step in *Will Rogers,* Tommy would order the number. For example, Keith Carradine sings a number with the boys called "Give a Man Enough Rope." Tommy says, "Do what you want. Remember, Keith Carradine's not a dancer. This is the number; make Keith look good." Keith is playing Will Rogers, so it's an absolute. In "Favorite Son," the number we spoke of earlier, there are eight girls on either side of Keith. He doesn't really move well, so maybe there's something we can come up with where he doesn't have to move a lot. So, Tommy has him sit down. He would order the number, and then I would create the steps.

CRAMER: Discuss the collaboration with your designers in preproduction.

CALHOUN: My favorite collaboration, without a doubt. It's also the most important collaboration that a director has. "What the show is going to look like" cannot be more important. The floor plan is everything. That's the hardest component, and my first area of focus when I direct. Once I'm confident enough to know I can do it and I've got the job, I look at the show and say, "Okay, how many scenes? Where do we go from here to there? How do we find a metaphor that best enables us to get from there sensitively, seamlessly, and cinematically." That's a very important question to answer because you have to live with that answer for the run of the show. I am not being overly dramatic; that can determine if a show is successful or not. I think many shows are sabotaged by bad design. So, that's the key, hands down.

CRAMER: Let's talk about costume design, because choreographers have a different investment in costuming than a director. On a show like *Will Rogers Follies,* costuming was key to the way the scantily clad women moved, and the way the men moved in their chaps and Western wear.

CALHOUN: My approach is much the same with the costume designer, although I must admit, my weakest links are costumes and women's hair. I just don't know anything about women's hair, and I'm not great with costumes. Tommy is impeccable with both. So, it was Tommy, not me, who said, "Let's put the tambourine in the hats."

CRAMER: I hope all our readers will go to YouTube and search for "Favorite Son" and watch any company do that number with tambourines in their hats. It was genius, and your choreography is mind-boggling. How did your collaboration with the costume designer for *Bonnie & Clyde* differ, since you were both director and choreographer?

CALHOUN: I had two different people, one in La Jolla, and one in Sarasota. I might add that's not unusual. My secret weapon is Tobin Ost. He designed the sets and costumes for *Bonnie & Clyde* in Sarasota. Previously, he designed costumes for my production of *Brooklyn* as well as the set and costumes for *Pippin* and *Shenandoah.* We spend extended periods of time together working on the sets. We'll take a trip away from the city to focus 24/7 on the project. Now, on costumes, after an initial exchange of ideas, Toby will "go away" and draft his ideas. He'll show me things for approval, but I'm pretty hands off when it comes to costumes, at least early in the process.

CRAMER: When you come in to rehearsal, are you completely blocked and choreographed on day one of rehearsal? Even if you know in your heart of hearts you're going to make changes, are you still prepared with the whole setup?

CALHOUN: I am prepared with the whole setup from day one, yes. Do I know what's going to happen every second? No. But am

I prepared? Yes. When I come in the first day of rehearsal, I have a model of the set which I've had with me for probably a month or so, and I know how to get from the first scene to the second scene to the third scene, through the whole show. I know that it's graceful and I know that it works, and I know why. From the directing standpoint, my job is to entertain and satisfy the paying audience. So, that's the first thing you're responsible for, just getting through the show. Like I said earlier, that's the magic, I believe; that's the success of a show. How did you get from A to B to C? Does it work gracefully, and does that support the text and the message of the show? So, yes, I come to work, and as a director, I know what we must do. Choreographically, I know why every number has to happen, and I probably have 70–80 percent of every number done, at least the beginning and the end.

CRAMER: Being prepared makes changes easier.

CALHOUN: It may change, but at least have Plan A. I believe it's the director's responsibility.

CRAMER: What's the shortest amount of time that you had to get a show up?

CALHOUN: Besides a crazy summer stock schedule that I haven't done in years and years, I would have to say *High School Musical*. I don't think I'm underestimating. I think it was two and a half weeks. And I don't like to say that because it's usually a bad thing. This time around, the process seemed to go without a hitch. The stars were aligned, and it was two and a half weeks that worked fluidly. I think there were probably three or four days of tech.

CRAMER: What's the longest rehearsal period you've ever had, where you felt you could sit back and have a cup of coffee?

CALHOUN: If you've done your homework, I really think it's like cooking. You can overdo it till it gets tough. I could keep tinkering on a show forever and never stop. So it's good to open a show and move on. But the longest rehearsal period had to be years ago, because today, with tight budgets, rehearsals are short. On *9 to 5*, the only reason the tour worked is because we made significant cuts economically. The producers came to me and said, "What can you do?" And I said, "All right, let's cut a week and a half of rehearsal and half a week of tech." I'd rather do that and put the pressure on me than take it from the stage. I want that drop, so I'll cut a week of rehearsal. I want that piece of scenery, so I'll cut four days of tech. I would rather put the burden on me than have the production compromised. I show up ready and prepared. I was a Boy Scout, and I think the greatest thing any young director and choreographer can do is come in as prepared as possible, and then be willing to change everything so that you can be successful in any situation.

CRAMER: Is the environment in your rehearsals collaborative for dancers and singers, as well as actors?

CALHOUN: It's collaborative as far as anyone is concerned. I walk in, and the first thing I say to everyone is, "Best idea wins." I don't care whether it's the accompanist or the custodian emptying the garbage with a good idea. I want, include, and hope I cast people that I know will bring something to the table. They won't stand there and wait for me to tell them exactly what to do. I think my job as the director is to put them into the best, most elegant, imaginative physical production they can be in, and then their job is to do something. It's not acting class, it's not dance class. You hire the right people, create an environment where they feel like they can be the best they can be, and you let them work. I think you get that from humor. We laugh almost all day long, and we cry because, perhaps it's a sensitive group, and I want them to feel like it's coming from love. The days of scaring people into good performances, that went out in the 1970s. No one does that anymore. I don't. If nothing else, I hope that my legacy will be that people love working with me. That would be the most important thing someone could say. We're the most blessed people in the world because we get to make our living creating musicals. I just feel so lucky, and with that good fortune comes responsibility. I think it's responsible to return that love and appreciation for our livelihood right back into the production process. That's a common energy that I create in every rehearsal.

CRAMER: Do you enjoy the casting process?

CALHOUN: Tap dancing and a good judge of character are my two God-given talents. I was lucky enough to discover some really major talent. I truly enjoy casting.

CRAMER: What are you looking for beyond technique and type?

CALHOUN: I'm looking for somebody that I want to date. I figure that's what a show is all about. If I want to hang out with somebody for a couple of hours, I figure the audience will want to do the same. Between the cast and an audience, you're on a two-and-a-half- hour date. So, not only do I care how well they sing, dance, and act; I watch them when they put their dance bag down. I watch them when they pick it up. I watch who they talk to, how they relate to the other people they're auditioning with. If I'm really interested, I go outside and pretend I have to go to the bathroom, unbeknownst to them. I watch and see if they are the same person in the room as they are in the hall. I don't want anybody to fool me, and I've been fooled very few times. There's nothing more important to the success of a show than casting. If you cast right, have good material, and the physical production is right, you're going to have a success. Absolutely.

CRAMER: How does your approach adjust in dealing with leads versus ensemble, stars versus "up and comers," or dancers versus movers?

CALHOUN: It just comes with the job. Different people need different things to be the best they can be. You're a parent, and diplomat, and it's important to figure out what they might need to achieve success. I don't find that difficult. It's just a matter of treating people with kindness and concerned interest. I think you treat everybody a specific way once you get to know them. If you're inquisitive and you get a sixth sense about who they are, you simply adjust your approach to make their life and rehearsal process better. That's human nature, and that's a responsibility that directors should assume. Now, there are performers that are insane. I mean, there *are* crazy people. The way you avoid that: don't hire them. Life is too short, and I don't care how talented you are; I'm not interested.

CRAMER: Here's a scenario for you. My friend and I are both in your audition and you're looking at our résumés. You find us equally talented and fascinating, and you want to date us, but you can't hire both of us.

CALHOUN: I would call people who have worked with you, and I'll say, "You know me. Which one? Give me the dirt." Meaning, fill me in on their reputation and work ethic up to this point.

CRAMER: You'd prefer to talk with people they worked with, as opposed to casting directors who know them?

CALHOUN: Oh, absolutely. I'll call Stroman or Jerry or Kathleen Marshall. I'll call other directors and ask what was it like working with a particular actor, and they will tell me. It is a small world. Once they get the job, an actor isn't fooling anyone if they become unpleasant to the company either on Broadway, in a regional theatre, or on the road. Word of a bad attitude or bad behavior gets around. I hear what happens. We check these things. Directors and choreographers talk. There is no escaping it. There are too many talented and kind people who need work, to put up with someone who is a problem.

CRAMER: What is the most important trait or characteristic of a good director or choreographer?

CALHOUN: Imagination and a sense of humor. It's a date, so I'm trying to think of it in those terms. Original thought is so important and so rare. There are thousands of directors that can direct your show, so who is the producer hiring? Hopefully you have a solid body of work and they say, "Oh, you know what, I like their taste." It comes down to the producers' taste and the taste of the director. They have to be similar.

CRAMER: Is there any advice you want to give to an aspiring performer coming in at this time in the business?

CALHOUN: I have so much that I'd like to say to them, but I think the most important thing is to be sure that this is really what you want to do. This is a career for people who wouldn't be happy doing anything else, because it's really hard. Very few people live the way they want to live, as comfortably as they want, doing this. There are many people who want to perform full time, and very few that can actually make a living at it. You need a specific disposition—a thick skin—because there's going to be a lot of heartache. You have to derive joy from the *journey* of being an artist. And if you can't square all that, you probably shouldn't be doing this. That being said, it's the most rewarding work I know.

CRAMER: Jeff, thank you so much for your time. It's been a pleasure.

CALHOUN: You're most welcome.

CHAPTER FOUR

Warren Carlyle

Warren Carlyle started choreographing at age 10. He made up dances for every dancer in the church hall, where he took his first class. Born in Norfolk, England, he would choreograph for any festival, studio program, or dance competition. It didn't matter. Warren just wanted to create movement.

His first job was portraying orphan number 11 in a touring production of *Oliver*. He made 52 pounds. At age 14, Warren left home to study classical ballet on a scholarship and never looked back. He is now a proud American citizen and believes strongly that the United States is the land of opportunity. Warren certainly seized his.

He has had a prolific career on stage and in film and television. A protégé of Susan Stroman's, Warren's career has spanned over a decade, having worked with some of the most respected names in the business, including Jerry Herman, Jerry Zaks, and Tony Walton, among them. Warren's work as both a director and choreographer has been seen on the Broadway stage in *Tale of Two Cities*, *Finian's Rainbow, Follies,* and *Chaplin*. He has worked for every major regional theatre in the country including Goodspeed Opera House, Asolo Repertory Theatre, and Paper Mill Playhouse. His work has also been enjoyed off-Broadway, at the Kennedy Center, the Old Globe, City Center Encores!, national tours in the United States as well as the United Kingdom, and throughout the West End.

CRAMER: Welcome Warren. It's truly a pleasure to meet you. Can you tell our readers about your dance background in England? When did you start dancing, and what types of dance did you study as a young man?

CARLYLE: I started when I was 10. I was a really hyperactive child. I had a lot of energy and my parents encouraged me to swim, run track, and horseback ride. At that same age, I saw the movie *Top Hat,* and I literally pointed at the television and said, "I want to do that!" My mom came from a tiny village, but she took me to the church hall and to my first tap class, and that was it. I was hooked.

CRAMER: Are you Billy Elliott?

CARLYLE: Yes, absolutely Billy Elliott, without a doubt.

CRAMER: For our readers, *Billy Elliott* was a hit Broadway Musical that tells the story of a young boy's artistic rise from a small village in North Eastern England during the United Kingdom miners' strike of 1984–1985, to his triumph as a professional ballet dancer.

CARLYLE: I took a tap class, loved it, and had an aptitude for it. A year later my tap teacher said, "You should take some jazz dance or modern dance." So, I took modern. I did that for a year and she said, "You should take classical ballet." So, I took ballet, and within six months I had a scholarship to a school in London at 14.

CRAMER: What were the rigors?

CARLYLE: I studied in a very strict classical ballet environment, and took four classes a day and very little else.

CRAMER: I'm assuming they also provide you with an education, including math and science and other rudiments.

CARLYLE: Yes, and I didn't do very much of that. I took a lot of classes in dance, art, and English. They were the only subjects I ever worried about. Honestly, I can't balance a checkbook or add or subtract anything.

CRAMER: But you appreciate a beautiful painting?

CARLYLE: Yes, I do. I love images, shapes, and colors as much as I love words. Now I'm combining choreography and directing, so both parts of my brain get satisfied. The visual part is satisfied through choreographic shapes and images. The language, the words, and the text are satisfied through the script. One of my first memories as a child was listening to music and imagining people dancing—visualizing dance—before I even knew what dance was. I wasn't aware. Nobody in my family had danced or been involved in theatre in any way. So, I have this memory as a five-year-old child with a Sony Walkman listening and imagining dancers in my head. Now, for a living, I sit in my apartment and listen to my iPod. I close my eyes and I imagine people dancing and I relive my first memory almost every day. It's a very powerful thing, and it makes me extremely happy. I think even if I hadn't had the classical training, I would still be doing what I am, in some way.

CRAMER: You began as a choreographer but you are now directing so much more. What is it about the creative process that turned you in that direction?

CARLYLE: I think it's the need. There's a need to communicate, and there's a need to tell a story. I think there's no difference in what I'm doing now compared to what I was doing ten years ago. Choreographing is often harder because you're handed a blank piece of paper, which is the music, and the director says, "Okay, go create a dance." In my head I say to myself, "Okay, go create a story." So, I'm constantly making a story. Directing doesn't feel any different than choreographing. Directing, in a way, is easier because the story is in the script.

CRAMER: So you think choreographers have a tougher job?

CARLYLE: At times, it's much harder. What's most difficult is to find a great story that's going to engage an audience, and to find a great choreographer or a great style that's going to fit the tone of the show.

CRAMER: I believe there is a misconception that choreographers simply make up steps. That's such a misrepresentation of a choreographer's job. You've raised the idea here, by describing it as story telling. Do you find that if you know what your story is, the steps come?

CARLYLE: Yes. A story always comes first, and in a funny way I can't create a step until I know why. So, it's like an actor. They have to know their motivation in order to say the lines. If I'm going to be ready for dancing and choreography, I feel the same way. I just sat behind the table for a week working through the script of *Camelot* in order to know who the characters are, how they move, and how they dance. Today I was working on "Lusty Month of May," and I was thinking about the knights, the clubs, and the gauntlets, and I suddenly found myself knowing exactly what to do. I'm going to dance with my right hand out because that's the symbol. That's the symbol I'm using. Take the little kerchiefs. Guinevere gives her kerchief to the three knights who are going to joust with Lancelot. I find a place in the dance where the girls dance with the kerchiefs, and the knights try to take them. So, if you read the script enough to go deep enough-and look hard enough, it's all there.

CRAMER: You are choreographing, and you're trying to help a director realize his vision. Let's use Guinevere as an example. Does setting a piece for her and finding the way she moves inform her scene work?

CARLYLE: Yes. That's the best thing of all—when the audience can't tell where the director leaves off, and the choreographer starts, or vice versa. That's also the great thing about working with someone again and again. There is an established language between director and choreographer.

CRAMER: How do you find working with a director that is brand new to you?

CARLYLE: Oh, I like it.

CRAMER: Do you?

CARLYLE: I like it a lot. I send pictures, leave voice mails, and send the director a list of things, or a costume swatch. I typed a three-page breakdown of a 3-minute intro to the director because I wanted him to know what I was thinking. I wanted him to know that I'm seeing apples as the forbidden fruit, and Guinevere as Eve. I wanted him to think about the parallels between the brightly colored scarves and the dark veils, scarves, and silks in Act Two for the enchanted forest. I wanted to point out those parallels because that's where I was going as a choreographer, and that would inform him as a director.

CRAMER: Do you communicate with your creative team any differently, regardless of whether you're choreographing, directing, or both?

CARLYLE: It doesn't matter. You talk as much as you can and with as much energy and passion as you can muster, because ultimately you have to lead the team into some kind of rhythm and some kind of creativity. Clearly, we all have to be doing the same show. The scenic designer has to be doing the same show as the costume designer, lighting designer, director, choreographer, and music director. Then if you're lucky, once in every 20 shows, everyone is in line and it works out. I think as a director that would be my biggest aspiration. It doesn't just mean blocking a scene and making sense of text, or picking up cues, or acting on a line, or any of those kind of one-on-one things. It truly means to all 250 or 300 people involved in the show, that everyone is on the same path, headed in the same direction. That is when I think art is at its most powerful, and creates an environment where people are free to do their best work.

CRAMER: Keeping with that thought, what kind of environment do you try to create in the rehearsal space?

CARLYLE: Happy. I like it happy. I think much of my training was very disciplined and English.

CRAMER: Rigid, would you say?

CARLYLE: Yes. It was uptight, rough, and very hard. If you couldn't cut it, you were done, you were out. Every month they would weigh you, and throw you out if you weighed too much. If you couldn't do a double tour, fifth position to fifth position, you were out. As a dancer I was trained in a fearful way, but now as a creator I can't create when I'm angry or when I'm scared. I can only create when I'm happy, and I also believe that good happy material finds its way into the work. I think *Finian's Rainbow* is a great example. It was such a joyous process, and you could feel that process in the show. I knew it was joyous from the first time I read the script and listened to the music. From creating the scenic valley, to creating a language with a harmonica player and a beautiful ballerina from American Ballet Theatre, it was joyous in every department. The costume designer and I looked at 2,000 costume swatches on my dining table, laughing, trying to figure out if "this goes with that" and when the skirts spin, do we need a circle and a half of fabric to make them spin beautifully? Then, I had to rethink chaine turns and pirouettes in the opening number, because now I had those beautiful skirts! Pure joy.

CRAMER: Are you completely prepared with every step and piece of blocking when you walk into the rehearsal room on day one?

CARLYLE: No, I like to make room for magic. Personally, if I plan every single step and every single moment, then I'm just a good boy, and I'm going to walk in the room and I'm going to *do* every single step and every moment. Sometimes I think I'm better with a big idea; I come up with a great concept. The details will work themselves out.

CRAMER: In the process?

CARLYLE: Yes. Quite often, I'm blessed because the people I'm working with are extremely talented. I like to leave room for them to bring something to the process too. I leave room for inspiration. I don't plan everything wall to wall, but, yes, I'll plan a dance break if I know I've got a big dance number to do, and I'll certainly know how I'm going to start and how I'm going to finish. Sometimes the glue—the getting to and from—the ins and outs; I can't paint without all the things in the room. In other words, I need everyone there.

CRAMER: So, you don't really use diagrams, pennies, or dimes to plan traffic; you're better on your feet with bodies in space.

CARLYLE: Yes. I don't plan traffic unless there's a very specific moment; for example, an English country reel. Then there are pre-established floor patterns in the traditional choreography, and I am forced to draw diagrams. Basically, I'm a stick figure person. I draw storyboards. Actually, I draw a lot of pictures, in my script, on napkins, on my hat, or on my hand.

CRAMER: Whenever you get an idea.

CARLYLE: Whoever is standing near me has to watch out.

CRAMER: Yes, because you're going to draw on them!

CARLYLE: Right! I loved arts when I was in school. I was very keen on drawing so I draw a lot. I've worked with the great director Jerry Zaks many times. I love him but sometimes he looks at me like I'm from another planet because I'll explain this amazing moment—this visual idea—and he doesn't understand it. So, I take my script and I'm able to draw it and show him, and then he's got it.

CRAMER: You've had a very natural progression from dancer to dance captain, assistant, associate, choreographer, and now, director. How did you get your start in England?

CARLYLE: I worked with Gillian Lynne, who is a wonderful director-choreographer. She did *Cats*, *Phantom*, and thousands of other wonderful things. Gillian represents the first time I was in a room with a choreographer, who did things for a reason. I started to be aware of her reason *behind* the step. I became fascinated by it. I've worked as a classical ballet dancer and I've done my fair share of shows as a chorus boy, but I was always interested in why. Then Gillian hired me as a swing on a show called *Pickwick* in London, and I swung 19 tracks. I started to develop my brain. Then I got a job assisting Arlene Phillips and others on lots of different projects.

CRAMER: Your first job with Susan Stroman was in *Oklahoma* at the National Theatre of London, right?

CARLYLE: Yes. I was in that production, and then after five months I stepped out of the show and became Trevor Nunn's associate director and Stroman's associate choreographer. When it moved from the National Theatre to the West End, I staged it there. Then, once that closed, Stroman said, "You know I'm doing this movie in New York. I'd love you to come for three months. It would be a great adventure." So I came for three months, and while I was here, Nick Hytner, who directed the movie, knew how much I loved America and knew how much I wanted to be here. So, he wrote me into the movie, literally gave me a little part and some lines so I could join the Screen Actors Guild. Then, of course, he arranged my membership in Actor's Equity, and that, it turn, helped me apply for a green card. Ultimately, I sponsored myself for a green card and was successful. Once you have the card for five years, you can become a citizen. Now, I'm a proud American.

CRAMER: I think that's great, and your career is just gathering momentum.

CARLYLE: I'm learning and I love it. There isn't a day that goes by that I don't learn something as a director.

CRAMER: Who has been the biggest influence on your career?

CARLYLE: It's tricky. Susan Stroman represents a big turning point in my life. She was a clear and sure turning point because for the first time in my life I had close-up, firsthand experience with that kind of genius. That force of nature that says, "Get out of my way. No one is better in the world. Watch out." I'm a generation away from Bob Fosse, Michael Bennett, and Jerry Robbins. I missed all that. Plus, I'm English, totally different culture. So the first time I was in the room with someone like them, I knew it was special. I knew I wanted some of that, and she was the one. She opened the door for me, and put her arm around me and said, "Look, if I choreograph from here to here, that goes from stage right to stage left because people read from left to right. That's the strongest cross you can make." Simple things like that. Simple things that opened my eyes and made me look at them in a way I never looked at them before.

CRAMER: So, you thought she was as much a teacher or a mentor than simply somebody who hired you to assist.

CARLYLE: Yes. She was an incredible mentor because she has humanity about her as well. She's a great woman as well as being a great director and choreographer. She's someone you want to have dinner with. She's someone you want to wake up next to and read the *New York Times*, or go on vacation with, and when you're in the trenches doing a show, you want to be with her. Jerry Zaks has become a great directorial mentor because he's an actor's director, and I never really trained for that. All of my directing is instinct or experience. I have no formal training which I think is interesting because sometimes I go at directing in a way that isn't conventional or textbook. I have no need to break things down to beats, or discuss the spine of a character. Also, once you get to a certain level with actors in New York, they're so far beyond that, they don't need it. It's all instinctive. I've been lucky. I kind of leap frogged over that part, but Jerry is someone who is very clear about what he wants, what he needs, and why he needs it. He's influenced my approach a great deal. Lastly, I would name Jerry Robbins as a major influence because I come from a classical ballet background like him. I aspire to be a great director one day, and I hold Jerry Robbins' career up as an example of genuine greatness.

CRAMER: How do you select your assistants and use them? Do you have different people for different projects?

CARLYLE: Yes and no. I've been through the creative process four or fives years now, and had the same assistant or associate.

But I do use different dancers in preproduction, depending on the project. If I am doing something classical, for example, I get classical, ballet dancers in the room. I like smart assistants and those who are not afraid to cock their head, look at what I am doing and say, "Are you crazy? Are you nuts?" Sometimes I like a sounding board when I'm working in preproduction, because I don't like it in rehearsal. I wouldn't ever want that. There has to be one voice in rehearsal, but when I'm in the safety of a preproduction studio, I need someone I can fall down on the floor in front of, because that's my most vulnerable creative time. If I try to do a double tour holding a gauntlet and a handkerchief and I stagger into the mirror, I need assistants who will tell me to put my other foot in front to make the step work. So, I follow their suggestion and it's perfect. It's a very trusted position and they are a representation of me. If I'm wearing both hats, and I'm in a room directing a scene, my associate choreographer will be teaching dance next door. I want that voice to my energy, creativity, and my positivity. It has to be my agenda, my vision, and my way of doing it. I demand a lot, and many times rely on an assistant to really see a movement. The first time I'm able to see what's in my head it's not on my body anymore; it's on the assistant's body. So when I say I need three pirouettes, a Broadway smack down, a layout, and a double tour, I need to be able to see if that dancer can execute it. It's a bit like shopping. You try it on and you know immediately if it's going to work or fit. If it doesn't, you can try something else.

CRAMER: How long do you normally get to rehearse a show? I'm not talking preproduction because you decide that on your own since no one is paying for it.

CARLYLE: Not any more. Now, I get preproduction time allotted into my contracts. It's a part of the deal.

CRAMER: And you decide per show, what you need?

CARLYLE: Yes, because it can cost 6,000 dollars to rent a studio in New York City for a week. It's expensive. For example, I did four weeks of preproduction for *On the Town*. Some producers have a lot of money and you know you can have as much as six weeks. As a director, you want to take care of the show either way. You want it to succeed. Normally you have limited rehearsal time once you begin with your cast. So you think, "If I could rehearse *Finian's*

Rainbow in four weeks and tech it in nine days, I should try and do that, because I know it will help the show succeed." It's always varying levels of compromise at either the front or back end.

CRAMER: *Finian's Rainbow* is unique because it transferred from City Center Encores! to Broadway. Did you bring a vast majority of the cast and designers with you?

CARLYLE: I didn't.

CRAMER: So you're working on a new set with new lighting and costumes, but you've put the show up before. Do you have more or less time in this example?

CARLYLE: We needed four weeks. We added new principles, and being under that Broadway spotlight, it's much different than a staged concert holding a script. At Encores!, it's an immediate disclaimer that says, we only have five days to put on this show.

CRAMER: So, did you have more or less time for your Broadway debut as a choreographer on *Tale of Two Cities*?

CARLYLE: I had a lot of time. We had six good, full weeks. The set of *Tale of Two Cities* was designed by Tony Walton, and I wanted to work with Tony because he was my link to Bob Fosse. He was Fosse's designer. Walton designed the original *Pippin* and he won an Academy Award for *All that Jazz*. The set consisted of six, two-story units that moved 48 times in the course of the show, and it was very cinematic. At the top of Act Two, they came together to form the Bastille. Here is my big debut and I'm not choreographing dances, as there is little to no dance in the show. I am choreographing stagehands moving pieces of Tony Walton's amazing scenery. The set danced as there were no dancers in this production. It was really interesting.

CRAMER: Do you read music?

CARLYLE: Yes, I do. I used to play piano actually.

CRAMER: Is it a valuable tool for you?

CARLYLE: Oh, my God, yes. Learn to read music. Learn to play the piano even if you just learn the right hand. Learn about the music because if you're going to be a choreographer, you're going to have a dance arranger. That person sits with you and you create the dance music. It's so helpful for me and for them if I can speak their language. I think it shows respect, just like going to a foreign country and learning key words and phrases. It's not any different when you're working with the lighting designer. I know what LX117 is when I'm directing a show. It's that special light that hits Charlie Chaplin when he becomes a tramp. I need to know the terms because it shows respect to other artists.

CRAMER: So tell me about doing something like *Finian's Rainbow* where I believe you said earlier you cut 45 minutes from the show. Your knowledge of music must have enabled you to sit with the music director and make proper cuts depending on what you wanted to do.

CARLYLE: In general, even before I get in the room I know I can look at the score and sing the melody through to the repeat. Then, I'm thinking, "I've heard that already. It's 2011. We're not going to see that twice." So, you know I'm going to take out the repeat. Then when I meet with the music director, I'm in an informed position. I love my choreography to "sing," You can dance it without a pianist. I can simply hum it while I dance. I like to be musical and thought of as a musical person.

CRAMER: Your career has now spanned over a decade. What changes have you seen in ensemble casting in that time?

CARLYLE: Shows have gotten smaller, so that means that ensembles have gotten smaller. Furthermore, that means you can't carry a person who only has one skillset. Everybody has to be able to say a line strongly and clearly and sing on pitch. Singers must move well and everyone must be an actor.

CRAMER: What do you look for in someone when they walk through the door at an audition? Is there anything that you feel you must have regardless of the show?

CARLYLE: Rhythm, because styles come and go.

CRAMER: With a dancer, it's easy to give them a combination to determine rhythm. How do you find that in someone who is primarily a singer or actor?

CARLYLE: You hear it in the dialogue. A good writer has his own rhythm as does a good old-fashioned musical. The dialogue has a rhythm, so I'll give them a page of text that has rhythm to it. I'll listen and know. Even the character and principle actors dance a basic movement combination, so I can see them change their weight. I can see if they hear the music the way I hear the music.

CRAMER: Have you disregarded someone based on the way they walk in the room, or stand, or carry themselves?

CARLYLE: No, I wait. I give them a chance. I listen, because they may teach me something. I avoid knee-jerk reactions. As I've gotten older, I consider things more. I'll think about it for a day and then I'll cut it.

CRAMER: In a casting session, tell me how you choose between dancer A and B, both being of equal talent and type and at the top of your list in every deciding category.

CARLYLE: Experience. Who has the most experience, or if it's a Broadway show, I would call someone I know on their resume that has worked with them before and ask for an opinion. That's happened to me a few times, actually. I have had people who are equal in ability, but their reputation varies in some way.

CRAMER: Have you ever had to audition for the job of choreographer?

CARLYLE: No, I haven't. I was asked once, and I declined because I didn't think I was the right person for the job. It was not the style that I thought I would be able to deliver.

CRAMER: How do you go about researching a show?

CARLYLE: Well, you don't have to go to the library anymore. That's always nice. I do quite a bit of research. I actually enjoy it, and wish I had time to do more. I do research text, but I also do visual research. With *Tale of Two Cities* I did a great deal of research in French Art. *Finian's Rainbow* gave me the opportunity to research not only Irish and Irish Americans, but the world of magic, unions, and music of the time.

CRAMER: How much of your research do you actually share with the cast?

CARLYLE: I share it in a limited way because I think I need to be the conduit. Not all of that information is going to be relevant to cast members, and it needs to be filtered through me and my lens. On *Finian's*, for example, I was clearly telling the story from Finian's point of view. The whole show was skewed in that the audience wasn't allowed to watch the show through an anamorphic frame. They had to watch it through a curve, taken from his telescope, which is how he first saw Rainbow Valley. He saw it through a curve. Not a single cast member needs to know that. They couldn't care less, actually. They just want to know, "Am I standing in the right place?" So, research is good, but I think I have to be the one who ultimately doles out little pockets of information. Sometimes you do have the luxury of a day to improve, or you might have a day where you can sit with the people in a given scene and share information about the characters. This often includes visual and textual things, as well as correlating music. That, however, is rare.

CRAMER: How do you rehearse productions for Encores!?

CARLYLE: Legally it's ten days. *Stairway to Paradise* was the first one I did. We planned for a year and I did a month of preproduction in the studio, and then set 28 numbers in 5 days. *Finian's* was five days too. But there's something interesting about the energy of that, because you can't sit back and judge things. You have to hold hands as a group—hopefully with talented people—and jump. So, there is a bit of frenetic energy, but I enjoy it.

CRAMER: Do you approach staging and choreography differently?

CARLYLE: Yes. In staging I know exactly what I have to deliver. With choreography there's a different kind of pressure to deliver pyrotechnics or fireworks—big lifts or four pirouettes. In really fine musical staging, no one will even notice I was there. It looks like the characters are moving through space doing what they should.

CRAMER: How is the dynamic different when you teach or instruct actors versus dancers?

CARLYLE: The dynamic is actually different from person to person. Everybody learns things in a different way. Some dancers learn with terminology, some with counts, and some with rhythmic syllables. I am careful with actors as opposed to dancers. I used to be one, so there's a universal language. With actors, it's a little bit more of, "How are you feeling? What do you want to do"? Even if, ultimately, I know exactly what I want from them, I'm careful with them. I am mindful that they have a process too.

CRAMER: Do you find yourself going back to make changes more frequently or infrequently?

CARLYLE: Oh, that's a good question. I think it depends on how good the material is. Honestly, if the material is great, chances are I won't need to do very much. If there are holes in the material, or if it's soft and doesn't make sense in some way, I'd better be ready to roll up my sleeves and make some magic so you don't notice.

CRAMER: Before the film *Center Stage* brought you here to America, you had done direction and choreography for film and television in England. Can you discuss the differences in your process for the stage, versus your process for film and television? .

CARLYLE: I think one of the things I love about film and television is having ultimate control of the focus. In theatre, you're in a wide shot for the whole show, so you have to use the girl in the red dress to focus the audience. Or, you have to use a spotlight, or someone jumping up and down waving their hands and yelling loudly. Then the audience knows where to look. But there is something about having a camera and an editor that can help me direct the focus specifically and clearly. When I do a close-up on that notebook, we're all looking at the notebook. I love being able to control focus in that way. I think there's something great about POV, or point of view. I can put the camera over my shoulder and shoot you, or vice versa, and we can have this really dynamic conversation that may leave me completely out of the picture, and simply be a 3-minute reaction shot of you. There's something really interesting about that to me. I think director-choreographer Rob Marshall (*Chicago, Nine*) has made that into an art. I think he's turned the camera into another character in the play—into another dancer in the show. I think it's choreography of the highest order when you can choreograph the camera, and I aspire to that level of film and television direction.

CRAMER: Your most recent choreographic work on film is the 2008 movie *Deception,* starring Hugh Jackman. Can you touch on that?

CARLYLE: So, Hugh Jackman, who I knew from doing the National Theatre production of *Oklahoma,* called me and said this circus act they booked for the movie had dropped out, and asked if I could do him a favor. I think I had five days' notice. I met with the director, the cinematographer, and the production designer. We scouted some places very quickly and found a club in Brooklyn with a basement and I had them spray it all black and create the catwalk. For *Deception* I had three dancers for preproduction, and I filmed from one point of view, from another point of view, and from a third point of view. I cut it together before we shot it and I was able to show the director and the cinematographer how I wanted it to look—these are the angles I think I'm going to look at it from, and this is the color I think it should be. So, I came fully prepared conceptually to deliver, and it seemed to be fine with the team.

CRAMER: What were the challenges of working on the movie *Center Stage*?

CARLYLE: It was interesting because we had company members from the American Ballet Theater and New York City Ballet. Traditionally, those two companies don't mix. Their approaches to work and technique are quite different. That was actually the biggest challenge because the actual choreography of it, and the day-to-day dealing with it, was fine. I guess I was like the referee ballet master. I was the one that was there keeping the peace. I was like the jolly English guy who just got off the boat. Thank God I had classical training. You know, 10 or 11 years ago I could still do 5 pirouettes and a double tour.

CRAMER: So both companies respected you.

CARLYLE: They respected me because all I had to do was dance, and I had them.

CRAMER: I watch your work and it may be classical in nature, but you do some powerhouse lifts that aren't necessarily related to classical ballet. Does that come from morphing what you've done classically with something else? I mean, is it all a derivative of a classical approach, right?

CARLYLE: No, I don't. I think it's a derivative of story.

CRAMER: Do you experiment on bodies and play until you get what you like?

CARLYLE: Yes, I do. I don't make the association in my head, and it's not linked at all with the classical training. I had a Russian teacher, and partnering was slow and deliberate, not the least exciting. The one person that did excite me the most was a woman called Doriana Sanchez. She was in the movie *Dirty Dancing* and choreographed a show called *Copacabana* that I danced in London's West End. Doriana staged Cher's show as Caesars Palace. She was a great choreographer for partnering and created the disco partnering work on *So You Think You Can Dance.*

CRAMER: So, you learned a great deal when you were dancing as a professional.

CARLYLE: Yes, and partly because I was a giant man. I was able to lift these girls. I was perfect for the task. Actually, when I did *Oklahoma* for Stroman, I had 21 lifts in one number. We used to laugh about it. I was the guy who would jete over to stage left and lift someone, and then I would roll on the floor to stage right, and lift someone else. Yes, I was the perfect person to do that.

CRAMER: As you have said, you are on your way to Canada to do *Camelot.* What's next?

CARLYLE: I'm choreographing *Follies* at the Kennedy Center starring Bernadette Peters, Jan Maxwell, Danny Burstein, Ron Raines, and Elaine Paige. It's great for me, and in a funny kind of way, I think it's because Michael Bennett was involved in it. There is more dance in *Follies* than there is in any other Sondheim show. Recently I spent a week exploring the script and the score. There are many opportunities for dance. It's going to be great, and I have a huge company with 41 people.

CRAMER: Oh, my goodness. That's unheard of these days.

CARLYLE: I have a great design team, and I've been working on a Duke Ellington project called *Jump for Joy,* which is a lost Duke Ellington musical. It's an all-black review from 1941. We've been restoring and researching it, and finding old bits of music in the Smithsonian. I'm working on a show called *Chaplin*. It's the story of Charlie Chaplin, a man who told stories for a living, without saying a single word. As a director-choreographer, the opportunity to translate his story with dance is vast.

CRAMER: Will you articulate the difference between approaching a revival versus a new work?

CARLYLE: The revival is so much easier because there's a road-map. The raw pieces are in place for you to rearrange, or for you to change.

CRAMER: Or put your own spin on it.

CARLYLE: Absolutely. Perhaps your spin is simply to give it the point of view of 2011. That alone might be enough. On revivals you've got book, music, and lyrics done. On a new show, there are so many elements that you must bring together. It's just a much harder endeavor.

CRAMER: How do projects come to you? Is it the same now as it was ten years ago?

CARLYLE: It's a little different now. I read lots of works and like to do everything. I moved here very clearly because it's the land of opportunity. I feel that there is an opportunity to be had in every project and every show. Now, I have to learn to be more discerning. I have fantastic representation and they know how to say "no." I'm the crazy one that says yes to everything because I think it would be great for me. I'm certain I'm going to learn something. But the reality is that I have to make considered decisions sometimes. It also becomes like backing horses. It's like the sweepstakes. In order to survive you have to have ten shows on the go, because you don't know which one is going to make it to New York. It's tricky. Then there are also some things that you, as an artist, connect with. You feel and understand the material deeply. Some shows you take because you have to make rent. Sometimes it's as simple as, "I need something for June and July; I'm going to do this." So, it's an interesting balance. It's a little bit feast or famine, I think, but there are certain things I connect with. The *Chaplin* piece is a good example of that. It was something that really appealed to me. It's a story about two English brothers, one of whom moves to America to follow his dream, the other of whom stays behind to look after their mother. I have a brother. I used to be English, and he stayed behind. We had that conversation. I said, "If I go and do this, are you going to be okay to take care of our parents, because I'm not coming back. I'm going to do this." Then I read something like *Chaplin* and was stunned by it. I'm so deeply moved by it, and if I can get the audience to feel what I feel, it will be great. So, there are some things that move me on that kind of level, and then there are others. It's art and common essence. It's a tricky balance.

CRAMER: Do you have a worthy theatre story you'd like to share?

CARLYLE: Ironically, with how much I'm sharing today, I must admit that, I'm not very social. I seem like a very happy, jolly person, but I don't go out very much and I don't party. I don't because every night is a school night for me. I'm still on that treadmill of working so hard, and doing so much, that I haven't come up for air yet. I feel I'm at the beginning of my life in the theatre. I haven't earned a good story yet. I could tell you about the time Uma Thurman got caught up on the lights, or the time the prop woman appeared in the movie of *The Producers* in jeans and a sweatshirt. There was the time I was in charge of cat wrangling for the day on the same film, and that I was in charge of the pigeons too.

CRAMER: All true?

CARLYLE: Yes, but not worthy. I want to give you a really good story. I want to overachieve.

CRAMER: Maybe you'll have one after *Follies* with all those theatre veterans, stars who have been around for such long time.

CARLYLE: I think it's going to be interesting for the more experienced people in the cast to meet their younger selves. In casting, you have a youthful, hopeful, 16-year-old girl who is going to play young Stella, then you have a woman who is in her early sixties, who's been homeless, a smoker, a drinker, on the wrong side of the law, married, and now in a different kind of a relationship, playing older Stella. Seeing those two people come face to face is going to be very interesting, and, for me, the thing that moves me about the show.

CRAMER: Well, I think that's key to the show.

CARLYLE: Oh, my God. The "what ifs" of both real life and life in the theatre are so many. What if Sergio Trujillo hadn't left *In the Heights*? Would Sergio have a Tony for choreography, not Andy Blankenbuehler? What if Sergio hadn't had a scheduling conflict and I didn't choreograph *Mame* at the Kennedy Center. Would I be doing *Follies* now? There are a million of those.

CRAMER: You got to work with *the* Jerry Herman on *Mame?*

CARLYLE: Yes, Jerry Herman. That was an incredibly special experience. To be able to sit next to Jerry on the piano bench with my arm around him, and cut that music was surreal. That goes back to what we were saying. If you want to be taken seriously, you have to know what you're doing. You have to be able to say, "No. I need those three measures out Jerry. It's longer than my career so far; we better get those out!" That's why you've got to learn to read music because those moments come up, and if you don't know, you don't know. Then your work suffers because of it. You have to know about the light cue. You need to know about a circle and a half of material for a skirt. You have to know about a hand light in 1952, and know what the shoes of the period are. You have to know that stuff.

CRAMER: What advice would you give to aspiring performers making their way in show business today?

CARLYLE: Say yes. Just say yes. That's all you've got to do. The rest of it will take care of itself. I believe that because, as a creative person, as soon as you say no, there is a barrier up. You're done. Fear and uncertainty does that to people. Not knowing what you're doing does that to people. But if you can find a way to say yes, even if every fiber of your being says no, say yes, because it will lead you somewhere. It will enable you to keep moving, and that would be my only advice. I think that's how I work with people. When someone asks me a question or asks me for something, I say yes. You got it. If someone asks you if you can do three pirouettes, you say yes, and then you go home and figure out how the hell you're going to do three pirouettes. If someone asks if you can be a Broadway director and you've never directed before, and it's an 18-million dollar show, you say yes, because you never know what's going to happen.

CRAMER: Warren, thank you so much for taking the time out of your busy schedule. It was very generous, and a delight to meet you and have a wonderful conversation. I look forward with great anticipation to all the things you have coming up and wish you huge success.

CARLYLE: Oh, thank you so much for asking me to do this.

CHAPTER FIVE

Christopher Gattelli

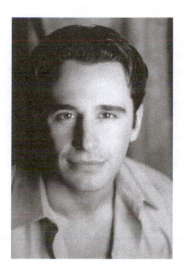

Christopher Gattelli began his dance training at 11 years of age in Pennsylvania. He claims he had to work hard because he wasn't naturally gifted. Through determination and perseverance, Christopher became a Star Search Grand Champion. He also won the title of Mr. Dance of America, a dance competition organized and promoted by Dance Masters of America. With those prestigious accomplishments in his back pocket, and further training through the Alvin Ailey School, Mr. Gattelli attended an audition for the Radio City Christmas Spectacular in New York City. There he earned his first professional job, and never looked back.

His performance career includes such dance-heavy hitters as *Cats,* the 1992 revival of *Guys and Dolls,* and the 1995 revival of *How to Succeed in Business Without Really Trying.* It was during

Cats that Christopher got his first taste of choreography, creating a number for the Broadway Cares/Equity Fights Aids benefit. Soon after, Christopher developed his talent for musical staging, choreographing *Godspell*—his first full-length production. Award nominations and wins followed with his choreographic work on the off-Broadway productions of *Bat Boy* and *Altar Boys*. Mr. Gattelli's illustrious and prolific Broadway career includes the choreography for *Newsies, Godspell, South Pacific, Women on the Verge of a Nervous Breakdown, 13, The Ritz, Sunday in the Park with George, Martin Short: Fame Becomes Me*, and *High Fidelity*. He is a multiple awards nominee and winner of the 2012 Tony Award for Best Choreography for *Newsies*.

Apart from being a resident choreographer for three seasons on *The Rosie O'Donnell Show*, Christopher has choreographed and directed regionally at La Jolla Playhouse, Goodspeed Opera House, and Paper Mill Playhouse. He also choreographed several special benefit concerts, including *Chess* with Josh Grobin, and *Hair* with Jennifer Hudson. He is also the director of the musical spoof SILENCE! *The Musical*, which ran in the 2005 NYC Fringe Festival, in London, and is still currently running off-Broadway.

CRAMER: Chris, you started dancing at age 11 in Bristol, Pennsylvania.

GATTELLI: Yes, I did.

CRAMER: You were a grand champion dance winner on *Star Search*. For our readers, that was a precursor to all the reality competition shows we now see on television. *Start Search* had singers, actors, dancers, comedians, and other types of performers. Were you a soloist, or in a group?

GATTELLI: I was in a group of five, and the only boy. We were called *Mirage*. It was this incredible period of my life. I started out in a dance studio and worked really hard because I wasn't naturally gifted. That same year, I got a scholarship to Alvin Ailey here in Manhattan. Since I lived in the Philadelphia area, I worked a schedule out with my school so that I was able to take my major classes in the morning, jump on the train to go to Ailey's, take three or four classes a day, and then head home. That intensive training sent me flying in terms of my progress and technique. I found a studio in Passaic, New Jersey, right on the bus route that was home to the former winning dance group, *America's Apple Pie*. I walked into her studio and the owner looked at me and asked, "A talented boy?" So, she put together a group of five, entered us, we got on, and we won. We ended up winning six shows, and we had the distinction of being the only grand-prize winners when the producers decided to compete different genres against each other.

CRAMER: Well, that must have been thrilling for a 15-year old! Your first professional job was at Radio City Music Hall here in New York City, and that led to incredible jobs and great connections. This story has some great lessons for students.

GATTELLI: I auditioned for the Christmas show when I was 17 with my best friend Laurie. We had our whole lives planned, and as new kids on the block, we were going to audition for everything in New York City, and give ourselves this finite amount of time to get a show. If we didn't get it, we'd move out to Los Angeles and try there. You know the story. Anyway, I auditioned for Linda Haberman, Scott Salmon, and Chris Chadman's assistant.

CRAMER: I'll remind readers that Chris Chadman was the choreographer of the 1992 revival of *Guys and Dolls* and Scott was the choreographer of the original Broadway production of *La Cage aux Folles*.

GATTELLI: Scott was choreographing the Radio City show. All the other dancers in the room were 5'10" and there was partnering. There I was, so short, but I went into every part with such determination. Linda tapped me on the shoulder, and I was so excited because that meant that Scott would see me dance. So, sure enough, Scott came in and kept putting me through all my paces. At the end of the day he said, "You look like a technician." He allowed me to do some of my dance and ballet "tricks" for him, and was very happy with my work. Based on what he saw that day, he created a feature, just for me, in the show. I was this little pipsqueak, you know, with all these big male dancers. It was so exciting and overwhelming at the same time.

CRAMER: Didn't that job audition parlay itself into jobs in both *Guys and Dolls* and *Cats*?

GATTELLI: Yes. That one audition literally made my career. That's why when I teach workshops and classes, I always encourage students to go to every audition. I could have waited for a Tommy Djilas audition for *The Music Man*. But you have to try. That was one of those situations where I went to this audition not expecting anything. I wasn't even right for the job at all and I got it! Then Linda, who assisted Chris Chadman on *Guys and Dolls,* was casting the first national tour. She said, "You should really come in; I think Chris would like you." Okay, sure. Went in, boom, I got the job. I didn't even go to the callbacks because I had a job out of town. Chris said, "You're in; don't worry." If, knock on wood, I ever get to stand up on stage and receive a choreographic award, I'm thanking them both because they were huge influences in my life. They left us too early. But in every project I do, I always think of them. To me, Chris brought the technical precision of Fosse to his creativity and storytelling, whereas Scott was like the showman, always 50 surprises in a number, with glitz and glamour. Being that my first exposure to those two talents happened at the same time, it influenced me so heavily that I always think of them when I'm working.

CRAMER: You got cast as Mistoffelees in *Cats* since the same casting director handled *Cats* and *Guys and Dolls*. However, you got cast in *How to Succeed* because of the Christmas show audition, once again.

GATTELLI: Right. Well, back in the day, Radio City did a Christmas and Easter show. *How to Succeed* choreographer, Wayne Cilento, played Easter Rabbit in the Easter show. Wayne remembered me from the show because, again, I had features. I went in for a replacement audition. Wayne said, "Oh, my God! It's you!" Boom. Got the job. It just keeps rolling, those opportunities. It's unbelievable to think where it started—that one fluke audition, I wasn't even right for, literally led to my entire career.

CRAMER: Talk about your participation as a choreographer in Broadway Cares/Equity Fights AIDS and who was in the audience that changed your life.

GATTELLI: I was doing *Cats* at the time, and a fellow cast member who I shared a dressing room with, wanted to do a number in the benefit to showcase all the talented dancers we had in our production. We were in long running show, and not many New Yorkers saw it anymore, just tourists. So I did a number for *Cats*. It was set to the song "Fever," but we called it "Feline." It was a sultry, jazz number. We wore red gloves and had tails. The story had some real wit. It was lots of fun. Broadway Cares' Tom Viola loved it and asked me to do the opening number for the Easter Bonnet benefit at the New Amsterdam Theatre. It was going to be the first performance in that space after the theatre's renovation. I was honored to be asked. The New Amsterdam opening was such a big, big deal. We asked five of the original *Ziegfeld Follies* girls to be a part of the number, which was an amazing experience. One still danced. She was 94 at the time.

CRAMER: Are you talking about Doris Humphries?

GATTELLI: Doris, yes.

CRAMER: Well, you know, Doris is from Norman, Oklahoma, home of the University of Oklahoma.

GATTELLI: Oh, my God!

CRAMER: Yes, Doris Eaton Travis is a hometown girl, and I knew her very well. She sat in the front row of many a show I've directed and choreographed.

GATTELLI: That makes me so emotional.

CRAMER: I've got little goose bumps.

GATTELLI: She got up on that stage at 94 and said, "I want to dance the same routine that I did 79 years ago." She launched into *Mandy* on the same stage, and literally stopped the show cold. People stood, cheering, and the dancers in the number performed behind her. It was a glorious moment. Rosie O'Donnell happened to be in the audience for that performance, and she said, "I want that number on the show. Somehow we have to get Doris and the dancers on the show." So we did it, and I staged it for the show, and it was great fun. *The Rosie O'Donnell Show* at that time was a very big deal. She gave so much to the Broadway Community by bringing so many stage shows on the air. At the time, Jerry Mitchell was the show choreographer, but his career was really taking off. *The Full Monty* had just opened. Jerry needed someone to temporarily take over for him, and he recommended me to Rosie. Though ultimately I was to choreograph in Florida at Disney World, I was first asked to do a test run at Nickelodeon. I knew nothing about camera work, and I had to do some serious homework to be prepared. It went quite well, and Florida was convinced I could do the big Disney job. To this day, it just baffles me that I actually pulled it off, because it was a full-on musical number that you would do from something like *Singin in the Rain*. They had the characters running down Main Street in Disney World, and we were in every part of the park doing shoots on rides. I mean, the dancing was crazy, and I thought my head was going to explode.

CRAMER: Talk about a fast education.

GATTELLI: It was unbelievable. The number was rehearsed, camera blocked, filmed, taped, and edited. Then we had to rehearse a live show that the taped version went into. I'd never done that in my life. It was staggering. After that, Jerry stayed busy, so for the last bit of Rosie's television show, we ended up switching off. I had so much clout when I was working on her show. I went in for a couple things, and someone always said, "Well, this is the choreographer for *The Rosie O'Donnell Show*."

CRAMER: What show got your choreographic career rolling?

GATTELLI: My first choreographic job on a full production was *Godspell* for Phoenix Productions, based on a friend's recommendation. The show was directed by *Godspell* composer, Stephen

Schwartz' son, Scott. Scott needed a choreographer, and we got along great. Stephen wrote some new material for the production, and it had a real family feel. I had never done a full-book musical before, but it went great. At the same time, Scott was in workshop mode for a new show called *Bat Boy*. At one point, he needed a little movement for one of the characters, and he persuaded me to do it. When it came time for the full production, he asked if I wanted to do it, and I said, "Sure!" It was a really great show off-Broadway, and I knew I had to do it. Through all of that process, I never stopped performing. *Cats* was great because management was so flexible with my schedule. They would let me go to Disney World to do the show for Rosie, as well as other projects. They were so supportive. I went from *How to Succeed* to *Cats*, and then right into *Fosse*. I was doing *Fosse* toward the end of the run when I got *Bat Boy*. I though to myself, "This is really serious now."

CRAMER: Was that the turning point where you thought, creatively, you had to make a choice?

GATTELLI: That was the thing. *Bat Boy* could have had a long run. I knew I really needed to prepare for that, because it could be a big stepping-stone for the next phase of my career. So, I left *Fosse*. That was the first time I stopped performing since I started, essentially. It was scary, but it was *Bat Boy*. Then came a string of amazing shows.

CRAMER: *Yes. Bat Boy, tick . . . tick . . . BOOM!, Martin Short, Altar Boys, High Fidelity, The Ritz, Sunday in the Park with George, South Pacific, 13, Women on the Verge* and *Silence!*. That's just Broadway and off-Broadway. That doesn't count the benefits—the *Hair* benefit with Jennifer Hudson, and the *Chess* benefit with Josh Groban. That doesn't count tours and regional productions either. You're just peddling as fast as you can.

GATTELLI: I'm so blessed. It's been the most amazing run. I still can't believe it.

CRAMER: I know projects are flying at you, but, humbly, have you become more selective? Are they picking you? Are you picking them?

GATTELLI: Yes, it's both. It's funny that we are talking about this because it's been a bit of a turning point lately with regard to what's coming at me. Much of what I've done to this point and what has made my career a success has been musical staging. And it's funny, because when I started, that wasn't my intent. My intent was to choreograph numbers much like I did for the benefits I mentioned earlier.

CRAMER: In other words, full-blown dance numbers.

GATTELLI: Yes. Jump, turn, and kick as high and as fast as you could because I wanted my choreography to reflect what I was doing in my performing life I suppose. You just want to blow it out. I remember feeling that I was ready to do the huge dance and big tap shows. Incredibly, the most gratuitous blessing out of all of this is that fate said, "Well, you need to learn this first." So, when I worked with Scott, he's the one who said, "Wait, wait, wait. Now what story are we telling through this number? How do we start? What do we need to learn? How do the characters need to turn? What changes them by the end of this number? How can we accomplish this without singing it, or how can we take some of that dialogue and put it in the middle?" It was literally like slamming on the brakes. I thought, "Wow, this is what it's really about. It's storytelling." Working with the companies of *Bat Boy*, *Godspell*, and *tick . . . tick, BOOM!*, was the start. Yes, there were dancers, of course, but these weren't shows with an ensemble of dancers. It was principal cast members who were acting, singing, and dancing. So, immediately I had to figure out, "How do you talk to an actor?" It's not like, "Okay, you're going to turn here and jump." The actor says, "Well, why am I turning?" I explain, "Because it looks great." Well, that doesn't work. You have to be able to say, "You're turning because you're so excited that you're going to reach for this stool, and you're jumping up on this stool and kicking, because you're happy!" As a choreographer, you are giving everything a meaning and everything a reason, and learning how to speak to an actor in those terms.

CRAMER: Then you are saying that you do approach actors and dancers differently?

GATTELLI: Absolutely. Most dancers want to be instructed and actors want to contribute. It's good to roll with the punches. If an actor says, "I wish I could do that because I'm feeling this," I want to try to work it in. Movement becomes more natural and character based. Take *Altar Boys,* for example. The boys came up with great and specific ideas at times. Because of working like that, I ended up becoming known for my musical staging.

CRAMER: You don't see musical staging listed separately very often, except when *your* name is listed. Directors are usually credited with musical staging when there is no perceived "choreography" per se. It's very interesting.

GATTELLI: Which is hilarious to me because it wasn't what I ever expected or intended. It was the best way for me to learn, because now that I am transitioning into directing, I have the skills I need. I would have never been able to do it, had I not learned the basics of the craft while staging.

CRAMER: You've done many shows with Scott Schwartz and Bartlett Sher. You must have a short hand with those artists.

GATTELLI: Absolutely.

CRAMER: Whether you create staging or choreography, as the lines are blurred between the two, do you find that you work so tightly with these directors, that you almost overlap what is created in a scene or a song?

GATTELLI: Well, it's funny. Yes, definitely with Bartlett. He is the most intense, amazing collaborator ever. You're always on your feet, thinking and going in the moment. I was terrified for *South Pacific*. There was no preproduction. None. He said, "Don't do it. Do your research, come in the room, and we'll go."

CRAMER: I am certain that normally, you come in completely prepared.

GATTELLI: Absolutely. Well, until that show, yes. That's all I ever knew because of the Rosie O'Donnell days.

CRAMER: Be ready.

GATTELLI: You have to be ready for anything, so you must have options A, B, and C done, because if she doesn't like that camera angle, you've got to reverse that section so that the kids can face this camera. You must be "uber" prepared. Working with Bart was trial and error and experimentation, and go, go, go, in the moment.

CRAMER: You were nominated for a Tony Award and a Drama Desk Award for your work in that show.

GATTELLI: It was a beautiful production. I'm so proud.

CRAMER: Have you been an assistant or a dance captain?

GATTELLI: I've never assisted, actually. I mean, that's the funny thing, because originally that was my plan.

CRAMER: I think it's every performer's plan if they want to be a choreographer or director. They assume they'll pay their dues and climb the ladder in a traditional way.

GATTELLI: Right. I'll be an assistant dance captain, dance captain, and then I'll assist someone. But for me it was just "poof," and I was there. It's crazy.

CRAMER: How do you select your assistants?

GATTELLI: Generally, it's someone different for every show because the requirements are different. If it's musical staging, my assistants must have the ability to speak and work with actors. I need someone who thinks more like a director but also has a dance or very strong movement background. My upcoming project *Funny Girl* requires someone with tap knowledge, who I really like as a person, so that we can have fun in the room, be silly and goofy. We need that sensibility and sense of humor going on for the show. We won't have to edit ourselves and be able to be open and free and in the rehearsal room.

CRAMER: Have your assistants danced or performed in shows for you, or been a dance captain for you?

GATTELLI: Yes, they have. I usually select someone who has worked with me in a show or worked for me on a project. But, I don't just have that one "go to" person. I might even select someone from an audition. My audition process is quite actor driven. I make the combinations more of an actor-dance piece. I never do the old pirouette, kick, and jump just to see the motors turn. I will try to set up the combo with intent. For example, we had a *Newsies* audition just last week. I tell the boys, "Ok, you are out in the street, the square, and you are drawing a line in the dirt with your foot." I am very specific about how I want something danced. So, the first time I say, "Remember, try to hit everything I told you. Try to nail that pirouette, but you're drawing with your foot in the dirt and your eyes have to communicate that. Try to get it all in. The second time, just have the time of your life, let it go, and take what I gave you and do it for yourself. I want you to have a great time." Well, I guess I'm telling all my secrets. But that really helps me. The first time is for me, and I see the focus and see them try to do what they think I'm saying, what they're trying to interpret. Then the second time, frees them from trying to perform for me and get the job.

CRAMER: You're not just getting dancers. You're getting actors who dance.

GATTELLI: Absolutely. It is always the dancer you just described, who ends up getting the job, nine times out of ten. So, it's like cutting to the quick. At this point, everyone should be able to do a double pirouette. I'm going for the dancer who's listening to what I'm saying. I don't care if you fall out of your double, that's what rehearsals are for. We'll clean and bust our butts in rehearsals to get it right. But in the audition, I want to see the dancers process the finer details. I don't care if you fall on the floor and take risks. Be in it and go. Then, usually, I can tell from that, from the way dancers perform my combinations, if they've heard my buzz phrases. Just like the line in the dirt; I want to know how they interpret that. Are they really listening, or are they just dancing the steps? So, if I am looking for a dance captain, assistant, or an associate, in terms of acting, I'm looking for someone smart. Let's face it, eventually that person is going to be taking over an entire room and leading the dancers. They have to be able to talk to them and communicate my acting intent for that number. They have to discuss the how and why of the number, as well as focus and other key elements. The assistant's job has to be more than just a "clean up" person.

CRAMER: I'd like for you to talk a bit about your process in pre-production. Do you have a standard process?

GATTELLI: No, it's different for every show, but I do always start out by listening to the music a million times, until it is literally a part of me.

CRAMER: Are you listening to piano or an orchestration?

GATTELLI: That varies too. Sometimes it's a demo that someone does. If it's a new work, it is usually piano. I try to imagine the hits in my head, and where it will go musically. For example, in *Newsies,* I'm listening to the workshop, which was just piano and drums. Then I'll also listen to the soundtrack, because it's fully orchestrated. Each version will inspire me in different ways. Then I will brainstorm with my assistant, and we get the big sections laid out—sections A, B, C, D, and so forth in each number. Then normally, just because it frees me up, I work by myself in my head, or as silly as it sounds, the shower. Not that I jump up and down, but because it's isolated and I can just be silly, I can really get myself into the heads of the characters, and just get it all out, no matter what it is. Then I'll clean it up and take it to my assistant. We'll refine it and put it on the dancers, and then mold it. My first big dance show was *Women on the Verge*. The audition was really important because it was my first time to put an impression out into the dance community of how I work and how I "do my thing." My assistant and I selected the music and mapped out the entire combination, complete with partnering at the end. It took hours. The morning of the audition, I came in and told my assistant that I redid the whole thing. I changed the song and taught him the combo in 10 minutes. I had to think about it on my own, and be in my own space to make it work. We had a live drummer and a great cut of the audition song, and decided not to partner until callbacks. That way, the dancers could really "throw it down" on the first day of auditions. To this day, I still meet people on the street that tell me they do the *Verge* combination in their living room. They had so much fun. That's how I want my auditions to be.

CRAMER: Do you dance anymore yourself, or do you hire assistants that can go beyond your imagination with their technique?

GATTELLI: I do dance everything I choreograph, but not "facility wise." When I kick, I don't kick to my head like I used to. However, when I tell the boys we will do a double pirouette to a double tour, I still whip it out so that I can say, "Come on kids!" I love that I still get to do it when I can. My assistants dance steps exactly the way they should look, so I love my assistants.

CRAMER: For our readers, most shows have what is called, a Bible. This is the entire show written in tracks (parts) so that the show can be re-created with the original artistic vision in tact. Who wrote the Bible for *South Pacific*, a dance captain, or an assistant?

GATTELLI: That was actually our genius dance captain. It was a very difficult process for her because our show was so much more organic and free. It wasn't strict enough movement to notate easily. Plus, we were working until the very last second, and constantly changing things. She wrote 40 tracks.

CRAMER: Do you have a great memory?

GATTELLI: I have a cuckoo memory. If I watch the show, I've got it. During run-throughs and clean ups, others always ask, "Why aren't you notating?" I've got it to the point that I could literally replay the entire performance in my head, then go back, go through all the notes that I was thinking as it was being performed, and write them down. I find that if I take notes for myself, I get lost. I can't really watch the stage. I need to sit and watch and absorb it all, instead of looking down to write, and missing something else. Even if someone takes notes for me, I miss something while I am communicating to the note writer. It's just best if I watch and capitalize on my memory skill. Anytime I have down time, I write out notes of whatever has just taken place. It is smaller pieces that way, and not an entire show.

CRAMER: That's really exceptional, and kind of fun.

GATTELLI: Yes. It's a fun little gift. You still need a good Bible if the show is going to have multiple productions, and we were lucky to have such a competent and left-brained dance captain.

CRAMER: How you go about research? Do you enjoy it?

GATTELLI: I think it's almost the best part of the process. My projects have been so diverse. I've been all over the map. I'm constantly being exposed to all these new forms and time periods. It doesn't even matter if it's dance or not, because I have gotten an education. There's a project coming up that I'm doing; it's like my secret weapon because there are many different forms of dance in it. I was actually in rehearsals for that, and I had to find someone who knew real Charleston, not Broadway Charleston—authentic down and dirty Charleston. Similarly, for *South Pacific*, we found someone whose specialty was swing dance of that time period. You can always simply take a swing dance class or learn a basic Charleston, but I found people who knew how the social classes of these time periods danced together, how people of different races moved, and what that means to their bodies. In *South Pacific* the Seabees, nurses, and soldiers might all move differently. Then add the African Americans in, and you have even more movement choices. It's both fascinating and complicated. You have one move and four or five ways to do it. It gives the show a unity and authenticity, but individuality, all at the same time. That's what made it so rich. The cast was phenomenal at picking it up and going there with it, because it was such a tedious process. I was just telling someone earlier that all the technique we work for in class, our whole lives becomes a bit worthless in this process. You take all that you have learned and throw it out the window. You can't point your feet, or straighten your arm, or keep your shoulders down. Literally, you have to retrain your body to look average.

CRAMER: Does your preproduction time vary for each show?

GATTELLI: Yes, it depends on the knowledge I have of the particular period. Preproduction is longer if I have to do more research because I am unfamiliar with a particular period. I Google search and look at hundreds of images to immerse myself in the period. If video is available, I watch all I can. Also, preproduction takes much longer if it is a dance-heavy show. I can spend two or three weeks in the studio creating stories, characters, and steps. I don't put a time limit or time pressure on myself, or my assistants. Some days we get nothing done. Some days we are laser focused and get a great deal done. It might be eight counts, but if it's quality work and it's right, then that is the days' goal. I never say, "Well, I must have this number completed by the end of the day." I can't inflict that much pressure on anyone in the studio.

CRAMER: Do producers normally cover costs of preproduction, such as studio rental and other expenses?

GATTELLI: Disney has been generous with *Newsies*. I have the time I need and the dancers and assistants that I need. With other shows, I have been completely on my own, so it does vary a great deal. Some producers just don't have the money for preproduction, and they are honest about it up front.

CRAMER: Once a show goes into rehearsal on day one, how much time do you have to get a show up?

GATTELLI: On average, it is about three and a half to four weeks before we get into the theatre and begin tech rehearsals.

CRAMER: How do you structure a number and work with a dance arranger?

GATTELLI: I dissect a number in terms of story. I'll bullet point the key elements and work from a character-based place. Take "Seize the Day" from *Newsies* as an example. The leader begins the number, and then the second in command is added, followed by different boys based on their character. Some are outgoing and would follow next; some are shy and would join later. Then I'll talk through all the story points with my arranger, Mark Hummel. I selected him because he was Chris Chadman's dance arranger for *Guys and Dolls,* and I wanted whomever Chris had. So with Mark, I went through the song and highlighted every acting beat we needed in the dance break, and arrived at the final pass where the boys are about to sing again and really own the number—everything detailed and laid out. Mark went away overnight, and came back and played through the most glorious dance break with every color that I asked for. It couldn't have been better. I do not choreograph first, and then ask an arranger to develop and create music around my steps. I must have music first. Music inspires me to move. Every sound you hear can't inspire an idea, and if you have created the music based on character, you can't miss. We then take the music, create the dance breaks, and based on dancers' abilities, we add or subtract what we need. Mark goes back in and adds hits, makes adjustments. Then, back to us until we fine-tune the entire piece.

CRAMER: Do you read music? Do you think it is a necessary skill for a choreographer?

GATTELLI: I have been playing the piano since I was four years old. However, I don't believe that reading music is a necessary skill for a choreographer. It helps me because I can more easily speak to a dance arranger, orchestrator, or composer. When you have the same vocabulary, communication is so much easier, and it expedites the process.

CRAMER: What kind of a rehearsal environment do you try to create?

GATTELLI: My ego or lack thereof is definitely a positive thing about my rehearsal environment. I will never say I have the best answer in the room. Never. We're creating this together, whether I'm directing or choreographing, we're all in the room together. If someone has an idea that's better than mine, just say it. If I'm choreographing something on someone's right side and they're better on the left, just tell me. It's not about me. It's not about doing exactly what I say because of my ego. I want what's best for the show, and if it means I change something because of another person's idea, great. Let's do it. When I was directing *SILENCE!*, the unauthorized parody of *Silence of the Lambs,* in its original run at the Fringe Festival, I was having a creative block. My stage manger came up with a really funny idea about the running sequence at the top of the show, and I was thrilled. I don't care where a great idea comes from. It's about putting up the best show you can.

CRAMER: *Newsies* must have been a monumentally huge draw. Can you estimate how many dancers showed up to audition for you?

GATTELLI: God, there were so many boys, probably 400. I can't even tell you how many girls there were.

CRAMER: Clearly they are not all going to get the job. Can you share your thoughts on auditions and the tough process so many go through?

GATTELLI: Clearly they're so talented, and it's not going to have anything to do with their abilities. I love giving people jobs; it breaks my heart not to. So, just dance and have a great time. You're either going to be right for the show, or not right this time, and that's okay. Enjoy it. Just dance. Try not to focus on the pressure. We put enough pressure on ourselves. I remember when I was auditioning. I was my own worst enemy—the self-critic. "I shouldn't have worn this. I fell out of my turn. I should have held that note and not cut it off," and so on. I want to see you at your best. I don't want to see you doing what you think *I want you to do*. Be yourself, because you are only right or wrong for this particular show this time. Just present yourself at your best. That's all you can do. That's my mantra, and that should be reflected in my rehearsal room. If people close up on you at a rehearsal because they think that you want something specific only, or you're trying to impose, they're not going to be creative. You need people at the height of creativity while you're working on a show, or you're not going to get what you need. Worse, you'll end up with what you started with and I don't want that. Like I always say, I go into a rehearsal room at 75 percent. I mean, unless it's Bart Sher. Then no percent.

CRAMER: So, your rehearsal room is very collaborative.

GATTELLI: Yes. I don't think anyone should be told and dictated what to do all the time. And again, this is just me. I know that works for other people, and there are peak performers that respond to that, because they just love to know specifics. But, I believe I get the best from the performer when he or she has a voice. They want to contribute as actors. So, I try to keep the room as open as I can.

CRAMER: Hypothetically, if you had an opportunity to talk to your cast before day one of rehearsal, what would you say to prepare them for the first day with you?

GATTELLI: Wow! That's a really good question. It depends on what it is, but I think I would probably say: do a little research on your own. Get in the head of the characters and the time period. Know something about it so you can have input. For example, when we start creating, and I start asking for things, you can say, "Oh, well, I saw Marilyn Monroe do this in a movie, and I loved the way that looked on her. I think that since my character is a bit of a vamp, I could try this." Here's a more tangible example. When we were staging *Alter Boys*, I would recommend that the boys watch videos of the Backstreet Boys and 'N Sync. That way they can get in the headspace of that kind of fun and bounce, because there's always a bounce to those boy bands. There's a natural thing that they do. So, when I suggest a reference, you, as a cast member, are already there. Communication is smooth and fast. Again, it gives the performers an opportunity to create, and not feel like each move is dictated. They have a say in what is staged. Most actors respond well, and it comes across on stage, right out to the audience.

CRAMER: I would like to discuss your collaboration process with scenic, lighting, and costume designers. By the time you are choreographing, the set is usually in its final stages or complete, but costumes and lighting are usually in earlier stages. When you visualize a number choreographically, do you also visualize costumes, or a specific lighting look?

GATTELLI: My collaboration with designers is really 50–50 in almost all scenarios. I learned early on that it is all a bit trial and error. Designers like to have their say and create first. I'll come in with ideas, and it is give-and-take based on what we see when we try something. I don't want anyone to feel like it can only work one way. I've found that when you give them too much, it makes them back off, and they may say, "OK," but they don't play ball. Whereas, if you go in with 50 percent, or maybe *secretly* have 90 percent, but you offer up only the 50, then you get to play ball a bit. I think this goes for all departments. If you don't have that balance with your creatives or your cast, again, I feel like you're not letting them rise to their game. Listen, I feel this way when I'm a choreographer, and a director says, "Can you add a tap step right there so they can cross downstage right?" I'd rather have the director say, "Chris, can you help me get the actor to cross downstage?" Then, it's a collaborative process. Designers are no different. Everyone is hired because they are creative geniuses, and can bring something to the table. I have worked with several people many times now. There are "go to" people in my life that have my same sensibility and aesthetic sense. There is a respect and a short hand that comes with repeated collaboration. You start feeding off each other creatively the more you work together and establish a team.

CRAMER: I have observed and experienced two different scenarios with directors and choreographers. The two can work in tandem, or the choreographer is asked to creatively realize the director's vision. I sometimes think that choreographers can be lower on the totem pole than one might prefer.

GATTELLI: It's not too far from the truth. I believe it completely depends on the director. When I did *Alter Boys,* for example, director Stafford Arima and I literally read each other's minds, and we did that show together. For as much concept and direction he did, I was there with him, and vice versa. It was a tag team effort, and that's the best collaboration. The best compliment I can ever receive is to be told, "I couldn't tell where your work stopped and the director's started." The work should be seamless, and the vision served. Now, there have been projects of late that I've walked into with the model already finished. Then you're limited creatively and it can be a bit stifling. Ultimately, the director has the final say. He's the captain of the ship, and I always respect that. But at least you know that you've had a say, and by the time I've choreographed the numbers, I know I've taken care of myself. I have levels and set pieces they can jump off of, and a place for them to get props. So, you know going in that you're protected, rather than when you're just handed the show in model form. Now, when you're directing, input is more like 90 percent. I'll use *SILENCE!* as an example. That production was a very specific concept because we got into the Fringe Festival, and you never have a budget for that. You only have 500 dollars to put on a show. So, here's the concept: You have a group of actors from a West Virginia summer-stock group, and you're all fans of the *Silence of the Lambs* movie. The subject of the movie comes up at lunch one day while you're rehearsing *Hello, Dolly!* during the day, and performing *Rent* at night. During lunch break, someone says, "Oh, I saw *Silence of the Lambs* on TBS last night. Wouldn't that make a great musical?" Then, everyone chimes in. "We should really do that." So this group writes the script, submits it to the Fringe Festival, and gets accepted. Then they pack whatever they can, get a van, and drive to New York to perform it at the Fringe. The set is literally four moving panels that do all these maneuvers. So, it's specifically created to be on the cheap. There's a great deal of humor in that. In this instance, I had a great deal of input, but I wore both hats as the director and choreographer.

CRAMER: Was the segue from choreographer to director-choreographer a specific choice?

GATTELLI: I think with any choreographer, directing is an inevitable progression on some level. As a choreographer, you are asked create to a story within a song. You have the tools. Plus, you work with inspirational directors. I've had the pleasure and good fortune to work with some of the very best including Bart Sher, Walter Bobbie, Michael Mayer, and Joe Mantello. You hear the way they speak to actors and how they communicate and tell stories; it's not that different than what choreographers do with music and steps. So, it was never a conscious choice for me. *SILENCE!* was the first show that gave me the opportunity to direct and choreograph. It came my way right after *Altar Boys.*

CRAMER: You have done four revivals: *Godspell, The Ritz, Sunday in the Park*, and *South Pacific*. Do you prefer rivals or new works?

GATTELLI: That's tricky. I love doing revivals because if the show is being done again, it is because the first run was such a success. Something about it worked, structurally or musically, and the audiences enjoyed it. As a creative artist, you get to go back in and do the show differently, with some new elements. Hopefully you can improve it on some level, or just give it a fresh eye. With a new work, the excitement is getting to put your stamp on it. Creatively, there is nothing quite like being a part of something brand new that no one has seen or heard. It's a pretty big thrill to answer questions like, "How many dancers do I want? How shall I structure this number? Shall I make it a tap number? Should there be a new song for this moment? How long shall I make the dance break? How is this section going to work with the scenic look?" It's such a remarkable, exciting, and nerve-wracking process to be a part of. The ride is thrilling, and it enables you to flex every creative muscle you have, putting everything on the table. So, forced to make a choice, I would say I prefer a new work, but there are pros and cons with either choice.

CRAMER: What has been your most rewarding theatrical experience to date?

GATTELLI: There have been so many, that I could probably fill pages with them. I'll probably become emotional talking about it, but one experience does stand out, and that is the creation of "Seize the Day" in *Newsies* with my boys. The show is about a younger generation trying to make their way, leave their mark, have their say, and sit at the adult table. "Seize the Day" embodies all these ideas. For the boys and me, it works on two levels. In the show, the number functions exactly as it should. It reveals the boys' ability, determination, skill, and passion to make their lives better. For me, it's electric because you watch those boys do it live, right in front of you, pushing ability forward and watching what they can contribute as artists. Amazing technique is still alive and well. Acting and singing crazy notes while you're dancing is still alive and well. To be able to create that number with that special group of individuals was beyond description. To top it off, the boys performed that number right after I won the Tony for Best Choreography. It was the juxtaposition of the award and the number that made it positively astounding. I'll never forget it.

CRAMER: Can you share some words of wisdom to aspiring performers?

GATTELLI: Can I share several thoughts? This question is so important to me.

CRAMER: Please. I am sure every thought you share will most certainly be an inspiration.

GATTELLI: First and foremost, if you love musical theatre, continue to pursue it. Don't let anyone deter you, no matter how many times people tell you "no," or how many times you *don't* get the job. Everyone has their day. Some people snap up a job within days or weeks of moving to the city. For others, it takes a little longer. It's definitely hard, but if you love it, persevere, you will have your day. That's a given in my book. Now, how do you make sure that happens? Be as prepared as you can for any job you are seeking—sleep, take class, stay in shape, study voice, come early, warm-up, and hone your instrument. Research the show to the absolute best of your ability. When you go in to sing, make sure you have more than one song. Be completely comfortable singing each song in your book. When you go in for a dance call, make sure you are not just learning the steps, but that you are listening to what the choreographer is saying to you while he or she is teaching the steps. Pay attention to detail. More than likely, the choreographer is telling you everything you need to know to act the dance combination, not just execute steps. In my world, if a dancer hops on a turn, I am not going to discount them as long as they are acting while dancing the combination, and trying to execute each nuance I have given. I will take the dancer who has picked up on every acting moment I have peppered into the combo over someone who nails a triple pirouette, when I have asked for a double. After the audition, when you have done your absolute best and given it all you have, walk out the door and let it go. I've seen too many people take things personally when they don't get jobs, and a lot of talented people leave the business because they let an audition experience swell into this idea of total rejection by the theatrical community. In reality, it's just one job and you might get the next one or one down the road. When I was a performer, I would have loved to have known then what I know now, sitting behind the table. You might think you performed perfectly in every part of an audition, but then you don't get the job and can't understand why. So much of the decision-making process is completely out of the performer's control. There are dozens of reasons why you might not get the job, like hair color, height, type, partnering, track positions, covers, costumes, you name it. Trying to figure it all out is pointless; 90 percent of the time, it has nothing to do with your talent. It has to do with the bigger picture, and the puzzle the creative team is trying to put together. Again, if you love it, stick with it. There will be rejection and disappointment, but your day is coming. Go into an audition and have fun, enjoy the process, and don't let it get you down.

CRAMER: Chris, thank you so much for taking the time to talk about the business and your creative career. Congratulations on your Tony, and best of luck with all your future endeavors.

GATTELLI: Thank you. It was my pleasure.

CHAPTER SIX

Kathleen Marshall

Kathleen Marshall's parents instilled the love of the arts in both her and her brother Rob at a very early age. Born in Pittsburgh, Pennsylvania, she began dancing at the age of 13 focusing on ballet. Her devotion and passion for dance grew throughout her teens. She graduated from Taylor Allderdice High School and received her Liberal Arts degree from Smith College. As a budding performer she could be found on the stages of the Pittsburgh Civic Light Opera, national tours, and regional theatres across the country. Arriving in New York City, she performed in several off-Broadway shows and made her jump to Broadway in 1993 to assist her brother Rob, the choreographer of *Kiss of the Spider Women*. The two collaborated on *She Loves Me, Damn Yankees,* and *Victor, Victoria.*

A multiple Tony and Drama Desk Award winner, she made her Broadway choreographic debut with *Swinging On a Star* in 1995 and choreographed many more Broadway productions including *Kiss Me Kate, 1776, Seussical, Follies, Little Shop of Horrors, Ring around the Moon*, and the West End revival of *Kiss Me Kate*.

As artistic director of City Center Encores! from 1999 to 2003, Ms. Marshall directed and choreographed *Applause, 70 Girls 70, House of Flowers, Carnival, Hair, Wonderful Town*, and *Babes in Arms*. She also choreographed *L'll Abner, Call Me Madam, Dubarry Was a Lady*, and *Boys from Syracuse*.

In 2003, Kathleen made her Broadway debut as both director and choreographer with *Wonderful Town*. Additional Broadway gems include *Pajama Game, Anything Goes*, and *Nice Work If You Can Get It*.

She directed and choreographed the Disney/ABC television movie musical *Once Upon a Mattress* starring Tracy Ullman and Carol Burnett and choreographed the television musical *The Music Man* starring Matthew Broderick and Kristen Chenoweth. Marshall served as a judge on the NBC reality series *Grease: You're the One That I Want*. Viewer votes selected the lead characters, Danny and Sandy, for the August 2007 Broadway revival of *Grease*, which she directed and choreographed.

Ms. Marshall is Vice President of the Stage Directors and Choreographers Society and is an Associate Artist of the Roundabout Theatre in New York City. For her body of work, she has received the Pennsylvania Governor's Award for the Arts, the Richard Rodgers Award, and the George Abbott Award.

CRAMER: I've got to begin by saying that I have read a great deal about you and your brother, Rob, first developing a real love of the theatre as a patron before you ever became a part of the profession. Talk to me about that, it's a great place to start.

MARSHALL: Well, you know, the fact that my brother and I are in this business, people think that maybe our parents were in it as well. But no, both are retired college professors. My father was an English professor at the University of Pittsburgh and my mother taught and also ran the elementary education graduate program. They were huge theatre fans and grew up in Boston so they saw all kinds of musicals when they were in out-of-town tryouts before the shows opened in New York. My parents took us from the time we were very little to see everything. I mean everything. We saw musicals, Shakespeare, and the ballet. We saw opera. I think I saw *Faust* when I was five years old and *The Tempest* when I was six. I mean they just took us to everything. And so we were fans before we ever thought it was something we could do or be a part of in any way.

CRAMER: So, you're a young girl and you decide to dance. I think you were a little older than the average beginner?

MARSHALL: Yes, I came to it a little late. I thought that ballet was for snobby little girls on Saturday morning. You know, with their hair pulled back and their little tutus. I'd already been dancing and singing around the living room and been in school plays and that kind of thing. So I tried to do gymnastics. This was back in the Olga Korbut days. I was terrible. I had no flexibility in my back. I couldn't do it. I could only do the moves in between.

CRAMER: The transitional steps.

MARSHALL: Right! So, I thought, oh, maybe I should try this part. So off I went to ballet class at 13 years old and it was one of those things. It just fit, you know? I had this wonderful dance teacher—Mario Melodia—in Pittsburgh, who just passed away a couple of years ago. He taught ballet and tap. He was my first teacher and he was wonderful because within a year he had me coming in three or four times a week but was only charging me for one class. My parents and I didn't know that. He just said, "Have her keep coming." A couple of years later when I was in high school, I was going to class every day. Faculty members from

Point Park College offered community classes and so I took advantage of those as well.

CRAMER: You have a college degree, right?

MARSHALL: Yes, I went Smith College in Massachusetts. One of the things that drew me to Smith was I knew I wanted a Liberal Arts education, but I also wanted to study dance and theatre. Gemze de Lappe was on the faculty there at the time. Ms. De Lappe was Agnes de Mille's main assistant and still stages *Oklahoma, Carousel,* and *Brigadoon* all around the world. She has danced with American Ballet Theatre, Fokine, and with one of Isadora Duncan's adopted daughters. It was perfect because I was completing a Liberal Arts degree, but at the same time, taking ballet technique five days a week, musical theatre choreography, styles, and history. It was great.

CRAMER: So I am guessing you got your start in summer stock productions, tours, and regional productions. Were you a dance captain or a swing?

MARSHALL: Oh, yes. I did all of that. I think every choreographer I know has made a similar progression. He or she was a dancer and was probably a dance captain or an assistant or associate choreographer before they started to choreograph on their own. Directors come to the job from all different angles. Some directors have always been directors. Some are actors who become directors. Hal Prince was a producer before he became a director. Every choreographer I know was a dancer at the beginning of their career.

CRAMER: How do you think being a dance captain or a swing impacts your role as a choreographer?

MARSHALL: I think it's either something you gravitate to or you don't. I think performers have tunnel vision about what they're doing. Choreographers are different. A wonderful director, Susan Schulman, who gave me my equity card when I was performing at Pittsburgh Civic Light Opera, said that I was always aware of what the whole room was doing. Mind you, she hadn't hired me as a choreographer yet. And I think you either have that sense or you don't. Who knows where that awareness comes from. You are aware of the whole at the same time that you're maintaining your own small part.

CRAMER: Do you think that awareness is the most important trait a choreographer can possess?

MARSHALL: I think curiosity is even more important initially. Both are of the utmost value and certainly go hand in hand. When I was doing summer stock, I would read the whole script regardless of the part I was playing. I would get the cast album and listen to it before we started rehearsals so I knew the story. I knew who we were going into it. I knew what the big numbers were and what we had to do. Many people just arrive at rehearsal saying, "Okay, tell me what to do." I think that being proactive and wanting to learn in what era the show takes place and what else is happening during that time in history is extremely helpful. I think that as a choreographer you're a perpetual student. You're always investigating. I did all kinds of research for *Anything Goes*, looking at movies from the 1930s, listening to music of the period, researching behavior, looking at costume designs, architectural design, well, everything. And so, whatever show you're working on, I think you become a temporary authority of that period. When I choreographed *1776*, I became an expert on the Declaration of Independence.

CRAMER: Do you think that your research impacts the show you are working on in a particular way?

MARSHALL: I think so. You want a show to be grounded and to feel specific. In turn, you give that specificity to your actors. Then on top of that, you need to create entertainment at the same time. And I think you have to be aware of that component. A lot of that detail may or may not manifest itself in the show specifically. It might just be a flavor or an attitude of something. But it feels like some kind of reality.

CRAMER: I've read many of your interviews, most especially the Lincoln Center series. You talk a great deal about a "vocabulary" for a show. Does this refer to all of the research that you do?

MARSHALL: Yes, you want to find the style of a show. It's great fun that on *Anything Goes* there are a couple of Fred and Ginger numbers. Of course, I've watched Fred and Ginger movies all my life. But then watching them again specifically with this shows' characters in mind, like Billy and Hope, you find their numbers are in the style of Fred and Ginger. Their relationship is all through dance. And you know, Fred never kissed Ginger on screen. All that

romance was through their movement. Ginger's upper body movement was not classical port de bra. It's not that kind of elegance.
Most of the time she has her elbows tucked, her shoulders raised
and her hands flexed, but it all had emotion to it. That's the style of
dance we want to do. You're not literally copying steps, but you're
trying to find that flavor and make it your own. For example, Fred
and Ginger never did big lifts or big extensions. But for a theatrical
piece, you may put in more of those bigger moves than you would
for film.

CRAMER: In New York you assisted your brother, Rob Marshall,
on *Kiss of the Spider Woman, She Loves Me, Damn Yankees,* and
Victor/Victoria. The list is so impressive, but what I find fascinating is your relationship with the creative team on *Kiss of the Spider
Woman.* That relationship got you your first job; is that correct?

MARSHALL: I love that you know that. I was actually touring
in *Cats* when my brother, Rob, was asked to come in on *Kiss of
the Spider Woman* and create new choreography for the show. He
asked me to be his assistant. Well, it's Chita Rivera, Hal Prince,
John Kander, Fred Ebb, and Terrence McNally. It's like, well, yes,
I'll do it. Then a couple of years later a friend of John Kander's, a
director named Michael Leeds, was doing a revue called *Swinging
On a Star,* based on Johnny Burke's music, and needed a choreographer. He asked his friend, John Kander, for a recommendation,
and I was fortunate enough to get it from John. *Star* played a couple of little regional theatres and then it opened in New York. It
was my first Broadway show as a choreographer.

CRAMER: Nice little segue.

MARSHALL: Yes!

CRAMER: Following *Swinging On a Star,* you choreographed the
Broadway shows: *Ring around the Moon, Kiss Me Kate, Seussical,
Follies, Little Shop,* and *Victor/Victoria* (creative consultant to
Rob Marshall). You were also the artistic director of City Center
Encores! in New York City. This unique venue showcases vintage
musicals in a "pared down" style. Delivered to the audience much
like a concert, the shows rehearse and open in ten days stripped of
the formidable technical and scenic demands of a Broadway show.
Your work at Encores! includes *Wonderful Town, Applause, 70
Girls 70, Babes in Arms, House of Flowers, Hair,* and *Carnival.*

It's an impressive list. *Wonderful Town* was the second show to move from Encores! directly to Broadway and ultimately your Broadway directing debut.

MARSHALL: Yes, the show opened at Encores! in 2000 and then we finally got it on Broadway in 2003 with Donna Murphy, which was so exciting.

CRAMER: You were the artistic director for four seasons.

MARSHALL: Yes, that was great. Also, Encores! is where I met and worked with Rob Fisher for the first time. He is really my creative partner in so many ways. Currently he's our musical director on *Anything Goes*. Rob Fisher has taught me how to have respect and reverence for these classic and vintage musicals by not treating them like museum pieces, but treating them like living pieces of theatre that need to be looked at in a fresh way. These shows, from the 1930s, 1940s, and 1950s, were created by showmen. They were creative people who were developing entertainment for the audience at that time. And those same creators, if they were working today, would shape their shows for a contemporary audience. And it doesn't mean to do anything anachronistic. It just means that, for instance, 40 years ago, if a show finished before 11:00, people thought that they weren't getting their monies worth. They wanted a 3-hour show, a big event. Now you go past 10:30; people start getting restless, looking at their watches and in their programs to see how many songs are left in the show. We're just on a faster clock these days. So, if Rogers and Hammerstein were writing today, they would write musicals that were two and a half hours long, not three.

CRAMER: After your tenure at Encores! and all the classics you've done on Broadway, I think you are sometimes given the title "Queen of the Revival." There are few directors out there that respect a vintage show, a classic, the way you do. It's easier to talk specifics, so let's discuss *Pajama Game*. I'm going to use this show as an example because many readers know Harry Connick, Jr. You took a show like that and turned "Hernando's Hideaway" into one of the most entertaining numbers I've ever watched, because you incorporated his strength as a musician. Could you discuss that in relation to how you give an older show a contemporary sensibility?

MARSHALL: I think a high priority is casting. That's important for approaching a show with a fresh eye. And you know, contemporary sensibilities are different and you have to take that into account. For instance, in *Pajama Game*, there was a character called Prez, who is the president of the union. In the 1950s version, he was a sort of married letch who chased all the women and most everybody turned him down. The only one that said yes was one of the big, round girls. And there were all these round girl jokes. Well, you know, that might have been fine humor in the 1950s, but it's a little distasteful for us today. So I worked with Peter Ackerman who helped us adapt it. And we had the blessing of George Abbott's estate to revisit those characters to make it work for a contemporary audience. So we turned Prez into a mama's boy who still lives at home. And instead of being a round girl, May was kind of shy and a little tomboyish. And so he finally found the right girl for him. We're not trying to change these things just for the sake of changing them. But we have to be aware of the contemporary audience sensibility. You don't want to have that cringe factor, something that's distasteful to us now. But it's also fun to take another look at the numbers. I remember I had a conversation with Harry Connick about "Hernando's Hideaway." I hadn't even met him in person yet. The conversation was on the phone. He was unsure about doing the show and I was trying to convince him to do so. He said when he does his concert he can go out there and do whatever he wants. He has an opening number planned and the rest of it they just make up as they go along. He has written Broadway shows so he understands what I am asking him to do.

CRAMER: He wrote *Thou Shalt Not*.

MARSHALL: Right, so he understands the discipline of that process. But he was thinking, as a performer, he couldn't go out there and do the same show eight times a week. So it started my brain thinking. Maybe he would say yes if I could create a place in the show where he could improvise and keep the show fresh for him every night. That's where the germ of the idea came from. In "Hernando's Hideaway" he's trying to impress the character of Gladys. It's like he'll do anything to get Gladys to loosen up so he can get the key, settle the strike, and get the girl. That sense of desperation to please this gal happens when he sits down at the piano. So we can imagine that Sid, who is a factory superintendent and isn't from this world, is going to sit down in his complete moment of desperation and all of the sudden play like Harry Connick, Jr.

CRAMER: You direct your revivals without blackouts and other accepted transitions that were critical in the original productions. Huge, complicated, time consuming scenic shifts had to be executed without all the technological speed we have today. The transitions of yesterday are useless in your revivals. You figure out a way to keep the production moving.

MARSHALL: Well, we try. The typical George Abbott musicals in the 1940s and 1950s are seen "in one." It was a drape in. Then pull the drape out and you have a full set scene and then you go back to a little "in one" crossover. That's another way to make a contemporary musical or a vintage musical fresh; you try to move things "a vista" (in full view of the audience), so that we're seeing every change happen. And the transitions are the real key in creating a musical that flows. It's something I think about right from day one with the designers and with the music department. How are we going to get from here to here? What are we looking at? How does it move? What's the story telling? How are we getting from one event to the next?

CRAMER: Discuss working with a music arranger; because you have also got to find a way to make the music fresh. I'm certain that you spent many a time trying to build a dance number with additional music. Do you read music?

MARSHALL: Yes. I can read music and also can read a score. Besides the great musical directors I've work with like Rob Fisher; I get to work with David Chase, our musical director and dance arranger on *Pajama Game*, and our dance arranger for *Anything Goes*. He's unbelievable.

CRAMER: When you work with someone over and over you get a real working rhythm together, finish each others sentences, and have many of the same creative thoughts; in other words, you two have real shorthand.

MARSHALL: Absolutely. And he does even more research than I do. He's incredible. He's a musicologist in his own right and an expert in the history of American music. What we do is look at what was there in the original, what the song is about, and then figure out the story we're telling. So the give-and-take goes back and forth. We say, "Here's the story we want to tell," and then he may come up with musical motifs and ideas and then say, "Oh, great, why don't we use that musical section to tell this." Then he'll play around a little bit and he'll say, "Oh, that feel is great. Can we expand that? Can we have a little bit more of that before we go to the next section?" We create a blue print first. We knew, for instance, that in *Anything Goes* we were going to have a first section that tells a little story about Billy and Moon. Billy's just been mistaken for public enemy number one and Moon's been mistaken for public enemy number two and they're being celebrated. So instead of the two of them exiting stage and having a group of tap dancing sailors take over, our first instrumental actually involves Billy and Moon and how they feel about the fact that they're being paraded around and made to feel like big men on the ship. Then in the following section after the next vocal comes back in, I knew I wanted to get the sailors on board. So it's a sense the ice has been broken and these two celebrities have strutted around the stage, which in turn gives everybody else permission to strut their stuff around the stage too.

CRAMER: Do you have a preference between revivals and new works?

MARSHALL: I've worked on more revivals than new musicals. But I love new musicals. There are several that I'm working on. But there's such a long gestation. Because the material exists, revivals are a quicker process, even if you're going to transform it a little bit. As somebody who directs and choreographs, the music is so important to me. When you work on some of these classic shows, you have a score in place that's just fantastic. You're trying to keep it fresh. But it's a very, very different assignment when you're starting from scratch with a new musical.

CRAMER: How do you select a project? Or have you had an occasion where the project selected you?

MARSHALL: *Anything Goes* came to me. Right after we did *Pajama Game*, the artistic director of the Roundabout, Todd Haimes, said they had gotten the rights to do the new production of *Anything Goes* and would I want to do it. I said absolutely. But I think it's very true when you first start off as a choreographer, many times you get hand-me-downs. Sometimes you're asked to go set a regional production of a show where you served as a dance captain or an assistant choreographer. You might be asked to re-create someone else's work. Then if you prove yourself and prove that you can run a rehearsal and get a show up and keep everybody happy, then maybe you'll be asked back to that theatre to choreograph something new. And I think that a lot of times the first job you get may be something somebody was no longer available to do and you step in. That happened to me on my first Broadway show *Swinging on a Star*. You have to be ready. It's like sitting on a bench in a game, you're suited up, and you got to be ready to go in whenever that happens. I think that sense of always being ready is incredibly important. I did *1776*, which is not a dance show. It's movement. But I worked very hard so it all made sense. I really learned how to work with actors and make them feel comfortable and not feel like, "Uh-oh, here's the choreographer. They're going to make me do something I'm not comfortable with." You have to make them feel comfortable. And it was Paul Gemignani, our musical director on *1776*, who recommended me to be the choreographer on *Kiss Me Kate*, which was a huge dance musical. This business is all about establishing relationships. It's all an opportunity. And you don't know when they're going to come. But when they do come, you have to step up to the plate.

CRAMER: Do you approach musical staging and choreography differently?

MARSHALL: There really is a difference when you're working with actors and when you're working with an ensemble of dancers and singers. We're teaching choreography for "Blow Gabriel" to the dancers you just say, here it is. You just start teaching steps right away. You may explain what the number is about, the style and the story, but you plunge right in with steps, at least I do. When you're staging an actor's musical number, you have to approach it very differently, almost gently. Even if you have a plan in your head as to how you think the number is going to layout, you need to involve them, listen to their input, and move slowly. Also, figure out who you're working with and how they best need to work.

CRAMER: What kind of rehearsal environment do you try to create?

MARSHALL: I like to do a lot of preparation because I find that the more prepared I am, actually the more flexible I am. If I have a sense of where the finish line is, we can detour a little bit because an actor wants to try something else. I know where we need to go. And, ultimately, I don't have to do it eight times a week. The actor has to do it eight times a week. So, if they don't like it, if they don't believe in it, if it doesn't make sense to them, it's not going to work. I may be in love with some steps or some idea that I come up with, but if it doesn't work on the actor or the dancer who has to actually do it, then you have to let it go. You have to throw it away.

CRAMER: Let's expand on your preproduction process and tell me how you use assistants.

MARSHALL: You know, when I first started choreographing, I didn't want anybody else in the room with me. I was just too self-conscious. And the great Peter Howard, who did the dance arrangements for *Swinging on a Star*, would make tapes for me. I would go into the studio by myself and put on the tapes and try to figure it out. You kind of have to make a fool of yourself. You turn on the music and just jump around. I was very self-conscious about that. But now, I'm used to the fact that I want assistants around me. On *Anything Goes*, I'm working with Vince Pesce who I've worked with for many years as a dancer and as an associate. We performed together years ago; he danced in two of my Broadway revivals and has been my associate on *Wonderful Town* and *Pajama Game*.

CRAMER: Oh, this is a lasting relationship.

MARSHALL: We've been together a long time. He's now choreographing and directing on his own. With David Chase, Vince Pesce, and me in the room; we all feel we can be loose and uninhibited.

CRAMER: Do you have additional assistants, for example, different people for different shows, depending on the requirements?

MARSHALL: I bring in a couple of additional people to work out some partnering and lifts or a number that involves a complicated pattern. When we created "Steam Heat" for *Pajama Game*, we brought in our dance captain who was going to perform the number in the context of the show, so that made it easier.

CRAMER: When you work on formations, do you draw, use coins, or some other prop to figure out traffic?

MARSHALL: I draw using yellow legal pads. I've got dozens and dozens of yellow legal pads with little x's and lines and ideas. I do something my brother Rob did. Other people I collaborate with have also taken up the practice. I work out an A, B, C list. The A numbers are the big company numbers, or the big ensemble numbers that need the most attention. Then the B numbers may be like rhythmic numbers that only involve a couple of people or smaller groups. They're something like "You're the Top." It's a number that's not going to have a dance break, but it's rhythmic and requires movement, choreography, and style. Then the C numbers would be ballads, something like "I Get a Kick out of You." You have to think the song through to understand the story that the lyric is telling, but you don't necessarily have to get up on your feet and figure it out, piece by piece. So with this formula, I'm creating a preproduction order of attack.

CRAMER: In the order of attack, do you try to teach big numbers first to get that choreography into people's bodies or do your work another way?

MARSHALL: As a director, I like to basically work sequentially. I do jump ahead to get the big numbers on their feet. The ones that have massive choreography need a head start.

CRAMER: Preproduction is done. You have a solid sense of what you want to accomplish, how you want blocking and choreography to move forward but some things just don't work out as planned. Is there a sense of being able to change things on your feet in the moment rather than having to come back to it?

MARSHALL: Oh, sure. Many times you may have an idea in mind, especially in terms of patterns and the like. But until you have all the bodies in the room to work those out, you have to remain flexible. There are some things that you know need to be tweaked and some things you can do fast on your feet. But sometimes you say, let's just woodshed later and bring it back in a better form. I think there are two steps in teaching choreography. The first step is simply trying to get people to do what you are asking them to do. Once they get it, you have to take another step back and say, "Have I asked them to do the right thing? Is there something missing? Is there something more we can do?"

CRAMER: *Wonderful Town* was your first Broadway show as director-choreographer. Prior to this was there a pivotal moment for you when you knew you must wear both the director and choreographer hat?

MARSHALL: Yes, it was my first Broadway show as a director and choreographer, but I had directed and choreographed it at Encores! as well as many other productions, so it's an interesting question. When I choreographed *Kiss Me Kate* for Broadway, Michael Blakemore directed. The scenes in that show were so complex, between the farce of the comedy and the Shakespearean scenes, that it needed sole focus. I think one of the reasons that that show was successful is because Michael was able to concentrate on those scenes to perfection and I was able to hone in on those big dance numbers. It's tricky, because even now with *Anything Goes* I feel like something gets neglected and we have to catch up. You get something on its feet and something else needs attention and so on. And I'm in that place now where I feel the scenes need to be pulled apart and reworked. The point is, there are some shows that should naturally have a separate director and choreographer and some shows where one person handling both jobs makes sense. If I have a vision as to how the whole show is going to move and feel, it's nice that you don't have to check in with somebody else. Although I think as a person who directs and choreographs, you must surround yourself with a really strong team of designers, writers, and musicians because you don't have the same checks and balances that you do with a director and a choreographer. You really need strong associates around you who are going to say, "Is that number too long? Maybe we should trim it a little bit. Is that making sense? No, it could be better. It could be clearer."

CRAMER: Is your rehearsal and preparation time frame the same length for each Broadway show or are there other contributing factors?

MARSHALL: It's interesting, on *Anything Goes*, we have a couple of fewer days in the studio, but a couple of more days of technical rehearsal compared to *Pajama Game*. *Pajama Game* saw two more rehearsal days but two less days in tech. With *Anything Goes* it was a deliberate trade-off because the set is complicated. It's a three-level set. There are so many characters coming and going and we needed to create the timing of bits, entrances, and exits on the actual set. So we have a little less time in the studio, but we're going to use that time on stage.

CRAMER: So you figure out what you think you might need for each show.

MARSHALL: Yes, and it's also what your producers are willing to give you. Hopefully you have five or six weeks in the studio, but for *Grease*, I think we only had four.

CRAMER: Well, that's a convenient segue to scenic design and the technical aspect of a Broadway show. When you are in preproduction, how do you communicate with your scenic designer?

MARSHALL: Well, I worked with Derek McLane on the set for *Anything Goes*. I've worked with Derek a lot, and again, it's that same sort of trust. We communicate in "what ifs." What if it's this? What if it's that? Last summer we started talking about it and he came up with some kind of basic ideas. And then we throw those around and he comes back with some sort of preliminary sketches and we talk a little more. I always feel like we spiral in. You don't know what the show is going to be yet, but you go around and around and around and you very slowly work your way to the center. With a spiral there are no shortcuts. You can't just cut right into the center. I feel that way about creating a show. You start to talk about the set and then you realize that set can inform this production number in a certain way. Or you come up with the idea in reverse and you try to figure out how the production number can be worked into the set. I had an idea to use a lifeboat in the number "Buddy Beware." So Derek jumps in and we trade ideas back and forth until we figure out how we are going to incorporate the lifeboat into that number.

CRAMER: Have you ever had a choreography reel? I'm guessing you never had the need for one.

MARSHALL: No, I didn't have one. When I started out there were stringent copyright restrictions about videotaping rehearsals and performances. It was tough. Now things are loosening up a bit and I think a lot of choreographers starting out are finding it necessary and even helpful to have a reel.

CRAMER: It makes it easy for producers and directors doing the hiring to go right to a website and look at someone's work.

MARSHALL: Sure!

CRAMER: You never had to audition or submit work for a job?

MARSHALL: I've interviewed for jobs but never had to create choreography on spec in that way.

CRAMER: That's even harder for me to imagine. How do you verbalize a visual art?

MARSHALL: It's hard. You have to understand that you are selling an idea. Okay, this is a hilarious case in point. I was being interviewed to choreograph a new television movie of *The Music Man*, starring Matthew Broderick. Producers Craig Zadan and Neil Meron and director Jeff Bleckner set me up at ABC with a video conference meeting as they were all in Los Angeles and I was here in NYC. So I was sitting at the end of the table and there's a screen there. But there was a delay in the feed.

CRAMER: Oh, sure, similar to when you are watching television and you have a foreign correspondent talking to someone here in the states.

MARSHALL: Yes and when you say something, there's no response right away. It was so hard on me because I had to have all these notes about the numbers and my ideas and how it would all lay out. So I described what I thought about doing for "Seventy Six Trombones" and it felt like two, three, or four beats went by and, dead silence. I thought, "Oh, God, they hate it, they hate it, they hate it." But because there was a delay with the video, there would be this horrible silence and then there would finally be a response, "Good, oh, that's good." It was this hour-long meeting that felt like forever. It was just deadly. But I was hired for the project, so it turned out well.

CRAMER: Subsequently, the same producers hired you to direct and choreograph *Once Upon a Mattress* with Carol Burnett and Tracey Ullman. Television direction and choreography must be a whole different world.

MARSHALL: Oh, yes. Talk about learning a new vocabulary.

CRAMER: So did you jump in innocently so that people around you knew that you had to have their help?

MARSHALL: Yes, I think you have to. It's like any learning experience. You have to acknowledge what you know and what you don't. I know how to rehearse scenes and how to create musical numbers. But I don't know what lens to use. I don't know anything about that. I mean I can talk to the Director of Photography about what sort of effect I want. You know, can we pull back on this? Can we zoom on this? Can we dub it? I don't know how to achieve those effects. So you really have to be open to the people around you.

CRAMER: How long did it take you to have a working knowledge of all aspects of the technical design of a show such as light, set, and costume design?

MARSHALL: I'll tell you, that's the one great thing about having been an assistant choreographer and assistant director before I became a director-choreographer. You get to be around everyone, you get to watch directors work. I got to see Hal Prince, Jack O'Brien, Susan Schulman, Frank Galati, Michael Leeds, and Scott Ellis in action. I got to see how they run a rehearsal, how they talk to actors, to writers, to designers, and to the music department. What notes do they give? What do they say in a production meeting after a preview? How do they run that production meeting, or a technical rehearsal? Those are things that unless you witness them, it's very hard to do.

CRAMER: You use this phrase—apprenticeship art. Did you just define it?

MARSHALL: Yes, it is learning the business by watching all these people in action and assisting wherever possible. There's no substitute for that.

CRAMER: Now, you're on the board for SDC (The Stage Directors and Choreographers Society) and they have the observership program.

MARSHALL: Yes, we have an observer on *Anything Goes*.

CRAMER: This offers a unique experience for an aspiring young director or choreographer to watch you and the artistic team firsthand.

MARSHALL: Yes, absolutely. Apprenticeship art at work.

CRAMER: When you are asked to direct a show, what kind of time frame reflects the initial phone call, conversation, or invitation to do that particular show through opening night?

MARSHALL: It varies. I mean this one, Todd Haimes and I started talking about *Anything Goes* four years ago. But it didn't really click into place until we had Sutton Foster on board. And then once we knew Sutton, it became very real. When Joel Grey came on board, Todd was ready to put it on the schedule. He wanted to get it in. That's actually the wonderful thing about working at Roundabout and at other institutional theatres. Once they decide to do something, you can count on them.

CRAMER: You're an Associate Artist at the Roundabout; is that correct?

MARSHALL: Yes, and that allows associates to bring projects to the theatre or vice versa and together we do readings and find our way.

CRAMER: Do you ever hear the phrase, "that's Kathleen Marshall's style"? Do you have a specific style?

MARSHALL: I don't know if I have a style. I admire somebody like Fosse, who created his own unique vocabulary. We all know if you hold your hat with those three fingers up . . . it's Fosse. He created and has ownership of his style. But hopefully I adapt to the show that I'm doing. I do love athletic, energized choreography, infused with humor. Anytime I can get a laugh in my choreography, it makes me happy.

CRAMER: Let's shift our attention to the audition process. Do you look for anything in particular when you are auditioning dancers? Is there something consistent you have found over the years that you look for each and every time?

MARSHALL: Vividness. I look for dancers who are vivid, dancers who are present. Of course, I want strong technique; that goes without saying. But I think many dancers that have strong technique don't concentrate on anything else. You want people who are alive, bright eyed, focused, and energized. I think dancers must be able to adapt to style very fast. I think many times there are dancers who can kick their leg quite high, they can execute triple turns, and leap and jump, but they can't absorb that style you're looking for. And I think that's a very unique talent. And here's the reality; I seldom put a triple pirouette in choreography; it happens only now and then. Often times, choreographers simply put a difficult turn in an audition combination because they need to see technique, but it doesn't necessarily end up on stage. But there's always going to be a style on stage. Dancers must know how to give energy and focus. There are people who have that brightness to them that I look for.

CRAMER: Today, casting directors and the creative team do not hire separate singing and dancing ensembles. It's all about money or lack of it. Dancers sing and singers dance and actors have to move and dancers have to act, it's a package.

MARSHALL: You bet. Absolutely.

CRAMER: Do you talk to the auditioning group in front of you and give them the story idea of the number?

MARSHALL: Yes, I usually explain something about the style of the show and the era of the show. For instance, on the audition combination for *Anything Goes*, we used "Blow Gabriel." I choreographed it from the point of view of the Angels (Reno Sweeney's four sidekicks). So they're doing something that's seductive and sexy. They give it just a little hot and just a little cool. They tease and they hold back, they tease and they hold back; consequently they have something to play. For the men, I teach something more athletic, but all the while they need to be saved (by Reno and the Angels). It went from highs to lows, but again, you give them something to play because you need to see that. And, you're right, you know, we don't have the luxury of hiring a "dancer" only. There used to be a dance ensemble of 16, a singing ensemble of 16 and then 10 principles on top of that. Now you're lucky if you get a total of eight ensemble members.

CRAMER: I am sure you have worked on multiple types of stage spaces over your expansive career. How does that work change when you direct and choreograph for film?

MARSHALL: It's very different because front doesn't have to be front in film. You have to choreograph the camera into it as well. The fun thing about that is that you can have in mind where you think the camera's going to be and what it's going to see. One of the issues that you always have on stage is transition. You have this 40' by 30' foot area where everything's taking place. If you're moving from one section to another, if the men are going to dance a section and the women are going to dance a section, and there's going to be partnering and a pas de deux, you have to build in the ways dancers are going to move from one section to the next. In film, you can just cut to it. You don't necessarily have to worry about it. You can start right in the meat of it. You don't have to do that transition from the men to the women.

CRAMER: Let's turn our focus to *Grease* and the reality television show *You're the One That I Want*. You were an official judge of that on-screen competition and I believe your associate Vince Pesce was the choreographer for the broadcast. Tell me what filming that television show was like for you.

MARSHALL: Laura Osnes played Sandy in *Grease* after she was cast from the show *You're the One That I Want*. She replaced Kelli O'Hara in *South Pacific* on Broadway and played Hope in *Anything Goes*. She left our show to play Bonnie in *Bonnie and Clyde*. It's all very interesting because the finalists on the *Grease* television show were not amateurs. They were all young and they all had various levels of training and experience, but they all *had* training and experience. I think that the television producers would have loved it if a waitress and a truck driver were suddenly musical theatre stars.

CRAMER: Sure, you turn over a rock and they appear.

MARSHALL: Right. But the skills required for musical theatre take time to develop. And I think that Laura and Max Crumm (the male winner cast as Danny in *Grease*) jumped to the head of the class by getting to star in a Broadway show from the television competition. On the other hand, they were playing Danny and Sandy. Max and Laura are both really skilled and have proven themselves beyond that. So, I think it was an interesting and wonderful experiment to bring a fresh look to Broadway. I remember we were in previews for the show and there were a lot of families in the audience. I'd be standing at the back of the theatre and people would come up to me and talk about the show. I had many, many families who said they were going to take their family vacation to Hawaii or elsewhere, but the kids saw the television show and really wanted to come to New York. It was their first time here and their first Broadway show. I said, "Would you come back?" And they said they would definitely return. It's so great because they've come at this from a different path, via television, and now they're seeing something they're familiar with. Maybe next time that family will return and see something that is brand new to them. So a new audience has been discovered.

CRAMER: Oh, I think that must be truly satisfying for you. You must feel as though the process was worthwhile.

MARSHALL: Most certainly.

CRAMER: Many of our readers are college students majoring in musical theatre. It's hard for these students to avoid becoming insular. Outside of liberal arts classes, students are primarily focused on musical theatre. I am sure this is true of seniors in high school trying to get into college musical theatre programs across the United States. Give some advice about how to experience life as a whole person and what it brings to the table as a director and a choreographer.

MARSHALL: Yes, I think that it's true. You can live in a bubble in a campus world. It doesn't matter where that campus is. People worry about whether they're in a big city or a small town or northeast or southwest or wherever. But the world of your campus is your world so much of the time. I think that what's available at your fingertips is astonishing. When I think about the fact that at Smith College I could just go into the dance studio at night and play around, I am flabbergasted. It was just open. The libraries were such great resources. There were lectures and happenings and free movies all the time. Once you are in the real world, everything is either hard to get access to or cost money to attend. When you're in college, take advantage of everything that's available. It's all going to inform you as a performer. Go to hear some author speak. Go to see a movie. Take a class you thought you'd hate. Expand yourself in that way. In any kind of creative field you have to keep your curiosity up and you have to keep expanding your world. That's a muscle that you have to exercise just as much as any other muscle.

CRAMER: Whether professional, college, or amateur level, there are many dancers who want to choreograph but they think they are limited in some way. Perhaps they've had limited experience with partnering or lifts or they aren't experienced in acrobatics or a particular style that is required. How can you explain to a dancer who wants to choreograph how you, Kathleen, go about visualizing or working out the specificity of a step or a lift when you might not necessarily execute them yourself?

MARSHALL: Yes, it's hard. I do as much of the choreography as I can because I also know that it has to feel good to dance. It has to feel fun to dance. There might be a section that you decide is awkward. For example, many times when dancers are choreographed to mirror steps, you've got to get the group on the same foot. You have to figure out who's going to do the cheat step and decide if that's going to be a hard moment. You don't want there to be an uncomfortable moment for dancers. So I just try to dance as much as possible. Now if there's something like lifts, partnering, or something really athletic or acrobatic that I can't do, you do envision it in your head. You must still work with your dancers to not only create *for* them but *with* them so that they're comfortable with what they're doing. I always say to actors, dancers, and performers, "I don't want you to have a moment in the show that you dread. I don't want you to arrive at some moment where you think, Oh, God, here comes that lift that I just can't do, or here's that high note that I just am not comfortable singing. Here's that acting moment that makes me cringe every time I get to it because I don't understand it and I don't like it, or here comes that joke that I just don't think is funny." I don't want an actor to have that moment. You might have challenging moments and moments that you have to gear yourself up for like a big note or a big jump or getting your breath to sing again after a big dance section. Those challenges are fine. But something that you absolutely dread, I just don't think actors should face that.

CRAMER: Once a show opens, how many times do you come back?

MARSHALL: Every couple of weeks usually, to check in, if I'm not out of town or so forth working on something else. And then if somebody new is going into the show, I come to one or two rehearsals or I come to their put in. (A put in is a process where news actors are added into a show.) You have to have a good team in place, a stage manager, a dance captain, a conductor, who can keep the show running, because it's a hard thing on Broadway to keep a long running show going.

CRAMER: Are there brush-ups?

MARSHALL: I've done that a couple of times on long running shows. We actually get back in the studio in front of the mirror.

On *Wonderful Town*, we did exactly that. They hadn't seen each other do this choreography in a while. It's one thing to give notes and say get it together on this. But to see themselves in the mirror again, that's what makes them feel like a company.

CRAMER: Do you reset your own work?

MARSHALL: Oh, yes. I've done national tours and London productions.

CRAMER: How does that work for you?

MARSHALL: It's good. It's funny because usually you've done something else in between and you're coming back to the show. Part of it is just remembering the work. When you move a show, whether it's going to be a tour or another production elsewhere, there are usually adjustments to the set. I tell you what, though. I would rather set an entire new company. I think it's much harder to put replacements in an existing company.

CRAMER: I've always been curious about this. What's the difference between auditioning ensembles in London and here?

MARSHALL: You know what? It's changed a little bit, but you have to remember that Great Britain is a small country. I mean when you think about New York, you know New York is filled with everybody who was star of their dance school or their college program or local community theatre. They all converge on NYC. London is a smaller pool of people to pick from. There are some wonderful dancers and some incredible people. But I found, especially when we did *Kiss Me Kate*, that we had to really pull it out of the dancers. It was very athletic and grounded style of choreography. At that time in London, the jazz was much more lifted and cool. It was huge effort to get people to bend their knees and really get into the floor.

CRAMER: So your auditioning pool is much smaller?

MARSHALL: Yes, but there are some really talented people, really good, strong people. The other big difference is that every actor up for principal parts have all been to some kind of strong academy or program. They've all had to do a little singing, a little dancing, a little stage combat, do a little more. Many of the actors in London are, as a whole, more well-rounded than American actors.

CRAMER: Can you let us in on your upcoming projects?

MARSHALL: I'm working on a new musical with Gershwin music called *Nice Work If You Can Get It*. We are hoping to open within the year. In terms of revivals, I'm working on a new version of *The Unsinkable Molly Brown*. Dick Scanlan is writing a new book for it and we've done a couple of readings. There are a couple things way down the line, including a new musical that's based on Toulouse Lautrec.

CRAMER: Well, I can't thank you enough for taking time for this and best of luck on your future projects.

MARSHALL: Oh, absolutely. My pleasure.

CHAPTER SEVEN

Jerry Mitchell

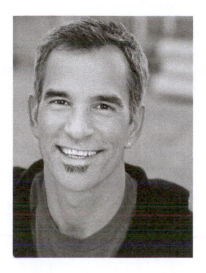

Born in Paw Paw Michigan, Jerry Mitchell was an athlete in his childhood when a neighbor took him to an audition for *The Music Man* with the Paw Paw Village Players. His theatrical career was born. He worked regionally in Michigan and toured in such shows as *A Chorus Line* and *West Side Story*. He was also a member of the Young Americans.

Agnes De Mille gave him his start on Broadway in the revival of *Brigadoon*. Soon to follow was *On Your Toes* and *The Will Rogers Follies*. Jerry has assisted such legends as Michael Bennett and Jerome Robbins. His choreographic career includes Broadway's *You're a Good Man, Charlie Brown, The Full Monty, Grease, Dirty Rotten Scoundrels, Never Gonna Dance, La Cage aux Folles,* and *Catch Me If You Can*. In 2007, Jerry took the reigns of director-choreographer with the mega hit *Legally Blonde*.

In addition, he founded *Broadway Bares,* a charitable organization producing shows with a touch of burlesque, dedicated to raising awareness and money to fight the AIDs epidemic. Twenty years later, this one show raises over one million dollars in just a single night. Mitchell's *Peep Show* in Las Vegas was a direct result of *Broadway Bares.* His lengthy film career includes *Scent of a Woman, In and Out, The Object of My Affection,* and *Meet Joe Black.*

In 2002, Mr. Mitchell founded *DanceBreak*, a New York City showcase for emerging choreographers. Nominated for multiple Tony and Emmy awards, Jerry won the Tony in 2005 for Best Choreography for the revival of *La Cage aux Folles.* In 2013, Jerry received the George Abbott Award for Lifetime Achievement in Theatre. His production of *Kinky Boots* recently opened on Broadway.

CRAMER: Jerry, your road to professional dancer, choreographer, and ultimately director-choreographer can be viewed as a bit of a "charmed life." Tell us about how you became a dancer.

MITCHELL: In a nutshell, I grew up in Michigan, and started performing in the community theatre when I was eight. I was in a production of *The Music Man*. My nextdoor neighbor asked me to go audition with her because she was in it and they needed boys for the boy's band. The director put me in the show and I said, "That's it. That's what I'm going to do for the rest of my life." Consequently I hung out with the Paw Paw Village Players for the remainder of my childhood. The choreographer Sammy Meeks had the only studio in town and offered me free classes whenever I wanted. It was identical to the story in the musical *Billy Elliott*. She kept asking me to come to class and I kept saying no since class enrollment was all girls. The only reason I ever took a dance class was because I broke my collar bone coming home from football practice one day and thought, "You know what? I'm going to go to class and keep my legs in shape for basketball." I played every sport so it seemed smart to seize the opportunity. I was 15 at the time, and a little more comfortable in my skin. I had immense natural ability as a dancer and had learned a great deal through show choreography with the community theatre.

CRAMER: Did you choreograph in high school?

MITCHELL: I'd already choreographed many school shows. I was choreographing the pompom team, the flag corp, and the cheerleaders. Sammy gave me all my classes for free and had me teach basic tap to the little ones on Saturday mornings. She paid me, took me under her wing, and basically let me fly. I was in a place where I belonged.

CRAMER: Did you attend college?

MITCHELL: That's hard to answer directly. I continued in community theatre throughout southwestern Michigan and at Hope Summer Repertory Theatre, knowing college was in my future. However, during my senior year, I ran into a friend of mine with the Young Americans. During their break between performances of *West Side Story* at Miller Auditorium, one of the dancers in the company was injured. My friend said, "Come back and audition for them as a replacement." I auditioned in the lobby and they hired me. Four days later I went on a non-equity national tour of *West Side Story* with the Young Americans. In 42 states, 260 cities, 3 dancers to a room, and 10 dollars a week, it was everything I had prayed for. After the tour, I was rehired at Hope Summer Repertory Theater to be an Associate Choreographer for their production of *West Side Story* and dance in the show. I'd met a lot of people from different universities when I apprenticed at Hope and I knew I wanted to pursue college. I didn't want to come to New York. I wanted to go to school. I was somewhat afraid of coming to New York at 18. However I was very competitive, so I applied to many schools and eventually I was accepted and attended Webster University. I was in the acting conservatory and was a musical theatre major, but as a freshman, I wasn't permitted to perform. I couldn't stand it. I had to perform so I joined the dance company.

CRAMER: At this point you never had formal training in ballet and you were 18, right?

MITCHELL: Right. So I signed up for ballet one. All I had taken with Sammy was jazz and tap class. The dance professor at Webster taught me once and said, "Come audit the ballet three level and I want you to audition for the dance company."

CRAMER: Many of our readers study dance as part of their musical theatre training. Can you give me a rough idea how many ballet classes a week you were taking?

MITCHELL: I was taking four classes a day plus acting classes and voice lessons of course. The daily schedule started at 8:30 and ended at 10:00 or 11:00 pm. Back then, I couldn't even do a glissade. I didn't know what a pas de chat was. I was completely clueless but picked up like a sponge and I loved it. It was heaven. During the summer following my freshman year, I auditioned for the Muny Theatre, got cast, received my union card from Actors Equity Association and came back for my sophomore year. Tony Stevens was coming through town casting a commercial for Dr. Pepper and I booked the gig. That was my first residual check. Spring break rolled around and I used the commercial cash to travel to New York City and visit friends who I had met at the Muny. I went with them to my first equity audition. It was for *Brigadoon*, choreographed by Agnes de Mille. She said, "I'll take him. He can dance. He can be a clan leader." She just picked me out of the crowd!

CRAMER: In front of everyone, right on the spot? She just pointed at you and said that?

MITCHELL: In front of everybody. So I got the show, went back to school and asked permission to leave since the NYC production needed me in the fall. Webster gave me credit and said I could come back after the show and complete my degree. Two weeks before my sophomore year concluded, *A Chorus Line* is playing at the Fox Theatre in St. Louis. I trotted on down to see the show and afterward decided to audition. I did, and got cast in the show.

CRAMER: And who did you play?

MITCHELL: It was 1980 and young kids from colleges would cover lots of parts. I played the boy in the headband (a designated role in the show) and covered Don, Greg, Al, and Bobby. So, I went on tour with the national company for ten weeks over the summer.

CRAMER: This is all before *Brigadoon*.

MITCHELL: Yes. I had to give my notice on *A Chorus Line* to do *Brigadoon*. This became a pattern. I would try to go back to school, but kept getting cast in shows. *Woman of the Year* came next. I faked being short enough for that one (6'2" and under was the requirement), by wearing sweat pants and never straightening my knees so that I wasn't too tall for the show. After that, Tony Stevens, who had cast me in the Dr. Pepper commercial, cast me in the movie version of *The Best Little Whorehouse in Texas*. Needless to say, I never went back to school. I did many television shows including the Tonys and several more Broadway productions before my next big show, *On Your Toes*.

CRAMER: It's at that point that your role as an Assistant Choreographer and an Associate Choreographer really began, correct?

MITCHELL: Yes, while dancing in *On Your Toes* on Broadway, Michael Bennett was doing an industrial for Jane Fonda Fashion Wear and I got invited to the call. When I showed up I was shocked to see that I would be auditioning with the dance elite of Broadway. Michael hired 40 of us and that was the beginning of my association with Michael Bennett. I got to assist him on a pas de duex in the show. He was so impressed, Michael decided I should dance it as well. I became one of two featured dancers, and the whole fashion show was choreographed around us. From there, Michael hired me to assist him on his new show, *Scandals*. When that show got postponed, Michael asked me to be his associate choreographer on *Chess* in London.

CRAMER: What was the time frame from the Jane Fonda Fashion show to *Chess*? In other words, how long did it take to go from dancer to associate choreographer?

MITCHELL: I think it was a year and a half, two years maybe. Michael and I were working on *Chess*. We cast in London and came back to New York and Michael got sick. It gets passed off as a heart problem but he had AIDS, of course, so the show was cancelled. Six months after that, Bob Avian (Michael's creative partner) asked if I would go back to London and co-choreograph *Follies*. The show was a huge hit and I headed back home to NYC. When I got off the plane I was told Jerome Robbins would be holding auditions for an assistant for *Jerome Robbins Broadway*. When I walked in, there are 40 or 45 dance captains in that room. We learned three dance sequences from his most famous shows. Jerome Robbins walked in the room. He sat down and watched us do the numbers and is literally there for just 35 minutes. "Thank you all. That was fantastic." Out he goes. That's it, we'll hear later. I go home and my phone rings. It's Jerome Robbins. He says, "I'm going to go into the studio and work today, would you like to come in and work with me? I'll pay you $100." And I said, "Absolutely. Where do I meet you?" I show up at the studio. I have no information. There was no contract yet, just $100 a day to start learning his vocabulary.

CRAMER: Can that situation even happen today?

MITCHELL: Yes, sure it can. There were two other assistants and we were literally going to dance with Jerome Robbins. Manny Azenburg who was producing *Jerome Robbins Broadway* said, "You like these guys. Let's give them a contract." So then they gave us a contract for three months at $1,000 a week. After those three months were up, he said, "You *really* like these guys. Let's give them a contract for six months." We got one for six months at $1500 a week. In the end, I worked with him for two years. I designed all the rehearsal schedules for more than 60 dancers. We did a workshop and then we rehearsed for six months. We took it out of town and then we went into Broadway rehearsal for another six months. It was literally two years of my life learning from him. Those were great experiences for me, working so closely with Michael, and then two years later working so closely with Jerry. My first solo professional job as a choreographer was *Jekyll and Hyde* in Houston, Texas. At the time I was working for Jerome Robbins and he said, "Go. You can always come back here." So I left to choreograph *Jekyll and Hyde*, and then I did a little show called *Hearts Desire*. I came back to New York and Jeff Calhoun was working on a show called *The Will Rogers Follies* with Tommy Tune. Now, I was really trying to focus on my choreography, but Jeff asked me if I would dance in the show and I agreed. I needed to get back on stage and dance. It was a spectacular show to be in.

CRAMER: That show connected you to your next job as an associate to Jeff Calhoun.

MITCHELL: Jeff asked me to assist him on *Grease,* followed by *Busker Alley* with Tommy Tune.

CRAMER: While you were working with Jeff you stumbled into a film career. This is a great story.

MITCHELL: I was in *Will Rogers* one night and I got a call to meet with a film crew on Seventh Avenue to help with choreography in a scene. The long and short of it was Martin Breast and Al Pacino were shooting a tango scene in the movie, *Scent of a Woman.* They had a wonderful tango teacher but he wasn't repeating a pattern, so choreographically the actor didn't have a story to tell from start to finish. I took the steps already created and stacked them up and made a choreographed piece that he could repeat. After all, he was going to have to do it in front of a camera 32 times. After the film came out, the calls started and I did *Meet Joe Black, In and Out,* and *The Object of My Affection*, among others. I was working with Meryl Streep, Kevin Kline, and all these stars who had to dance. Meanwhile, all I wanted to do was a Broadway show! Luckily for me I finally got to do a regional production of *Follies* at the Paper Mill Playhouse and director Michael Mayer saw the show. He offered me my first job as a Broadway choreographer on the revival of *You're a Good Man, Charlie Brown.* I say this to so many young choreographers who want to work on Broadway: "It's not about how many numbers you choreograph in a show, it's about getting your foot in the door. Once it's in the door, suddenly you have a calling card." After doing *Charlie Brown*, director Jack O'Brien called me to choreograph *The Full Monty*. Over the years, we've continued to collaborate on *Hairspray, Dirty Rotten Scoundrels,* and *Catch Me If You Can*. I have worked with Jack more than any other director.

CRAMER: During *Will Rogers Follies* you created *Broadway Bares*. Tell us what it is, what it does, and why you created it.

MITCHELL: I was a choreographer and I was trying to showcase my ability. In addition, I had lost too many friends to the AIDS epidemic and my volunteer work wasn't enough. I didn't feel like I was doing my part. It seemed reasonable to combine the two. Influenced by a New York Cable TV show and my love for bur-lesque, I decided I wanted to do sexy, hot choreography. Somehow all of that surfaced in *Broadway Bares*. We got our start at a lit-tle strip bar doing one show with all men. The owner asked for another, we did it. We made $8,000. As soon as the show was over, I said, "I can do this better." We can add girls. So I added them and we made $17,000. I knew the show could be better with a theme. We added themes and we kept building more into it: costumes, lights, and higher production value. Dancers were calling me. They wanted to be in the show. They'd seen it. It's hot. It's sexy. It's not what they got to do on stage in a Broadway show and in this pro-duction they were the *stars*. It snowballed. To this day, performers, crew, everyone generously contributes their time and talent free of charge. We made a million dollars last year, *one* million dollars in *one* night stripping for charity. We've got a book, a CD, and a website. We did it in London, Vegas, and outside of NYC on Fire Island. It's become a brand. Our little charity show also spawned *Peep Show*, which is produced in Vegas.

CRAMER: The *Broadway Bares* "calling card" opened the door for you in Vegas as a director-choreographer. I have spoken to many established artists in this book who, like you, knew they must showcase their work. Most were relegated to a studio with an invited audience, but you were able to share your vision and work on a vastly larger scale complete with production value.

MITCHELL: Yes. *Bares* helped me in more ways than one. Producers and directors could see that I was capable of putting a show together and creating something from scratch.

CRAMER: So, you had that show under your belt when director Michael Mayer asked you to choreograph *Charlie Brown*.

MITCHELL: The show was already in its tenth year. I was so happy to get each job as they came along. I was taking one step at a time and slowly building my resume. I was not trying to jump or get ahead of myself. I was happy to do each gig and learn from it and go forward. This profession takes patience and diligence.

CRAMER: *Charlie Brown* was a big hit, but your next show *The Full Monty* made people sit up and take notice. Your choreography was exceptional. The show is about Buffalo steelworkers low on cash and prospects who decide to strip for money after their wives are smitten with a touring show of Chippendales. Who better than you Jerry, with your *Broadway Bares* track record to choreograph this musical? Besides the final strip number, the basketball number is unique because, as a dancer, you had specific tools to create the piece. It is your background as an athlete and a ball player that made the number "real."

MITCHELL: The basketball number was a career changer for me but all of the staging in the show was crucial. I said to Jack O'Brien, the director, "First things first. We cannot make these boys do a pirouette. If they do a pirouette, we sink the ship." These are guys like my brother who not only look like they can't dance, they can't. They are going to play basketball and actually take their clothes off and it's going to be fun for the audience. David Yazbek, the composer, had written this great Michael Jordon ball number. During rehearsals, the end of Act One just wasn't working and I got to thinking, "What if we took the ball number from Act Two and moved it to the end of the first act?" The idea was that the lead character gets the boys psyched up by taking them through a series of basketball drills. They actually think they're going to be able to accomplish the strip number because they're translating basketball moves into striping moves. The boys come back at the top of Act Two and realize they're just basketball players. They're not dancers yet. Consequently in Act Two, there is still another place to go, another level to achieve. That number got a scream from the audience when the curtain came down and it's become something I have continued to try to do with each of the shows I work on. I want the audience to go out at intermission on a high. I try to make sure I get a little scream, a thrilled reaction from the audience. I also did this on *Legally Blonde* at the end of Act One. The audience leaves the theatre actually cheering and screaming for Elle Woods to make it into college. The audience becomes so involved in the success of the characters. It happens in *Hairspray* with the march against segregation, as well as in *Dirty Rotten Scoundrels* with the game changing Act One conclusion. The audience is completely invested and so excited to see where the story will take them in Act II. It's such a high. You always want the audience to be buzzing when the lights come up for intermission. That little scream always delivers.

CRAMER: How do you select and work with assistants on your shows?

MITCHELL: Almost every single assistant I've hired has been a dancer for me first or has been a choreographer or dancer in *Broadway Bares*. I have to see them perform. I need an assistant who can get up and out dance me. You have to show me that you can do that double pirouette better than anyone else in the room or at least have an attitude about it. They need to be able to do whatever I do as well as bring their own bag of tricks to the party. The story and structure of the choreography and conceit of the idea is always mine from start to finish; but I invite my assistants to take the journey with me because I trust them and I believe in their talent. They always bring their "A" game to the room. I was a swing for two shows. I was fast. Show it to me once—boom—I had it. I was like a computer when I was a kid. I could do every step. I can still do most of the steps today from all of the shows I danced in because I have that memory. These tools and abilities are absolutely necessary when you are a swing, a dance captain, or an assistant. I was hired in Vegas to retool *EFX*, a big show at the MGM Grand. I wanted to create an aerial number with dancers, so there we were all in a room together with this apparatus hanging from the ceiling. My aerialist was choreographing and he goes up to do this pass on this aerial machine. He did it once and I watched, sitting in a chair. I said, "Well, what if you turned to the left?" He said, "What do you mean?" I said, "I'll show you." So, I get on the aerial apparatus and the crew takes me up 12 feet in the air. Now, no one in the cast knows that I can even do a pull up, let along suspend myself in the air. I started executing the whole routine. My aerialist's jaw was on the floor. First of all, he didn't know that I could do anything like that. Second, he was unaware that I could pick up what he did by watching it one time. I watched his body twist and turn upside down. It was mostly gymnastic dance in the air. He wasn't doing flips or anything like that. Safe to say that during the whole routine I had my hand in one loop, so I couldn't fall or be seriously hurt. My aerialist couldn't believe I could do it, but that's choreography. It's the ability to recognize physical motion, clock it, and show someone else what you just did. Assistants should be spectacular at that. When I turn around now and say, "What did I do?" I look to my assistants and they say, "You did this." I say, "Okay, show it to me," because I'll forget it and somebody has to remind me what I did. Not always, but their job is to dance and watch you. That's the assistant you want. You want somebody who can actually watch you do it and then give it back to you.

CRAMER: Do you and your assistants work in a more improvisational atmosphere or do you come in completely prepared for the day?

MITCHELL: Once I am involved in a show, the first thing I do is listen to the music again and again. I do a lot of research on the period and then get in the room and start to work on vocabulary, the steps that actually belong to the period. How do I want to move when I hear the music? During this process I'm thinking about the story constantly. Where does the character have to go? Then I begin to structure and fill it in. Today was the second day of *Catch Me If You Can* rehearsals. I've worked for two weeks in a room creating all the numbers with my assistants, so I have a basic shape. I have the steps for everything, but now I've got the full company of dancers. I often say to them, "I'm going to teach you this section and then I'm going to do patterns later to get you to the next section. I'll teach you both sections but don't worry about the patterns in between. Just walk to the places I give you. Eventually I will give you a step pattern but right now I'm drawing the outline." Then I'll take my colored pencils and I'll start shading it in. Once I get it the way I want it, I'll spray it with hair spray and it'll stick, you know? I don't want to waste time if it's not exact. I want to get the rough structure and see if it holds. Once the structure holds for me then I start to shade it in.

CRAMER: Have you ever had to choreograph a large portion of a number on the spot or in the moment in a rehearsal?

MITCHELL: Yes. When we were doing *Dirty Rotten Scoundrels* we were two or three weeks into rehearsals and we had no number for our supporting leads. Our composer David Yazbek had started the number "Like Zis, Like Zat" but it was never completed. One day he walked in and announced he'd finished the number, so we escaped into the next room and in 20 minutes I choreographed the entire duet start to finish. I had been waiting, you see, and I knew everything about the characters. I knew what their story was, where they had to start and finish, and I knew where the number had to take them. When you're doing a musical, it always depends on the story, always. It doesn't matter if it's a word, a step, or a costume; it's all about telling the story. The more information you have, the better. If you are capable of applying that information to the number, then you're home free. What does the number need to deliver? At what point in the story do I have to get this character from here to there? That's really what you're trying to figure out.

CRAMER: What do you look for in a dancer, beyond technique?

MITCHELL: My favorite dancer is an actor. You can turn until you're blue in the face, but if you can't tell me why you're turning the way you are, or what you're expressing and what you're feeling when you're doing it, I'm not going to be interested for very long. That'll last about 16 counts and then you have to actually make me feel something when you move. An actor who dances or sings is always going to get my attention. We were doing the ballet "Billion Dollar Baby" in *Jerome Robbins Broadway,* and in the number the cast gets drunk and exits a speakeasy and they all bust loose. There's one meek and mild flapper girl in a shimmy dress who comes out, raises her arms, screams at the top of her lungs, shakes her dress so all the fringe is moving, goes crazy, and does the Charleston. Mr. Robbins cast Suzanne Fletcher as that girl in the Broadway show. Now, Suzanne Fletcher is really an actress who sings and dances, but is more of a character actress. It was spectacular when she performed that moment because she was acting and it's the only way it would work. It had nothing to do with being a "dancer." It was such a great lesson to learn, so valuable for me. One day I brought my dog to rehearsal. Jerome Robbins loved my Golden Retriever. He sat under the stage manager's table on his leash. We were rehearsing another number called "Make Your Dreams Come True," which was a pantomime ballet. It centered on three fantasy dance numbers done by one female dancer and three male silent movie stars. In rehearsal I was playing the last male star, a Valentino type, and I had to die dramatically after I was poisoned by the actress. She emptied the poison from her ring into my drinking cup. I took the cup, drank, and I died on the floor. Jerry says, "Stop, stop, stop, stop, that's terrible. I didn't believe that and nobody else will either. You teach that to a dancer, it's going to take me six months to get it out of their body and reteach it to them right." And he says, "Give me that cup." Now, remember, I didn't have a cup in my hand because it's a pantomime; but he said, "Give me that cup, play the music, watch." He grabs the imaginary cup out of my hand, drinks it and dies. My dog starts to whimper and crawls towards Jerry. He convinced my dog! Ultimately, it's about commitment. That is another great lesson learned.

CRAMER: What do you look for in a dancer or performer at an open call?

MITCHELL: Once dancers have learned the combination, I talk to them. I say this to young performers all the time: "Look, I know you just learned this so I don't care if you make a mistake. I can teach you steps. What I can't teach you is to dance full out and to dance like you've never danced before in your life, or like this is the last time you're ever going to dance. You've got to show me what that is. Show me this means more to you right now than anything else. Your energy and focus is *here*, nowhere else. If I see that quality in you then I'm going to watch *you* not the person three down from you."

CRAMER: There was a time when casts were made up of principals, the singing ensemble, and the dance ensemble. That no longer exists. Financial constraints have forced producers to use smaller casts. Performers must be actors, singers, and dancers to be hired today. That being said, do you make any delineation between musical staging and choreography?

MITCHELL: Oh, yes. When you're working with a cast in a musical, you're going to have a huge variety of technical levels. I have a huge variety right now in *Catch Me If You Can*. It's day two and I'm thinking, "What am I going to do with these guys? How am I going to make them look good?" Ultimately, that's my responsibility. My job is to make everybody look fantastic. If they don't look good, I don't look good, and neither does the show. I have to remember why I hired them and utilize their strengths for the good of choreographic structure, as well as the good of the show. If everybody had exactly the same talents, you'd be bored; so you figure out how you're going to put the puzzle together.

CRAMER: How much do projects overlap for you?

MITCHELL: I think what's interesting is, you find yourself working on multiple projects at once. All of them are in different stages of development. I'm working on two projects right now. One is *Kinky Boots,* based on the film by the same name, and the other is *Ballroom,* a remake of the Michael Bennett musical. I've done two readings and one reading—workshop with *Ballroom.* With *Kinky Boots,* I've done two readings. We're working on the script and preparing to do a full workshop on our feet. I have to keep primary focus on *Catch Me* until opening night, but until then, I can multitask on upcoming projects.

CRAMER: Do you have preference between new works or revivals?

MITCHELL: I always prefer a new show. It's not that I don't appreciate or dislike revivals. I won a Tony Award for choreographing a revival, but I will always prefer to do something new. If you're going to do a revival, why do it if you don't approach it in a brand new way? What's the point, otherwise? I haven't directed a revival yet. I'm working on *Ballroom* and it's quite different. We have new songs by Marvin Hamlisch. The script is almost completely restructured. I've lost characters and brought new ones in. It's a very interesting piece because we don't have a reference to ballrooms today. It's not in our psyche. Our reference is *Dancing with the Stars.* So, it's a tough story to tell and you have to approach it fresh.

CRAMER: Your first job as director-choreographer was *Legally Blonde.* Were you approached by the producers to direct?

MITCHELL: Yes. The producers asked me if I'd be interested in telling the story and I said, "Absolutely. I love the story. I love the movie." I thought it was a no-brainer turning the film into a musical. The producers didn't have a writing team, so demos (a sample of work) were requested from many composers. I asked them to put the demos all on one CD with no names. There were four groups and I listened to the CD of every group doing the same three songs:

the opening number, the *Legally Blonde* ballad, and another song of their choice. What is so fascinating about this story is that I chose a team of composers who had written dance music for me years before on a film called *Geppetto,* that I did with Drew Carey. We found our book writer, Heather Hearne, out in Los Angeles. She had written a couple of great movies and I thought she really knew and understood Southern California. Heather knew El Wood's vocabulary and was her spitting image, so we were off and running. *Legally Blonde* was a huge hit in New York and London. We are mounting a tour in the UK as well as a German and Australian company.

CRAMER: Will you be involved in any of that?

MITCHELL: Yes, all of them.

CRAMER: Did directing seem a natural segue to you?

MITCHELL: Yes. I knew that I was going to end up directing. *Legally Blonde* was the perfect show for me because I went into it completely confident. I was not afraid. I knew how to tell the story and I surrounded myself with the greatest team in the world to help me tell it.

CRAMER: Some industry people feel like choreographers have secondary status. They have to fulfill the vision of the director while trying to maintain their own voice.

MITCHELL: It shouldn't be hard to maintain your own voice, but you do have to fill the vision of the director. The director's got to be in charge. There can only be one captain of the ship. If you're lucky enough to have a director like Jack O'Brien, you have a generous collaboration and you learn. He invites you to a seat right next to him and allows you to have a say in the scene. In other words, if he's going to tell you something about your choreography, you can tell him something about the text in those scenes and he welcomes it. Think about the musicals that you think are brilliant. Most of the time, they were directed and choreographed by one person. If they weren't, then the team had an amazing alliance.

CRAMER: You've worked with Jack many times as referenced earlier, including *The Full Monty, Hairspray, Dirty Rotten Scoundrels*, and *Catch Me If You Can.* You must have a sixth sense about the other person.

MITCHELL: We don't even talk. We look at each other and we know. We're both from Michigan and we have the same upbringing. There's so much that seems easy and familiar about our collaboration and relationship.

CRAMER: The shows you have done together are seamless.

MITCHELL: That's the point. It has to be seamless. You can't see where the director's work stops and the choreographer's starts. It must flow. It needs to be one idea coming from the same brain. We're all individuals—the writers, the director, the choreographer—but we must present one clear idea.

CRAMER: How many different styles of dance would you say you studied in your lifetime?

MITCHELL: I've studied ballet, tap, jazz, ballroom, acrobatics, gymnastics, and tango.

CRAMER: Your answer is pertinent to all students who ask why they must take a form of dance they do not like. It's not always ballet. It can be all different forms.

MITCHELL: I think the most important thing in my life was ballet.

CRAMER: And you didn't start till you were 18.

MITCHELL: If I could, if I had the time, I would take a ballet class every day.

CRAMER: Do you feel that any one style or genre of dance has influenced your choreography more than any other?

MITCHELL: I don't know. Style is a very interesting question. I'm not the one to say that I have a style because it's not what I'm concerned with. I'm concerned with telling a story. So I do the steps that are required to tell the story. For instance, when the Jets in *West Side Story* dance at the gym, do they move like the bottle dancers in the wedding scene in *Fiddler on the Roof*? No, I don't think they do. Those styles are so foreign to each other. They are completely unique and honest to the characters. Now, on the other hand, Fosse was a style master. He had a very limited bag of tricks, which were brilliant, but you saw them in all of his productions.

CRAMER: You can visually identify a show of his immediately.

MITCHELL: Yes. Not all of his shows have the same steps but there's a group of steps that we identify as "Fosse." There are other people who have used them but he was the one who put the white gloves on and suddenly it became a style. I don't know if he was thinking that when he did it, but it's definitely a style that defines him. You can't say the same thing about Jerome Robbins. He had amazing humor in his choreography but you can't label him "a funny choreographer." Michael Bennett had a bit of a style, yet his choreography had great contrast. *Dream Girls* doesn't have anything in common with *A Chorus Line*. For me, it just depends on the show. *Hairspray* isn't going to have a whole lot to do with *Catch Me If You Can* but they're almost the same period. They're three years apart.

CRAMER: When you go into the studio to begin working on your vocabulary for a show, you are listening to the music over and over, as you said. Are you listening to piano tracks or are you listening to complete orchestrated tracks?

MITCHELL: It depends on the composer.

CRAMER: Do you read music, and if you do, do you find it helpful?

MITCHELL: I do read music, but never when I'm choreographing.

CRAMER: So it's all from an aural perspective?

MITCHELL: Yes. What do I hear? How does it make me feel? Mark Shaman (composer of *Catch Me If You Can*) will give you the entire score before you start rehearsing. He will give you a track with everything orchestrated exactly how he hears it. Cindy Lauper (composer for *Kinky Boots*) has also been providing me with complete tracks. Marvin Hamlisch (composer for *Ballroom*) played his tracks on the piano. So it depends on the composer.

CRAMER: Do you find that you ever have to backtrack in any way to add things that you may not have heard initially, musically, to compliment what you hear later down the road?

MITCHELL: Oh, yes, absolutely. You'll hear something and then the real orchestration is played and it's either not there or something's there that you didn't hear before and you say, "Oh, I've got to fix that."

CRAMER: Are you ever in a situation where you have no music, where you start from scratch?

MITCHELL: Sure. When I start preproduction and I don't have anything to listen to, the key person in the room for me is the drummer. The composer is giving me a song on the piano but usually I'm consulting with the drummer first. When we put the basketball number together for *The Full Monty*, I got to a section and said, "Write something that sounds like the drum section of a big band number. This is what I want here. I'm dribbling the ball." The drummer improvised something on the spot and I said, "Yeah, write that. Go home and write that." When he came back the next day we started to tool around with it and really made it work. He got the idea of what I needed to make the ball bounce, and make the audience see it bounce. All I said was "big band" and he knew exactly what I wanted.

CRAMER: What kind of atmosphere do you create in your rehearsals?

MITCHELL: Today was the first day of *Catch Me If You Can* rehearsals with the dancers. It was 10:00 a.m. and I said, "Okay, let's go. Full out. Ready. . . and five, six, seven, eight," and they all laughed. Many of them know me. Some of them are working for me for the first time and I said, "Look, gang, if you don't know me, here's the truth. I have to start at ten full out because from ten to two, I'm a maniac. In the afternoon I'll do less crazy stuff." You know, I'm a little more relaxed in the afternoon, but I'm an early riser. I'm very concentrated. I'm like a horse in the gate, ready to go. I get in there and I go full out. Today I did this opening number from start to finish. It's huge. It's not finessed, but my goal was to get it done and on its feet.

CRAMER: You'd rather get everything up and on its feet, and then clean and fix.

MITCHELL: Absolutely.

CRAMER: Let's talk about your TV show, *Step It Up and Dance*. Your role was mentoring dancers. Did you enjoy the project?

MITCHELL: Yes, I had a good time. They didn't really understand what to do with me in the show. Oddly enough, it was more about the dancers than it was about dance. Do you understand?

CRAMER: Oh, I do. Producers prefer the backstage drama. It is reality television after all.

MITCHELL: Yes, it was all about drama. I've learned so much about the good and bad in reality television. It was a wonderful experience and I'd do it again. I would do anything that promotes dance in a positive light, and the show did just that.

CRAMER: Do you think that directors and choreographers face any particular hurdles or obstacles these days that they didn't necessarily face when you were starting out and assisting others?

MITCHELL: Well, I think it's incredibly hard for a director to break in, and I think it's equally hard for a choreographer. It's the reason I started DanceBreak in 2002 with Melinda Atwood. Each year, DanceBreak produces a series of presentations in New York City to showcase the work of emerging choreographers for an audience of producers, directors, artistic directors, writers, institutional managers, and agents. It provides invaluable networking opportunities to early and mid-career choreographers. Melinda and I wanted to support and advance the careers of these artists. I now serve on the Foundation Board. When I got my start it was very important for me to be a dancer first and work under choreographers who I admired. I often tried to audition for choreographers that I wanted to work for and observe. When I was in the room with Agnes de Mille, Jerome Robbins, Michael Bennett, Ron Field, or any of those people, I would sit and watch them. I learned so much by watching them and I wanted to be their assistants. I couldn't just go up to them and say, "Let me be your assistant," because why would a choreographer ask you to be their assistant if they don't know whether or not you can dance? You must prove yourself physically first. It all goes back to the qualities I described earlier for any assistant, dance captain, or swing.

CRAMER: How does the role of choreographer differ from the role of director-choreographer?

MITCHELL: The role of director-choreographer is easier because your story is clear. You don't have to talk through every beat of the show with the director. You do have to come in with your own ideas and then sometimes put them on their feet and show them to the director. Either he'll say, "I love that," or he'll say, "That's terrible. Start over." You know, I've had instances with directors where I felt the director didn't understand movement. He didn't understand how choreography can help tell the story. I've always emerged in a positive light because, ultimately, I'm a collaborative person when I'm choreographing. When you're the director-choreographer you know the story and you are asking the creative team to help you. It's all coming out of your head, so if you don't have to tell the choreographer what your idea is, you've actually saved time. When I was doing *Legally Blonde*, I had a hat on the desk and I'd say, "If I put this hat on, don't ask me questions about direction. I'm the choreographer today. We're doing steps for the next two hours. Don't ask me anything. Just learn the steps." It was a great joke. We had a ball.

CRAMER: It appears you have transitioned into director-choreographer for the long haul. Is that a fair assumption?

MITCHELL: The work drives me. Where there's a good story, there is rewarding work to be done in either hat. However, on my next two projects I am serving in both capacities.

CRAMER: I would like to wish you the best of luck on both *Ballroom* and *Kinky Boots*. It was so nice to chat with you.

MITCHELL: Thanks Lyn.

CHAPTER EIGHT

Casey Nicholaw

Casey Nicholaw began dancing at the age of 13. He joined San Diego Junior Theatre and took classes in tap every Saturday. Since that was his only formal training, Casey learned to dance and to choreograph performing in shows all through his childhood. After just one and a half years in college, Casey packed his bags and headed to the Big Apple. His hard work as a performer and the support of his family had a direct impact on his career path once he arrived in New York. Casey performed as a dancer, singer, and actor in eight Broadway hits including *Crazy for You, Steel Pier, The Scarlet Pimpernel, Saturday Night Fever, Seussical, Thoroughly Modern Millie, Victor/Victoria,* and *Best Little Whorehouse Goes Public.*

Casey has been nominated for Tony and Drama Desk awards for his Broadway work as a choreographer for *Spamalot*, and as a director and choreographer for *The Drowsy Chaperone* and *The Book of Mormon*. He shared the Tony award for directing *Mormon* in 2011 with Trey Parker of South Park fame.

City Center Encores has seen Mr. Nicholaw at the helm of two productions and he has directed regionally at such prestigious theatres as Carnegie Hall, the Old Globe, Good Speed Opera House, and Radio City Music Hall. He brought new shows to life such as *The Night They Raided Minsky's, Robin and the Seven Hoods, Aladdin*, and *Elf*.

CRAMER: Casey, your career trajectory could be a text book example for most students pursuing a Broadway directing or choreographic career. Share with us some of the finer points of your journey.

NICHOLAW: I began as a dancer. I was an ensemble member in eight Broadway shows. In seven of them I was an original cast member and for one show, I was a replacement. This means that when a cast member left the show, I was placed in their track or part. The most important thing I could do as a cast member was observe. I watched everything happen. I was so interested in the process—what worked and what didn't work. By the time I was cast in *Seussical*, one of my last Broadway shows, I was filled with my own ideas on how to improve every aspect of the show. I paid attention all the time. That's exactly where my training came from. With *Seussical*, I told myself that I didn't want to be that person sitting backstage silently declaring how different I would do things if given the chance. I decided to man up and do something about it. I rented studio space Wednesday and Saturdays between shows and said to myself, "I'm just going to be creative." I didn't know what that meant, and for the first few weeks I was just sitting there eating a sandwich in a studio thinking, "What the hell am I doing?" But before I knew it, I decided to do a presentation or showcase of my own. I spent all the money I had in savings—close to 4,000 dollars, and asked 25 dancer friends to participate. I choreographed three pieces and invited every writer, director, and producer I ever worked with to the showcase. There was a tremendous amount of people in attendance because of all the Broadway shows I had been a part of. The showcase went really well. I was so proud of myself for being able to pull it off, and that's how it all started for me. I got into other people's consciousness through that effort. This led me to jobs at theatres like Fifth Avenue in Seattle and the Ordway in St. Paul. Many producers loved my work even though I was really green. Most wanted to discuss future projects. Two years after my showcase, I participated in DanceBreak. But in essence, I had already done DanceBreak on my own.

CRAMER: For the benefit of our readers, let's explain your use of the term "green" and what DanceBreak is all about. The term "green" means a beginner lacking choreographic experience. Here's where DanceBreak enters the picture. Each year, DanceBreak produces a series of presentations in New York City to showcase the work of emerging choreographers for an audience of producers, directors, artistic directors, writers, institutional managers, and agents. It's basically a showcase, but choreographers compete by videotape for one of the six spots on the program. There is no winner from the six who participate. Hopefully, the showcase leads to job offers.

NICHOLAW: When DanceBreak happened, it threw me over the top. Many of the same creative people present at my independent showcase were in attendance, and DanceBreak served to reinforce my previous work. Producers and directors could see that my creative effort was no fluke.

CRAMER: You were getting better and better.

NICHOLAW: I got several jobs specifically from DanceBreak. Two of them were productions for City Center Encores! I was high on the "choreographic radar," so to speak. *Spamalot* came right out of that. I got a call from director Mike Nichols saying, "You know we've got your name." Jerry Mitchell was actually too busy to do *Spamalot* and recommended me to Nichols. Jerry is the nicest guy alive. I think that's how it should be, established directors and choreographers encouraging new directors and choreographers, instead of constantly operating in competition mode.

CRAMER: That's not the first I've heard of Jerry Mitchell's big-heartedness. I find that amount of generosity remarkable, and of course, you'll do it for someone else one day.

NICHOLAW: Yes, I am already starting to do that with my associates. I recommend them for anything I can't do. Not only did Jerry Mitchell put in a good word for me, but the director on *Bye Bye Birdie* at City Center Encores!, Jerry Saks, did as well. Nichols called Jerry Zaks and said, "What do you think of this guy?" So, I met with Nichols, resume and DanceBreak video in hand, and we talked for an hour. I never got a single thing out of my bag, and he just said, "So, you want the job?" I said, "Yes!" and Lyn, I sobbed my way home in the cab! I had my first Broadway show.

CRAMER: In keeping with our conversation about working for the sake of experience, did you ever help out a colleague by dancing for free if he or she was presenting a showcase or choreographing?

NICHOLAW: Yes, when I was starting out, my friends and I would do preproduction for each other. I would say, "I'm doing this show. Will you come work with me?" He or she would say, "I'm doing *Footloose* over here, will you come work for me?" We would trade off and help each other out.

CRAMER: I would like to restate that your career has taken a traditional path in the sense that you have gone from an ensemble member to Broadway Director-Choreographer.

NICHOLAW: Absolutely and my life has kind of been like that. I'm more grateful for the path than anything in my life, quite honestly, because I didn't get everything really fast. I waited tables in New York. Over the years, I've worked my butt off to get to where I am, and am so lucky it happened that way because I'm so much more appreciative of absolutely everything.

CRAMER: Have you ever been an assistant or a dance captain for anyone?

NICHOLAW: I haven't. My training came from watching everyone at all times.

CRAMER: Keeping your eyes on the show process.

NICHOLAW: Absolutely. Also, I got a good reputation as a performer. I was creative and did my job. I was trustworthy, you know, and fun to have around.

CRAMER: Performers do ride on their reputation.

NICHOLAW: There are many performers that don't observe and focus only on themselves. You know what I mean. It's a comment on their work ethic. Word spreads about those kinds of cast members. There are people I won't hire again because of that. A bad work ethic angers me more than anything. It really does.

CRAMER: You now have several Broadway shows under your belt and many award nominations to back up your work. Selecting a project must be completely different now, right?

NICHOLAW: Totally different, because now people come to me and say, "We would like to commission you to do this project." Or, "are you interested in turning this movie into a musical?" There is some material I'm just not interested in, but I make the decision to accept the project based on something else that appeals to me about the show. Oddly however, I sometimes pick something just because it's offered and it turns out to be a project I adore.

CRAMER: Can you give me an example?

NICHOLAW: There is a musical version of the children's book, *Tuck Everlasting,* that I'm currently working on. I don't know if you know that book at all, but I knew nothing about it beforehand. I read it and thought, "Well, that's a nice book," but once we started working on it, I was in love with it. We're doing another reading of it this spring and hopefully it will be in New York sometime within the next few years. Occasionally you select a project because you like the people involved, or you like the concept of it as opposed to the material itself. The process can also work in reverse. You like the material going in, but eventually, it takes on a life of its own, and once you add your own sensibility, it doesn't work for you any longer.

CRAMER: Tell me about assistants and associates you hire. How do you select them?

NICHOLAW: Well, I like to surround myself with people I know. The associates that I have are my friends. For me, that's the best way to go because they know you so well. But an associate who is your friend can be a tricky line to walk at times; you never want it to get ugly. I'm lucky because it's worked out pretty well.

CRAMER: You have different people for different projects depending on need, so tell me how you use them, and how much freedom you give them.

NICHOLAW: I use Jen Warner, Casey Hutchings, and John McGinnis, among others, as my Associate Directors. They're all fantastic. Normally, I will have one Associate Director and quite a few associate choreographers. They really have their eyes on choreographing, so you're not going to keep them as long. Quite honestly, this is because they want to do their own thing, make their own way. It's totally understandable. Meanwhile, some associate directors are happy doing just that—being associates. They sometimes have children and families, and the associate role is the right fit. Most of the associates I work with were performers with me at one time. Again, it's really worked out nicely because it's personal. We're a team and because I do both jobs, director and choreographer, and have two rooms running at the same time, it's extremely important that I have someone I can depend on, who can function on their own while I'm in the other room. All my associate directors are dancers as well. Since I am a Director-Choreographer, it is imperative that they function in both roles. For example, if someone is having trouble with tap steps, Casey can take them while John is in the room with everyone else doing a big dance number. I'm over in the corner doing a scene, and we know we'll stagger the union breaks so that on my 10-minute break, I'll run in there and take a look at the dance number. I will always start the number myself and then when an associate starts cleaning I move on to something else. I've got someone I trust well enough to say, "You know, I don't know what the ending of that is. Just put an ending on it and let's see what it looks like." My associates know my sensibility well enough to decide whether I will like something or not.

CRAMER: That's so great and quite a time saver. Now, when you have auditions, do you bring in your associates to assist in the selection process?

NICHOLAW: I handle casting, with my musical director and casting director, but I certainly have associates there to help because I don't like to dance around anymore. When I first did *Spamalot* I was so excited to do it all. I danced all the combinations, but it's better for me to be able to sit back and watch the instruction and how people are picking up the combinations.

CRAMER: Do you find over the years that you look for anything in particular in someone auditioning, something that has become consistent for you in each audition process?

NICHOLAW: I just want people that are present, who aren't putting it on or mugging. I want someone that has warmth to them.

CRAMER: What size ensemble do you normally cast?

NICHOLAW: You basically get six guys and six girls and they all have to sing and dance, depending on what the show is. Sometimes you also get a couple of character actors. Each show calls for something different but you know the ensemble has to do it all. I prefer people that have a little character to them. I respect shows that require more character types. *Robin and the Seven Hoods*, based on the 1960s Rat Pack movie, a project that we just did at the Old Globe in San Diego, had the sexiest cast alive. They were great character men, and such good dancers. I really hope that show comes to New York, because I've never been prouder of any of my work. I believe choreographers improve exponentially with the amount of creative work they do. I am very lucky in that way because I have had so many jobs within the last few years.

CRAMER: When you are prolific it makes you better. I think the more work you are generating, the more creative you become.

NICHOLAW: I agree. I think, sure, there is a burnout point too.

CRAMER: Let's speak to that point. You have put up five or six different companies of *The Drowsy Chaperone* and at least four companies of *Spamalot* beyond Broadway. I assume you were at the helm of all these productions. What is it like putting up your own work over and over again?

NICHOLAW: It's really fun the second time. It was a joy to do *Drowsy* in London because I felt like we had improved upon it, big time. Some of the things I wanted to improve I wasn't able to do in New York because of talent limitations or other obstacles. It felt more like a dance show in London than it did here. Then, the US tour followed and my associates took on that responsibility because I was doing something else.

CRAMER: You turn the entire production over to them?

NICHOLAW: That is where they really come into play, and you have to trust them more with the spirit of the show than with just the steps. Most of my work contains huge amounts of comedy. If my associates do not impart that spirit toward the work as they teach, then the show is in trouble. I have to trust them completely.

CRAMER: How is your creative process different for a revival versus a new show?

NICHOLAW: I don't have much interest in revivals. I like creation and developing a show from structuring and problem solving and working with the writers to build something new. That is exciting to me. However, I'm sure that after a few new shows in a row, I will be really happy to do a revival. On the other hand, I have to say that two of my favorite experiences have been with City Center Encores! This is a venue that specializes in scaled-down revivals. I did *Follies* and *Anyone Can Whistle* and those are two shows I didn't know at all. They didn't feel like revivals to me. I knew the music but I'd never seen a production of either one.

CRAMER: Is your process different if you're just choreographing, versus directing and choreographing?

NICHOLAW: It's the same. I was so involved with every aspect of *Spamalot*. Nichols and I worked side by side, and I don't feel like I worked as "just a choreographer." That was certainly my title, but Nichols was completely inclusive in the process.

CRAMER: What was it like working with someone of that caliber?

NICHOLAW: It was incredible, but when you are working on a show you don't think of them in a different way; they are just your creative partner.

CRAMER: What is your input with scenic and costume designers?

NICHOLAW: Oh, just about everything you can think of. It's collaborative from the start.

CRAMER: Do you write post-it notes, make charts, send ideas via e-mail, or have in-depth conversations on the phone when you get an idea?

NICHOLAW: Well, it is a combination of all the things you mentioned, but then there are lots of meetings once you get rolling. I will meet night and day with the set designer and costume designer. I prefer in-person, face-to-face meetings because you have to look at things, and two people work better together having everything in front of them.

CRAMER: Do you do a great deal of research for a show?

NICHOLAW: Sure, I research like crazy, but the funny thing is: accurate research doesn't mean theatrically worthy research. For example, 1920s dance research is a bit boring and there isn't a great deal of it, so I end up using an idea from the research and simply doing my own creative thing. It's a great way to start, but then let it go.

CRAMER: You trust your instincts.

NICHOLAW: Just go with your gut, yes.

CRAMER: Do you have associates with you in preproduction?

NICHOLAW: Yes.

CRAMER: What is the first thing you think about when you are about to choreograph a particular number in a show?

NICHOLAW: It depends. Basically, the first thing that happens is: I live with the music for a while. I set up time with the dance arranger. We talk through the dance break and I let them come up with some musical ideas first so that I can get inspired and start to talk specifics. Then, when you get to preproduction, the first week consists of my associates and me, working with the arranger, so that we can add speed or change things up a bit. Week two, we invite dancers. Before actual rehearsals start, we'll have four to six dancers hired to come in and help us see what it looks like on bodies in space. It is so helpful, and that is where the numbers come alive.

CRAMER: So, you would prefer to work with bodies in space as opposed to visualizing everything in your head?

NICHOLAW: No, I am a pretty big visualizer. Associates have discovered me sitting against a wall with my eyes closed. I feel like I picture it as a movie first. If we've dubbed steps to a certain point, but I don't know where to go next, I will just close my eyes and imagine where I would want to see it move. That is when I start visualizing it. Once you get the structure and visualization down, the steps are really easy. If you are step-wise, you can come up with almost any kind of movement if it serves the story.

CRAMER: So, at this point you've got a few dancers for the second week of preproduction, and you've got some kind of an idea of what you are going to do when you go in for the first days of rehearsal. You still leave yourself open for improvisation, right?

NICHOLAW: Oh, totally.

CRAMER: Is the whole show loosely structured?

NICHOLAW: It's like I have a really solid ground plan, but then it will change at the drop of a hat because it doesn't feel right. All of a sudden we're deciding those steps don't feel right or the story-telling stops cold.

CRAMER: How do you feel about allowing your actors to contribute ideas in rehearsal?

NICHOLAW: I let actors contribute, absolutely. Often it is some-thing like, "What kind of lift would you like to do here? Where do you feel you would want to go next?" You do some of that, but it's a tricky thing. We are all taught that there is a hierarchy in the creative process. There are times that if you let everyone go wild, you're simply not going to get anything done. More than likely, you'll lose respect and whatever vision and structure was in place. Then you start feeling bad for telling people "No, I don't like that." It's too much. People want to be told what to do—they really do. There are many ways to handle actors with respect. You learn tricks over the years. It's not deception, you know, but you learn how to have it all planned out in your head and make actors feel like they are developing it, and are coming up with ideas them-selves. You make them feel like they are contributing something that is very important, because an actor wants to be told what to do, but they don't want to feel like it is completely rigid, that they are being forced to do it a certain way. If an actor says, "You know it feels kind of funny, it would be better to do this," I'm fine with that. I'm not that rigid in the least, but I think it is important that they are making a contribution to the process.

CRAMER: In your work, does a difference exist between staging and choreography?

NICHOLAW: No, I think it has to feel like one process. For me, the spirit and energy of the scene has to feel one in the same with a dance number or sequence. This is why I like doing both direction and choreography. Many times you see a show and the minute you get to a dance number, it feels like a completely different produc-tion. Then the number is over and you're right back to where you were. Literally, you are watching two different shows.

CRAMER: When you sat in the studio with your sandwich and thought, "Why am I here?" did you already know, in that moment, that you wanted to direct?

NICHOLAW: No, I didn't. In fact, I was choreographing a show in San Diego called *Lucky Duck* right before *Spamalot* happened, and John Rando was the director. He said, "Well, you know you're going to direct soon." I felt very comfortable as a choreographer but deep down I really wanted to direct. His words gave me new inspiration because I felt I could do it, given the chance. Then lo and behold, a producer of *The Drowsy Chaperone* called and asked me to direct and choreograph the Broadway production after *Spamalot* and knew I could do it.

CRAMER: You were ready.

NICHOLAW: Now, of course, I have no desire to be a choreographer on a project. I need to do both jobs, wear both hats.

CRAMER: Right, so having control of the entire vision is the key?

NICHOLAW: Yes, for me it is. There might come a point where I won't want to choreograph as much and direct only, but right now, I love choreography. I like telling stories through dance, and I like the energy of the process. That gets me really excited.

CRAMER: You have done productions at City Center Encores!, regional work, and Broadway shows. Explain some differences in the time allotted for different venues and productions.

NICHOLAW: First, you work completely different in each venue. Encores! productions are so tricky but I love it. I thrive on how quickly it has to happen.

CRAMER: The time frame is really short, right?

NICHOLAW: This is Encores! Basically, you have a meet and greet on Monday, and you have a read through if there is time. The music director teaches the music Monday, you start staging it Tuesday, and complete staging Wednesday and Thursday. You perform a run through of the show for the producers on Friday. The sitzprobe, the seated rehearsal with orchestra, is on Saturday and then you have Sunday off. Monday you space the show on stage. Tuesday, you rehearse with costumes and props and then Wednesday night is your first audience. So it's fast. But I love it, I thrive on it, and I know how to do it. The thing is, it's all a bit backward from the process of a regular show. You have to plan an Encores! production three months ahead of time and write it all down exactly as it is going to be blocked and choreographed. You're not allowed a process. There is no time, and setting it is completely different from a regional or Broadway show. So an actor will ask to try something different or experiment and you just have to say no, because of your time factor.

CRAMER: That's hard but that's the way it is.

NICHOLAW: But it's so rewarding to me! It's like the joys of summer stock: seeing everyone in a hallway, or corner-working on their dialog, music, or choreography as efficiently as they can. It is really fun for me. I just love it.

CRAMER: In a regional theatre, what kind of time do you have?

NICHOLAW: Regional theatre is sort of in-between Encores! and Broadway; at least it varies depending on the show. Regional theatre is three or four weeks of rehearsal and a Broadway show is four or five. It used to be six but now we are living through this tough economy.

CRAMER: Yes, how much time did you have for *The Drowsy Chaperone* on Broadway?

NICHOLAW: *Drowsy* had five weeks, *Mormon* had four, and *Elf* had three. But the thing about both *Mormon* and *Elf* is that we had six-week workshops in New York pretty close to our rehearsal start dates. With *Elf*, we did a six-week workshop in the summer. It was preset with the same cast and three weeks was certainly enough.

CRAMER: How were you asked to join the creative team for *The Book of Mormon*?

NICHOLAW: I got a call in the summer that they were looking for a co-director to join Trey Parker, as well as a choreographer. I was in the middle of *Robin and the Seven Hoods* in San Diego, so I just drove up to Los Angeles to meet them and they said, "Great, Let's do it." Seriously, this was only four weeks before the show was going to start rehearsals. I opened *Robin and the Seven Hoods* on a Saturday, flew to New York and started rehearsals for the workshop of *Mormon* on Monday. The dance arranger for *Mormon* had to fly to meet me in San Diego and we had two weeks of preproduction on the numbers in the mornings, while I was in previews for *Robin and the Seven Hoods*. It was actually fine. You know, I'm pretty good at compartmentalizing.

CRAMER: Most director-choreographers are working on multiple projects simultaneously. It seems to be the nature of the beast.

NICHOLAW: It is a little exhausting sometimes wearing five hats each day. By the end of one day, my brain power is just zonked.

CRAMER: Do you read music?

NICHOLAW: Not really, a little bit, but never had much training in music.

CRAMER: So, working with a dance arranger is particularly helpful to your process.

NICHOLAW: Oh, yes. They are creating the structure of the numbers with you.

CRAMER: Even though you don't read note for note, you must still consider yourself musical because you've danced your whole life.

NICHOLAW: Oh, completely, and I'll even sing what I think the dancers should be doing choreographically to the music arranger. We have our own language. Reading music doesn't really help with an arranger anyway because they are creating music from scratch.

CRAMER: But, you can easily follow a score?

NICHOLAW: I can totally follow the score, yes.

CRAMER: In casting your shows, you most always need a comedic quality from a dancer, singer, or actor. How would you go about finding what you need?

NICHOLAW: I find it in their singing audition more than in their dance audition. I usually have everyone read a side from the script. Many times you will just give them a few lines and see if they can act at all, or how comfortable they are with speaking. Obviously, you will get a glimpse of their sense of humor as well.

CRAMER: Let me ask you about growing up in San Diego. You are the oldest of three?

NICHOLAW: Yes.

CRAMER: When did your dance training begin?

NICHOLAW: I didn't start dancing until I was 13. I got into San Diego Junior Theatre where there was a yearly show. We had a little dance class every Saturday, and I focused on tap because I've never had much of an extension, and I've never been supertechnical. But that's how it happened, doing shows in San Diego.

CRAMER: And you went to UCLA, is that correct?

NICHOLAW: For a year and a quarter, then I was out of there.

CRAMER: You came straight to New York?

NICHOLAW: Yes. I came here with 50 bucks and nowhere to live.

CRAMER: Brave.

NICHOLAW: Nineteen.

CRAMER: Oh, very brave. Once you were here, what was your path?

NICHOLAW: I did some summer stock, and watched all my friends get their Equity cards while I didn't. I spent my time waiting a lot of tables and losing my hair. You know, just the normal actors' life. I finally got my equity card working at Beef and Boards Dinner Theatre in Indianapolis. When I lost my hair, I started working more than ever. I was more of a character man.

CRAMER: So you came here with 50 dollars in your pocket, you couldn't afford a voice coach or teacher, and you couldn't afford dance class. How did that progress for you?

NICHOLAW: Well, I did end up affording all those necessities, because I got a job right away working in a movie theatre. I also worked in a restaurant. I took three dance classes a day when I got to the city. I got a voice coach. Coaches are more expensive than class so that wasn't as consistent. I went to lots of classes because it's also a really good outlet to curb spending. I spent all my money on dance classes, and then every Saturday night we would have a game night with friends. It was the way to socialize for free.

CRAMER: Who is the biggest influence on your career?

NICHOLAW: Actually, a little bit of everybody I've worked with, just watching them. I definitely think I have my own style and always have, but, of course, Susan Stroman is a big influence. *Crazy for You* was my first Broadway show. She and I share the same love for old movies and MGM musicals. But I've learned from everybody whether I like what they did, or didn't. I often find myself saying, "I will never do that," or, "I will always do that." This is based on what I observe, or what I learned from other directors and choreographers in the eight Broadway shows I've danced in. *Crazy for You* director, Mike Ockrent, is a huge influence because I was very impressionable during my first Broadway show. I loved working with him, and he treated all the ensemble artists with such respect, and with an attitude that we were more than ensemble members. We felt so important in that show. So much of that is attributed to him.

CRAMER: So you were that kid in southern California, the one with your eyes glued to old movie musicals?

NICHOLAW: When I was a kid you had to wait and see if it was going to play at a revival house because we didn't have DVDs or Blockbuster. We couldn't even afford a Beta Max. But if *On the Town* was playing at the Camden Theatre, off I went.

CRAMER: Were you a singer in school? Were you in choir?

NICHOLAW: I was in high school. I was pretty much a triple threat, which made me a valuable performer. Quite honestly, you know, every time I auditioned for a show, I never got the role I wanted, which meant I must not have been that good. I must have been really energetic, and that's about it. But yeah, I was able to do it all.

CRAMER: Were your parents an influence in any way?

NICHOLAW: No, not really. But my parents were great. They recognized my love for theatre and my interest in it. My mom bought me the cassette tape of *A Chorus Line* and she took my friend and me out of school and drove us to LA to see it. My parents were really supportive.

CRAMER: Have you ever had to audition for a choreographic job?

NICHOLAW: I think I only had to do that once and it was for *A Little Princess*, which never happened. I think it was between me and Andy Blankenbuehler and he got it, but it's okay, I like him.

CRAMER: What was the process like?

NICHOLAW: It's a lot like DanceBreak, but you are given the music, of course. You have to round up your own dancers. I auditioned for a film but the producers were looking for an African American choreographer. If I had gotten the movie, I couldn't have done *Drowsy*. *Drowsy* is basically what made me, you know.

CRAMER: Are you interested in becoming cinematic?

NICHOLAW: Sure, and to be honest, you have to look at things cinematically anyway. When I am sitting against the wall with my eyes closed, I am thinking cinematically. It's funny; I don't feel like I'm rushing to do film because I don't have the experience. I love theatre so much. If that is something that came up, I certainly wouldn't say no.

CRAMER: In casting, do you find that you go back to many of the same people?

NICHOLAW: Oh, yes, absolutely, of course, I do. If I can give any of those people jobs, I will, because I trust them and know them, and love having them in a room.

CRAMER: Once a show opens, how often do you go back and watch it?

NICHOLAW: Oh, it depends on the show and the length of the run. You have to go back quite a bit. *Spamalot* was open for four and a half years, and every couple of weeks to once a month, I was there. Of course, there are periods of time when I am out of town, but once you start replacing people, it really changes. It's this person's first show, it's this person's last show, and this person is going on for the first time in an understudy role. I am asked to watch this person, or that person, or just to come in and take a look at something in particular.

CRAMER: And are you involved in replacement auditions?

NICHOLAW: Yes, I try to be. Sometimes you can't when you have so many other irons in the fire and you have to stop a new project in order to go to a replacement call. Listen, after three years, there are songs you don't want to hear any longer, you know? Once a show has been running for a while, and there's been a tour out, you can start mixing and matching cast members. *Spamalot* was like that after a while. It was fairly easy to replace people because so many people had done it. Some cast members go on to another show that completes its run, and then they come back to *Spamalot*. It happens all the time.

CRAMER: Once you get a show up, do you worry yourself silly with changes that you should have made or concern yourself with things you should have done? Do you let all that go?

NICHOLAW: You let it go, but usually you get a second chance with the tour. And then you play with it a bit, and decide it's much better. Then sometimes you'll actually put that into the newer version. It's good to keep people a bit fresh.

CRAMER: When you get into tech rehearsal, does your focus shift from your actors to everything technical?

NICHOLAW: I love tech because you have to put the creative part with actors on hold for a little bit, and spend time on a different kind of movement from dance steps, the movement of lights and scenery. It's one of my favorite parts of the process.

CRAMER: Have you ever had to go in and direct or choreograph a show that you did not cast?

NICHOLAW: *Mormon.* I would say that when I first started there were perhaps people that I wouldn't have cast to begin with, but I'm so glad it worked out. I love the cast, and I think they are the right people for the roles. It is not an issue in the least.

CRAMER: What about casting in regional theatre?

NICHOLAW: I choreographed a production of *My Fair Lady* at Fifth Avenue Theatre is Seattle, and it was all cast. It can be tricky since you don't know all of the dancer's capabilities. You just force yourself to work in the moment and not do too much preproduction when it comes to choreography.

CRAMER: How does a choreographer even break in to the business today?

NICHOLAW: What's tricky is that a lot of the beginning jobs aren't around anymore. There are less summer stock and regional jobs out there. I think the most important thing in life is just be the best person you can, make the most honest journey, and meet lots of people. I think what brought me here is that I wasn't angling for it. It happened in the steps that we've been talking about. I didn't have to be a choreographer. I made a choice. It just happened naturally, and I think you never know where you are going to get a job from in life. It can come from any walk of life, or any connection.

CRAMER: How is the work ethic different from when you started in theatre years ago?

NICHOLAW: It's quite different. I don't think there are many people these days that want to go work somewhere for little or no wages or that will go to a theatre and participate for the experience alone. I just don't think people think that way anymore. They want it all, and they want it now. It's Broadway or nothing. You know my best experience was as a performer at the New London Barn

Playhouse. We did ten productions and made a 150 dollars for the entire season. We cleaned the toilets, we built the sets, sewed the costumes, and I wouldn't have traded that for anything in the world. I know students are coming out of school saying that they would never do anything like that. Boy, it is a different time.

CRAMER: It is a time of entitlement.

NICHOLAW: It is, isn't it? It's so depressing to me and it affects people's work ethic. People's lives are more difficult when they aren't open to all experiences. You must network; just meet people. You never know what may come of it. Take a less prestigious job. Take a chance.

CRAMER: What was your first paid job as a choreographer?

NICHOLAW: It would have to be the New London Barn Playhouse, again, because the choreographer was so bad, they asked me to finish choreographing his show. Then the producers asked me to choreograph two more. Remember, I was hired as a performer!

CRAMER: Did you audition for the performing job at New London Barn Playhouse or did someone you know hire you directly?

NICHOLAW: No, I auditioned for that job. While at UCLA my freshman year, I decided to travel to NYC for spring break. So, I saved up my money from my job, and I had enough for one week. I saw lots of shows, and I thought it would be fun to audition while I was there. I remember picking up the trade paper, Backstage, at a news stand. I went to Lincoln Center to get music, but I really didn't know what I was doing. I auditioned for five different theatres. I got the job at New London Barn Playhouse without anything, no resume or headshot. I got a couple of callbacks while I was in New York, and honestly I didn't even understand what I was doing.

CRAMER: It was dumb luck.

NICHOLAW: Right. So, my first summer after my freshman year in college I went to New London, loved it, and wondered why I would want to go back to California. I wanted to move to New York and start working, not stay in a school lacking a musical theatre program.

CRAMER: Casey, you appear to be a very happy human being. Is that the environment you try to create in rehearsals?

NICHOLAW: Yes. That is what I try to create. Life is too short; it really is. I'm not a yeller. I will get a little angry sometimes, actually two times with my performers, and one of the times happened two days ago.

LYN CRAMER: Really?

NICHOLAW: Yes, and all students reading this should pay close attention. Seriously, there was an actor in *Mormon* on stage and he wasn't giving it his all. We were in tech and he didn't look good doing a number, and I walked up to him and said, "You need to give me a little more there." He said, "I'm sorry; I'm just not quite here. I'm doing my taxes today and I have a lot on my mind." It irked me so much that I went to my associates and stated the problem, and was told to pull him aside. So I did and said, "You know what? I don't care what you are doing. This is your job. If the director asks you to give more because you don't look good, you give more." I have no patience for that. I work my butt off, and so I expect people that are working under me to do the same. I do create a really great environment that's fun and easy and a bit laidback. I'm not someone that drills people to death, but I expect them to work as hard as I do and I expect them to do their work. I hired them because I liked them and I trust them and I expect them to do it. I don't want to be someone who is always watching over them nudging and nagging them. I'm very respectful. There is always a point in my rehearsals two weeks in where it's a little out of control and everyone is goofing off a lot because I do create a fun work environment. However, there is still structure. There must be because I work really fast. We're going at a quick pace. These *Mormon* boys did not know what hit them, they really didn't. When we got into rehearsal for the workshop, most of the boys were in a panic because they were not hired as dancers. The first workshop had a different director who didn't dance. Now, with me, the boys are dancing their butts off, and they had to get it together fast.

CRAMER: Right. I bet you were just a wall of energy they didn't even expect.

NICHOLAW: They didn't, but they love it now.

CRAMER: Oh, I'm sure they do. There is nothing like a good kinetic actor/singer who gets to dance in a big number. That is a reward like no other.

NICHOLAW: Yes, totally.

CRAMER: Do you have advice that you would like to pass on to students?

NICHOLAW: Yes. Be as good at your job as possible. Be present and really absorb everything. That to me is the single most important thing. Take every opportunity to observe. You still have to goof around, have fun, and enjoy the camaraderie; but observe everything. I feel its how I learned all I know. Be a good worker, and don't burn bridges because if you're not doing your job, it gets around. It absolutely gets around.

CRAMER: You are in a casting session and are looking at two resumes of actors you do not know personally. All things being equal, on what would you base your decision?

NICHOLAW: It would completely hinge on the person's attitude. When I started working on *Spamalot* and would be in a casting room with the casting director looking at all the headshots, the casting director might really love someone and I would say, "Not a chance. I was in a dressing room with him or her. He or she is not a nice person to be around every day." That is why I say do your best job always, because you never know who you are in a room with, and what they are going to end up doing that can have an effect on your life and your livelihood. I've had many, many people's headshots cross my desk where I said, "No, they are trouble backstage. I don't want to work with them. I don't care what their talent is."

CRAMER: Do you pick up the phone and call anybody for a reference or information on someone?

NICHOLAW: I have. It's a small business, really. There was someone I really did not enjoy working with in a show, and a director recently called me and asked what I thought about this person, and I had to tell them the absolute truth. A director is not going to call unless there is already negativity being circulated about someone. Normally, I am just confirming what is already out there.

CRAMER: Is there an upside to these situations?

NICHOLAW: Yes! What I love about the situation is that I can recommend someone that is the same type, and who is a good worker. Usually the recommended actor steps up to the plate and gets the job. It's all karma.

CRAMER: Speaking of karma, who have you worked with in a show, a fellow performer, who has gone on to greatness?

NICHOLAW: Sutton Foster and I did *Thoroughly Modern Millie* together. She played one of the leads for me in *The Drowsy Chaperone*. Also, Beth Leavel who I performed with in *Crazy for You* was the title character in *Drowsy*. We met doing a production of *Showboat* in North Carolina. When I jumped into new territory directing, I wanted to be surrounded by people I know and love. Everyone associated with *Drowsy* were friends and associates, and it was a very special experience.

CRAMER: As was this. Casey, I can't thank you enough.

NICHOLAW: Oh, absolutely, are you kidding?

CRAMER: Is there anything you want to add or?

NICHOLAW: Everyone do your job and have fun doing it.

CRAMER: Thank you so much.

NICHOLAW: My pleasure.

CHAPTER NINE

Randy Skinner

Randy grew up in Columbus, Ohio, and graduated from Ohio State University. With his parents' encouragement, he began dancing at the age of 4, taking classes in tap and jazz. Although he didn't start formal training in ballet until his college years, he credits his teachers with giving him strong ballet technique in his classic jazz classes, a tradition he continues in his own teaching.

He began his career with the Kenley Players, a summer theatre directed by one of Randy's mentors, John Kenley. Mr. Kenley hired the biggest names from the MGM musical era and put them onstage. Randy credits his ensemble experience and friendships made there with instilling in him the desire to perpetuate the classic dance style of the great MGM musicals. He carries that torch today.

Randy moved to New York City in 1976 and eventually met Gower Champion. His life changed. Now a choreographer, director, and teacher, he has helmed productions on Broadway, off-Broadway, in Europe, in regional theatres from coast to coast, and staged innumerous productions for City Center Encores!

He has been nominated for three Tony Awards and two Drama Desk Awards for his unique choreography. Randy is a guest master teacher at colleges and universities across the nation and continues to teach at both Broadway Dance Center and Steps in New York City.

CRAMER: I am so delighted to be speaking with you Randy. I first became familiar with you and your work when I saw *42nd Street* on Broadway. You co-created all of the dance numbers in Gower Champion's original production in 1980, right?

SKINNER: Yes. I did.

CRAMER: I know you're from Columbus and you attended Ohio State University. And I was delighted when I heard you were a communications major, because that was my major as well. My degree was in communications with a theatre emphasis.

SKINNER: Yes. We called it "speech education." That was the degree. I don't even think that term exists anymore. It was an emphasis then. So, if you graduated with that degree, which I did, you could teach debate, public speaking, drama, oral interpretation—all of the things under the umbrella of what, at that time, was referred to as "speech education." It was a great degree.

CRAMER: I'm sure it has served you invaluably when communicating with performers.

SKINNER: Yes, and my minor was psychology. I've actually used the knowledge from that degree more than anything else I've ever learned, dealing with people and with meetings, how to play the room, be a leader, and get people to do what you need, etc. It was a great education. I actually went through something called the Honors Department. Besides having the main degree, I was able to eliminate courses that I didn't think were going to be useful, and pick up courses I never would have had time to take—all this with the help of my own individual advisor. I got to create my own degree, which was great.

CRAMER: You started dancing at 4. Tell us the circumstances surrounding your first dance class.

SKINNER: We lived in the Midwest, so boys didn't dance. But there was a little neighborhood girl taking, and our families were real close, so I went with her. Then, she dropped out, and I stayed. I had great parents that understood childhood self-expression. My brother and I were able to take whatever kind of lessons we wanted. They had a rule that once you started something, you should try to stick to it. But I think if we had tried something and didn't like it, we would have moved on to something else. My brother took clarinet and I took dance, and we both happened to like what we chose and stuck to it. My parents were really in touch.

CRAMER: Are your parents musical or artistic in a specific way?

SKINNER: They both sing. My mother plays the piano, and my dad was a great woodworker in his spare time. He loved working with his hands. So, they were both artistic, but neither one of them ever had a thought of doing it for a living, or even getting up in front of people. I think my mom and dad had the best of two worlds. They had the normal life with my brother, who got married and had kids, and then they had this other life with me traveling to New York and LA, seeing musicals and plays. It was a great balance.

CRAMER: Now, when you first started dancing, did you begin like a lot of boys do—taking class in tap?

SKINNER: Yes, tap and jazz. Then I added ballet early in my college career. Of course, when I was younger, my teachers gave a great traditional jazz or theatre dance class that included lots of ballet training. So, I really grew up getting ballet and not even knowing it. And then when I went into a formal program in college, I thought, "Oh, I know most of this, but it's just formalizing it all and seeing it done in a specific structure."

CRAMER: I have taken many classes with you. That's exactly how you teach.

SKINNER: Yes, I pass that on now because I realize that many performers don't take hardcore ballet classes. I'm trying to promote traditional jazz—the pure Broadway style of jazz from the 1940s, 1950s, and 1960s film dancing. When you take a class from me in theatre dance, you get a traditional warm-up that's gentle to the body, and you get basic exercises across the floor that concentrate on purity of line, purity of arms, and long, thorough, stylized combinations. So, you're getting a good taste of ballet class while you're taking it.

CRAMER: You have said that you are a student of film. Explain the influence that movie musicals have in your life and career.

SKINNER: Sure. My parents always took me to movies—I can't even remember the first one. I had a television in my room when I was growing up, and I was always watching movies in my room and sneaking it on at night. I fell in love with film. While you watch, you block the world outside, and it becomes a private experience. And, of course, films can take you on a journey in a way that theatre can't, because the camera can manipulate you. It pulls you in so powerfully. I discovered Fred Astaire and Ginger Rogers and the musicals, and somehow that spoke to me. I went into their world and something touched me. I watched all of their movies and was very fortunate to get to work with Ginger twice. Sometimes, I think about my place in time and how I fit. If I had been born at any other time, I never would have crossed paths with some of these iconic film stars that I grew up watching. I have John Kenley to thank. He had huge theatres in Columbus, Warren, and Dayton that seated upward of 5,000 people. And at that time, he brought in the biggest stars from movie musicals.

CRAMER: Rattle off names of stars, who you performed with at his theatres.

SKINNER: Sure! Cyd Charisse, Ann Miller, Ginger Rogers, and Mickey Rooney, to name a few. The great MGM people would come and do musicals in Ohio because they simply loved doing it. They also acted in plays and movie dramas and comedies. It was quite inspirational, and no one realized how fortunate we all were.

CRAMER: So that's where you "cut your teeth," so to speak. I mean you were performing with the Kenley Players, so you were meeting the best in the business from the moment you started as a young man.

SKINNER: Yes, that's right. John was from Ohio originally, and he loved giving Ohioans their start. He enjoyed giving us our equity cards.

CRAMER: Did you perform multiple summers there?

SKINNER: Yes, it was always my home. I had apprenticed with him when I was in high school. I turned professional my third year in college. Then he hired me officially, and from that point forward, I would go back every summer. Not only was it great experience and valuable work, but it was a trip home to see my family. It was security, because he was a very loyal producer. Most of the MGM stars picked up on my training, and realized that I loved the movies and the dance styles they represented. They all encouraged me to "carry the torch" and continue to pass these styles on to younger people. It really is our American way of dancing. An MGM dancer could go from ballroom to jazz to tap to ballet, equally well. They were handpicked by the studios and trained. The chorus kids were under contract at the time, and the studio was paying for everything. So, you got the best training. It makes sense why they grew up and became really wonderful performers. Now performers have to do it all on their own and pay for it out of their own pocket.

CRAMER: You're one out of a handful of director-choreographers who continues to teach class. You teach consistently and your classes are filled to capacity.

SKINNER: They are.

CRAMER: Randy, it must be thrilling to know that students want to immerse themselves in this traditional style in today's hip-hop and commercial jazz climate.

SKINNER: It is. The energy and spirit that comes out of those classes is empowering. I still get joy out of going into the studio and creating every step. Now, I'm not going to kill myself and do a trick in a combo at this point in time. And I'm not going to do heavy lifting and that kind of thing. But I choreograph in a specific way. Whenever I have something in a show, whether it's an acrobatic trick or a lift, I will always go to my principals or dancers and say, "Can you do this eight times a week, joyfully, without any fear of injury?" So, that's a mantra of mine, and I take that very personally, because I still dance. I remember those days. If you were nervous about a move coming up, it could really make your whole show a little off, because you're frightened of it. It's not any different for a singer. You never want to be worried about hitting a note. So I've always been really protective of my dancers, because I want them to feel like I do when they reach my age—injury-free and fabulous.

CRAMER: How do you help dancers stay injury-free in your classes?

SKINNER: I teach a warm-up based on my own training. This is a name many young students don't know, but should know: Juliet Prowse. She was a very special performer—a great dancer. My warm-up is a combination of Juliet's warm-up that she did every night before her show, as well as moves from the American Dance

Machine. I performed in the world premiere of that company. Juliet invited us to warm up with her. It wasn't required. You could join her onstage, and she would lead this warm up, which takes about 20–25 minutes. You really do feel entirely ready to dance after that, and yet you've not killed yourself.

CRAMER: Your shows require great versatility from your dancers, much like the MGM dancers of whom we spoke.

SKINNER: Correct. Plus, of course, dancers have to be able to sing today, too. Today you have great jazz dancers, great ballet dancers, and great hoofers. You do have some people who have blended it all together and do all three pretty well. But, when you do a show where maybe the tap level is pushed a little higher technically, and the stakes are higher, then you sometimes lose a dancer or two, because they haven't really dedicated themselves to tap. Then, of course, if you have a show that has a great tap number plus a great jazz number, you sometimes lose your hoofers at the auditions. They wipe the floor clean with the tapping, but then you ask them to do something with great style in jazz or a combo that involves many turns or pirouettes and they don't always have that capability.

CRAMER: What do you look for in a good assistant?

SKINNER: My assistants must be equal to the best dancer in the room, and hopefully better. They have to demonstrate flawlessly. Choreographers can theorize. They can talk about it. They can demonstrate with their hand. But there's nothing like either the choreographer or the assistant getting up on their feet and showing the group how it's done. It commands this respect in the room if somebody is still doing everything flawlessly. Now, as you get older, that is going to go by the wayside, and that's natural. So, my assistants must have that ability. My assistants must know the terminology correctly in all the art forms. They must be able to say the right word for the right step if somebody asks. They must know how to count properly. They have to be able to break down a piece of music, and know how to impart it to counts. And they must be good teachers. They must know how to break it down and teach it properly. The rehearsal then takes on a level of respect and decorum, because dancers are saying, "It's very clear, there's no misunderstanding." They also must be kind to people. Not only are we passing on our work and our work ethic, we're passing on a basic theory of life—which is to create a positive work environment. I like to work all sorts of ways, and it's great when your assistants can do that. When I teach class, it's great to be able to teach with counts or teach by speaking the lyrics. Sometimes it's fun to switch music on dancers, thereby training them to demonstrate real versatility. I try to create real intelligent dancers, and that's what I need in my assistants. They can reverse everything. They can partner either way. They can be the boy or the girl. That's a big requirement for me. I want freedom in the room, so that whatever might come up, somebody is there that can handle the question, or demonstrate whatever is needed. That's tricky, because you're asking a lot from people. But I do have great people that work with me.

CRAMER: Many of your assistants have been with you for a very long time. You must have a great shorthand.

SKINNER: Yes, and I keep looking for new people, because a lot of my assistants are moving on, into their own careers as choreographers.

CRAMER: What additional characteristics make up your rehearsal room environment?

SKINNER: Discipline. If somebody starts to act up, we call them aside. You see a lot of this today, because dancers are from different generations, or they were raised and trained differently. Some will ask ridiculous questions, or will ask questions that have been answered five times already. So, my assistants know that you have to nip things in the bud, and you have to make sure the room is focused. This is challenging today. As you well know, you see differences in students over the years, and it's nobody's fault. You don't ever want to sound like an old person saying, "Oh, this young generation." Everybody's a product of their generation, of their times, of what's going on in the world. So, we're all coming from different places.

CRAMER: Do you approach staging and choreography differently?

SKINNER: Yes. There are book songs, or you're dealing with duets and solos, and that is quite different from big production numbers.

CRAMER: How would you approach an actor who moves, as opposed to a dancer?

SKINNER: With actors who move, I always have something mapped out, as if I was playing the part. That's where I start. Then, we get in a room. The solo or duet might come naturally because they're so gifted—because the text leads you. If you're dealing with a book song that really is a story moment, then you have to gear into the text very heavily. Some actors are very good at that. They can practically stage themselves. Others actors stand there— they have to be given every gesture and every nuance. It just really depends on the person.

CRAMER: Do you have a different personal approach in the same situation?

SKINNER: It depends on their personality. Some people are fear-less, and they have such a great sense of humor, and they're very secure. And then there are people who get a little afraid of move-ment because they might feel awkward. So, you have to handle them a little bit differently and give them positive reinforcement. When you choreograph a show that requires partnering, you have to teach people how to hold each other, how to lead, and how to follow. I take that for granted, often skipping ahead, and my assist-ants say, "No way. We have to stop. We have to break this down, and you have to tell us what you're doing!" I have all these subtle nuances that I do personally when I partner. A good partner can take a novice and get them to do anything you want.

CRAMER: Yes. Look at Dancing with the Stars.

SKINNER: Absolutely. And those are skills, so I have to teach that. And then, of course, dancers love it once they learn it. There's always these extra elements of the art form that you take for granted if you were brought up in the traditional way, or at a time when partnering was promoted in shows.

CRAMER: What is your time frame in preproduction? For exam-ple, are you completely choreographed and staged on day one when you walk in the door?

SKINNER: No, not at all. I have an idea of everything, and I usually have a vocabulary of steps. I like certain sections totally done. I never have an entire number finished. I usually have the arrangement pretty well mapped out, but that changes in rehearsal too, when you're doing an original show. I do a great deal on my own. I don't really get into a room with a lot of assistants in preproduction. Because of my tap background, I've always been able to hear rhythms. So, I can literally sit in a chair and choreograph an entire tap number and never stand. I hear it and I can see it. Like an orchestrator who assigns instruments based on how he hears them in his head, I can do that with dance because I can see patterns. I've always been able to see where people should move on a big stage, and I've done many big shows with large casts.

CRAMER: What additional components must be considered when building big dance numbers?

SKINNER: You have to have an overall arc of the show so that big numbers are placed properly within the entire show itself. You can't give it all away in the first 10 minutes. The whole evening has to fill. You have to keep topping yourself, or knowing where you're going to place moments so that your audience goes on the journey. Then, each number has to have its own individual build. If it's story driven, you build it in a certain way. If it's just a big production for production's sake, you still have to build something within it, so there's a beginning, middle, and an end. There is also what I call "overpeaks." You find that sometimes a number overshoots its stay, or there's no inherent build in the number. You don't take the audience on any kind of journey. So, it's tricky. I think that's the hardest part of choreography. Step creation is not the hardest part, as most people think. I have danced my whole life and still take class. Steps are always around. My head is full of them. I think the whole idea of creating the journey is where I have to place the most thought. I focus on how I'm going to get the number cooking, then pull back, and then hit the audience at the end.

CRAMER: How do you decide which numbers to tackle first?

SKINNER: There's no formula for me. Sometimes the ending will happen first because I'll see an image in my head. I listen to the music a great deal.

CRAMER: Needless to say, music is your number one motivator, correct?

SKINNER: The music is everything. Dance *is* music. Music can be a cappella if it's a tap number. If it's a book moment, the lyrics are crucial. But if it's just a big dance number following a song or something, then music is everything.

CRAMER: Do you completely visualize or do you draw, write, or chart?

SKINNER: I visualize first, and then just let it filter. I keep paper for little notes, or if an idea hits me. I've learned to keep paper everywhere, because you never know where or when something great will come to mind.

CRAMER: Your assistants are more responsible for graphing, charting, and making sure you have a hard copy.

SKINNER: Yes. I also don't rely on my assistants to pick up things from me. I go into a studio and can create a step and remember it. That's why I can work alone. I think a lot of choreographers need to have the assistants there just to remember things. As a matter of fact, many use a video camera today.

CRAMER: I know you read music because you were your own dance arranger for a project called *After the Night and the Music.* Do you play the piano?

SKINNER: No, that's why I need a pianist there.

CRAMER: So how do you work with a dance arranger, and how did you become one?

SKINNER: I can hear the orchestration. I can hear what I need. I know when I need a key change. I certainly know when I want a build in a tap number, or if I want stop time. Then, I prefer working with the pianist and the arranger together. In *After the Night and the Music,* there was no actual dance arranger present. There was just an accompanist. So, he basically took exactly what was in my head and put it down on paper, and then they arranged it. When I work with a true dance arranger, it's a real give-and-take.

CRAMER: When you cast, what do you feel is the most important trait you're looking for when a dancer or actor auditions for you?

SKINNER: What you hope to find in the ideal world is the technical dancer that you need. And then style is equally important, if not more. Lastly, the shape of the dancer, depending on the show and what's required, must be considered. Those are the three items. When you're lucky to find all three, it's just glorious. Now, when you're looking for 16 of those dancers, that's tough. If you're looking for a smaller chorus, it's a little easier. Today, you also have to add in the singing, of course, because you don't have the luxury of separate choruses as we once did.

CRAMER: Do your associates or assistants handle replacement auditions?

SKINNER: Depending on the show and the content, I am usually there to hire all of the replacements. Assistants put them into the show.

CRAMER: Replacement performers have to be specific in height, weight, and build. Can you explain why?

SKINNER: They are going into existing costumes. You don't always have the luxury of building new clothes. If a show involves partnering, you can't suddenly cast a 5'7" dancer to replace a 5'3" dancer, or vice versa. It will adversely affect the choreography. So, you set your picture and then you try hard to make sure that picture stays the same throughout the run. It's simply easier.

CRAMER: You have worked regionally here in the States, and also done extensive work overseas. What's the difference between an American performer and a European performer?

SKINNER: An American Broadway style. We have it, and the English, particularly, love it. You have great dancers over there, great technicians. But if you're looking for aggressive high-quality Americans, that real hardcore power sell, or dancers that just hit that stage and take it by storm, that's a bit harder to come by. It's a societal difference. Sometimes, you have to give them permission to cut loose or coach it out of them. It's just a different world. They have their tea breaks. All kidding aside, you stick it out and it's all very civilized, and everything's incredibly polite. It's quite refreshing. It would be nice to have a little bit of that balance over here.

CRAMER: You tell a wonderful story and theatrical life lesson about being involved in the first show about Al Jolson. Would you share that with our readers?

SKINNER: Yes. It's a great lesson for students, because you never know if you've made good choices and the right decisions. I think we beat ourselves up a whole lot about that, always second guessing. In 1979, there was this big musical floating around called *Sugar Babies* that was going to go on the road for six months, and then hopefully, come into New York. It was starring Mickey

Rooney and Ann Miller. I had worked with both of them by that time. Ann called me on the phone and said, "I'm doing this new show called *Sugar Babies*, and I'd love it if you could be one of my boys." There were going to be four backup boys: two would dance with her. I had already been cast in this musical about Al Jolson. It was trying out in a theatre on Long Island, and ultimately moving to Broadway. It meant I could live at home in New York, in my own apartment. That was a big deciding factor for me. So, I basically chose that show over the *Sugar Babies* offer. *Sugar Babies* went on the road for six months, came into the Mark Hellinger Theater, and ran for eight years. The Al Jolson musical closed out of town on Long Island. So, yes, I'd walk by the Mark Hellinger Theater and see Ann with her four boys, and say to myself, "Whoa, what a decision." Then fast forward about six months. I'd gotten a call from Gower Champion. He was doing this new show called *42nd Street*. Now, dancers everywhere had heard about that one, too. And I thought I might have a good crack at being a dancer in that show, because I knew the movie and figured it was going to be a big-time tap show. It was common knowledge that Gower already had an assistant. I couldn't imagine why he was calling, but it turned out that he had a position to fill. That February, I spent an entire day dancing with him, and he hired me that night. Actually, what had *really* happened was, the dance arranger for *42nd Street*, Don Johnston, had been the dance arranger on the Al Jolson musical. So, when Gower was in preproduction, Gower said, "I need a male assistant." He already had a girl on his team, and he needed a guy. Don said, "I have just the guy you should meet." Now, if I had not done the Jolson show, I would never have met Don. I would have never had a direct contact to Gower, unless I had gotten into the show as a dancer. Even then, it would have been a different relationship. So, that really was one of those breaks that changed my life. I'm a walking testament of somebody being offered what is called a "break," and then meeting the challenge. I think many people get breaks, but they're not the least ready for them when they happen. Luck is preparation meeting opportunity.

CRAMER: What set you apart, do you think?

SKINNER: When that call came to me and I went in, I was completely primed from my training. Well, I owed my teachers, of course, and my commitment to the training. I was a dedicated student. I was able to walk in and deliver what he needed, and that was one of those breaks that you can say is life altering, because Gower Champion died on opening night of *42nd Street* in 1980. That show became an enormous hit, which meant there were going to be other companies. I had no idea what had really just happened. I was still in dancer mode—only 27 years old. I was just thinking about dancing and singing and performing.

CRAMER: At this point in time, you did not have choreographic aspirations. It landed in your lap, so to speak. Had you choreographed at all in your youth?

SKINNER: I did a lot of choreography in college along with my performing, but it wasn't ever a goal. My dream and my goal was to come to New York to sing, dance, and act. I never gave choreography too much of a thought at all until, as you said, it literally landed in my lap.

CRAMER: How do you work with a creative team?

SKINNER: Well, I meet with each person, particularly with the costume designer. I have meetings and explain each number and what's in my head. I think like a producer because I spent 12 years with David Merrick, traveling the world with him by his side. I started watching and listening, realizing this man knows how to budget. I understand how valuable the dollar is. So, when I have meetings, the first thing I do is say, "Now, tell me what has to go into the shop right away because of schedule." Then we try to get clear on what I want, because I don't want to waste money. I know how hard it is to come by. You don't want to waste money on a set of costumes that might be tossed out because the number's in flux. That money could be buying a television commercial. So, if you've blown your budget on a set piece that got tossed out in the alley because the number was cut, that money could have gone to the cast album. You must have meetings about the style of the number. I often know that I want the dresses to really move, and you have to be careful with the show's period, because sometimes you've got to manipulate the period a little bit to get the movement. Perhaps you have a big set that you really insist on, and the scenic designer might say, "Okay, I can give you this, but it will be a little different than the truth." You have to work hand in hand. For example, the staircase in *42nd Street* required many meetings with designer Doug Schmidt, because I knew we were going to dance on it. We had to be very specific about the depth and the width of each stair. We'd say, "Now, do you think this is safe? Do you think this is doable?" There were no guardrails or anything.

CRAMER: Do you test set pieces first before you ask your performers to dance on them?

SKINNER: I will always go first. I will dance on it full out. Also, if I can do it, then I expect my dancers to do it, unless they have some fear of heights or something. We have run into that. In *42nd Street* we told everybody there's going to be a 9-foot staircase. We did have a couple that really had trouble with it. Often, they don't think they will. They say, "No, no. I'm fine." Then they get up there and they have problems. It's a drop-off. *White Christmas* was the same. We had a very tall platform that moved up and down. I do test everything first. I have to map it out and decide if my dancers can dance in the confines of the structure comfortably, and not feel like they're going to fall.

CRAMER: How much time do you have to get a show up after preproduction?

SKINNER: We probably had four full weeks in a studio and two full weeks in tech for *42nd Street.*

CRAMER: Is that a luxury now?

SKINNER: No, I would say that's probably typical.

CRAMER: Like most of the directors and choreographers in this book, you have also choreographed for City Center Encores! Your shows include *Do Re Mi, Face the Music, No, No, Nanette, Gentlemen Prefer Blondes,* and *Of Thee I Sing.* You have to put those up in record time.

SKINNER: Yes, ten days. A Broadway show put up in ten days.

CRAMER: Do you prefer working on new shows or revivals?

SKINNER: Both. New shows are challenging because it's untested material. You have to think a different way. Revivals can be interesting, because you've got to find a way to reinvent them to a degree. I don't believe in changing something if it doesn't need to be changed. There's just different steps and challenges. I think any time you do a revival, you really do have to pay respect to the original source. But you do have to find a way to make it speak to a modern audience.

CRAMER: Can you give us some examples from *42nd Street*?

SKINNER: We had three new songs that weren't in the original. About 75 percent of the show was all new dancing. It was really more of a girls' show in 1980. The men were out there, but the women were much more prominent. The revival was much more equal in involvement between men and women. The men had big sections that never existed before. I learned a great lesson from Ann Reinking when she did the revival of *Chicago*. When I saw it, I thought Ann really paid respect to her mentor, Bob Fosse. But then she did something quite effective. She made it current for today's audience, and yet you knew there was true respect being paid to Fosse. When the *42nd Street* producers approached me, they said, "We want to pay respect to Gower, but we want you to use your imagination and do your own work, go with it." And I don't know if I would have thought that way, were it not for Ann's version of *Chicago*. I've learned another lesson when I saw—I believe it was 1985–the revival of *Mame* with Angela Lansbury. Producers made a choice to re-create the exact show from the 1960s. All costuming, choreography, staging, and sets were an identical replication. That was one of the first shows I ever saw when I was in high school. I came to New York on a field trip with my class. I went home and said, "I have to come to New York. I'll never see anything bigger than *Mame*." Flash forward to 1985 and I saw the revival and said, "This can't be the same show that I saw. It just can't be." Your memory plays tricks. What seemed so big in 1967 seemed less so in 1985. And, of course, the revival was a terrible failure. It was a very well-done production. It was just 20 years later. So, that lesson stuck in my head, too. I thought, "Okay. How do we make the revival of *42nd Street* just as good as I remember, just as big, and hopefully bigger?" That takes money.

CRAMER: And you had it.

SKINNER: We did. We had great producers who gave us exactly what we needed to compete with people's memories. It's also challenging when you take a movie and put it on stage. And, of course, I've done that three times now with *42nd Street*, *American in Paris* and *White Christmas*. If you were transferring a movie that was not dance driven, or a movie that was not a beloved iconic film, it would be totally different.

CRAMER: What was your biggest worry, bringing these iconic films to the stage?

SKINNER: My biggest fear was would we be cutting numbers that were audience favorites. With *White Christmas*, I tried to talk it up with many people and ask what their favorite numbers were. It's interesting that I would hear, "It's my favorite movie," and when asking the same people what their favorites song was, they were nebulous about it. I truly felt we were safe. We could do it.

CRAMER: A great example is the addition of "I Love a Piano" in *White Christmas*. That number is not in the film, and you added it into the stage version with great success. It was a big, big dance number and the audience reception was tremendous.

SKINNER: Sure, every time you enter a project like that, you aren't completely confident with your choices, but you think it through carefully, and you have meetings and you talk. There are reasons you eliminate certain songs and add in others.

CRAMER: Another example is the choice to cut the *American in Paris* ballet from the 18-minute movie version, down to 8 minutes for the stage.

SKINNER: It's a big challenge, certainly. But those are the choices you must make. It's highly unlikely that modern audiences today would enjoy an 18-minute ballet in a musical. We decided on a length based on the longest possible amount of time, because it was a challenge to cut the music down. We had permission from the estate, of course, as they were very enthusiastic about the project. We wanted to honor the great themes in that piece. Since I read music, I was able to go home and review the recording. Then, on my own—without outside influence—I could sit down and mark in the score what I wanted. Then, I could take it to my musical director and say, "Now, these are my ideas. What do you think?" He would bounce ideas off of me and vice versa. He would make segues smooth. But if I didn't read music and have the score in front of me, there's no way I could have taken 18 minutes of music and tried to keep cuts straight in my head. It is a bit of an advantage to read music.

CRAMER: You are singularly carrying the torch for a very specific time in our dance history. With that in mind, do you think you have a signature style?

SKINNER: Let me address the style of that era. I can say two things. First, it all looks like it is just happening. Dancers worked hard for that effect, but that's the appeal of it. It's so uncalculated. It just looks like it's happening at the spur of the moment. All the arms look natural. Look at the background dancers in many of those movies. They all look like they're together, but it's not robotic. Therefore, second, they all have individuality. I think much of that comes from the fact that they would be on set all day, and then they'd go out dancing at night to the clubs in Hollywood. Ginger Rogers used to tell me great stories about it. When you're dancing as part of your social life, you bring another element to your art form. That has to account for why those dancers were doing all those great moves that just looked so natural. It's something you can't teach in the classroom. You have to help people tap into it and try to coax them along. I am keeping that style alive in the classroom and onstage.

CRAMER: Gower Champion and David Merrick were iconic craftsmen who had enormous influence on your life and career. Did you have other people that were big influences on your work?

SKINNER: Certainly. John Kenley, of course, and all of my teachers. It's a bit of a hodgepodge of many people. Gower *is* my mentor. We went out to lunch one day during rehearsal and he sat me down and said, "You really need to do this. You need to start right now and think about choreographing. Think about getting on the other side." My reply, "But, Gower, all I want to do is dance." And he said, "I don't want to hear that." He said, "You can still dance, but I'm telling you. Do it right now." Now, I didn't think too much about it admittedly, I was at an age where I didn't quite take it to heart. It happened anyway because of his death on opening night, so the segue was natural. When I hear students talking, when I see a gift in them, or if they mention to me that they would like to choreograph or teach, I tell them exactly what Gower said to me, "Start now. Explore it. You don't have to give up anything, but open up that door." And I realize what he was saying. You don't always get a chance if you wait too long. Take the talent you have and start wearing more hats. He knew it was a difficult business, so it gives you more of a chance of sustaining a livelihood if you are able to wear more than one hat. Now I pass that on. I think about that smart man. He knew what he was saying to me. We live in a country that doesn't always let you start over. People at the top can make moves, but not people starting out; it's tough.

CRAMER: Do you find assistants or dance captains in your classes?

SKINNER: If I see great talent, I'll often call over students and say, "Have you ever been a dance captain?" They'll be picking up my work exceedingly fast. They can just do anything. And then I will often say, "Have you assisted? Do you have a desire to do that?" And if they say yes, then I tuck that away. Often people will call me and say, "I would love to assist."

CRAMER: And you appreciate that tenacity, do you not?

SKINNER: Yes. Exactly. I think you need to put your desires right on the table in the best way possible. I tell dancers, "Write letters to the people you've worked with. If you are friendly, call them. Don't be shy about expressing your desires if you think you might want to be on the other side-if you would like to observe." I mean, really, what's the worst that could happen? They say no and put you off? You have to be tenacious.

CRAMER: After an audition, have you had to get on the phone and call another director, choreographer, or casting agent and say, "I have dancer A and B. They're both equal in technique and performance as well as the same type. What can you tell me about A"?

SKINNER: Oh, that goes on all the time. I've actually done it, and I've had many people call me. We all respect each other. I mean, there are so many great people working behind the scenes today. You do check up on people if you detect something or need to make sure you're hiring a hard working, generous, and kind talent. If you see any problem in the audition, or you pick up on something, yes, you always check it out, because nobody wants to have that behavior in the room. It happens with principals, not just chorus people. And it's very helpful, because you do take the word of other people that you respect. There is too much talent in the world to put up with bad attitudes or uncooperativeness. If you are not a good company member, unless you're a star that sells out the house, you will get on a "do not hire" list quicker than anything. I'm always amazed in a business where it's so hard to get work, why anybody would not be aware of something inappropriate that they might be doing in the rehearsal hall, or an attitude that might come across.

CRAMER: When you research a show, is your research directly applied, or do you use it to simply enhance your own work?

SKINNER: Well, both actually. For instance, I just saw a fascinating piece of footage on Irene and Vernon Castle at Lincoln Center a couple of weeks ago. It was a costume exhibit, but they actually had some very rare footage of them dancing. There's hardly anything out there on those two iconic names in history. I saw a move that they did, and I thought, "How impressive. I want to put that in a show some time." It was a move that they obviously created, and I'd never seen it. It involved a couples' turn in ballroom style. I stood there and watched that tape three times in a row. It was a 10-minute little blurb. That's an example of where I might take an authentic step and use it. Other times you do research, but then you have to theatricalize the moves for the stage. You might not want to put up an authentic square dance, for instance. It might be visually boring.

CRAMER: Do you prefer an out-of-town tryout with a legitimate audience, or an in-town workshop?

SKINNER: I would always prefer to stay home. Now, there is a reason. You can't go out of town quietly anymore. Everything's on the Internet by intermission. You also can't stop word of mouth from getting to New York. Those days are gone. An audience can tell you so much, there's no doubt about it. But I also am a big believer that if you do a workshop or a reading in New York, and you bring in the right people to look at the show, they are going to tell you the truth and not feed your ego. You can learn just as much in a workshop setting. You have to be savvy if you're going to do that in New York. You can invite your friends, of course, but you have to have those key people you really trust that are highly intelligent, and know the commercial world, the kind of people that can come to you and say, "Let talk about it. Let's dissect this together." Now, a lot of people say going out of town makes your cast and creative team very concentrated, because that's all you're working on. There is some validity to that. You have nothing to do except the show, and it's very intimate. When you're in New York, you have your lives. So, I think a lot of people like going out of town, because they feel that focus is right.

CRAMER: Do projects come to you now more than you seek them out?

SKINNER: I like working with producers. So, I will get an idea and call someone I have worked with before. Other times people call me. Again, there's no real method. As choreographers, we all get typed into a certain style or genre. It's inevitable. Sometimes I think people presume I might be not be interested in a small show that doesn't have a lot of dancing, because of *42nd Street* and *White Christmas*.

CRAMER: That must be frustrating.

RANDY SKINNER: Well, I like those shows, of course, but I like small shows, too. I just did the musical version of *Lend Me a Tenor* in England. We're waiting on a West End theatre.

CRAMER: The play is hilarious.

SKINNER: The play screams for musicalization because of the subject matter. That was a show that mainly had staging. It was not a big dance-driven show. And I enjoyed it. I had a great time.

CRAMER: Do you have any future projects coming up that you can share?

SKINNER: I've got some great things on my desk that I think would be commercial, because you've got to think about that when a project is in development. I think several would be appealing to a wide range of audiences, and that's also a good thing to have. I think we're in an era of big stars again, at least the shows that seem to be doing well and running long. There's no doubt that the shows that have stars in them are bigger draws, because people can't come to New York and see ten shows anymore. You used to be able to come and see everything. Now you come and you might see one or two shows, so people are choosy about what they spend their entertainment dollar on. If you have a big star in a show, it might be a bigger draw. Many times you're in meetings nowadays where that's a big topic of discussion. "Are there stars out there that could do this show? Should we take the time to explore that?" It can take a great deal of time when you send a script to a star. Then, two months later you get an answer: yea or nay. If it's nay, you go to the next one. You can spend a year looking for a star.

CRAMER: You've given so much advice through the entire interview. Are there additional pearls of wisdom you'd like to share with aspiring performers?

SKINNER: I would say the most important thing is to constantly learn and study. That's why I still take class and still offer class. As long as you want to perform or choreograph, you owe it to yourself to constantly learn. You must take care of yourself. It's your instrument. It's your voice. It's your body. You have to treat it with respect. Take care of your health. Feel good about yourself. Your mental health is just as important. There's a lot of stress and disappointment when you hit a city like New York or Los Angeles. A lot comes at you, a lot of chatter. Now, with the Internet, information is all out there. There are many things that go on that can make you feel bad about yourself, because everybody's putting information out there. They're blogging when they do or don't get jobs. You have to really know how to go into that quiet place with tunnel vision, shake it off, and be good to yourself.

Don't beat yourself up. Work hard. Look in the mirror and admit to yourself quietly what you do really well. Don't have false modesty about yourself. Be able to have that inner dialogue and say, "I do that damn well. I am good at this." Look in the mirror and know what you're not so good at. Hopefully it is something that you can correct, or work hard to correct. Don't force something that's not in your instrument. If you're a bass, you can't be a tenor. People have ruined their voices trying to be tenors that don't have that range. If your body is not ready for a certain kind of movement, then you've got to learn to gracefully let that go and concentrate on what you *are* good at. That's the biggest advice I can give to people. I had coaches and mentors who said, "You're good at this. We're going to get you there." And the same people were also very helpful saying, "This is not in the cards for you. This is not in the stars." You hit the city thinking you can be everything to everybody. It's part of youth. Just be true to yourself. Also be generous. There is room for everyone to be a success.

CRAMER: Well, again, thank you. It's been great having this time to share.

SKINNER: Yes, you're quite welcome, from one teacher to another.

CHAPTER TEN

Susan Stroman

From the time she was 5, Susan Stroman was creating dances. With her father at the piano, she visualized movement to the show tunes he loved. While working toward her degree in English Literature from the University of Delaware, she worked in community and regional theatre before making her move to New York City. No other director-choreographer working today has had a career teeming with such diversity. Her professional work includes Broadway, off-Broadway, television, film, concerts, and extensive work in opera and ballet.

Stroman is the recipient of five Tony Awards, five Drama Desk Awards, eight outer Critic Circle Awards, two Lawrence Oliver Awards, a record four Fred Astaire Awards, and the Lucille Lortel Award. She received the George Abbot Award for

Outstanding Achievement in the Theatre, an Elan Award for her choreographic work, and the Drama League's Distinguished Achievement in Musical Theatre Award. Susan directed and choreographed *The Producers*, winner of a record-making 12 Tony Awards including Best Direction and Best Choreography.

Highlights of her prolific stage and television career include *Crazy for You, Showboat, A Christmas Carol, Steel Pier, The Music Man, Oklahoma, Young Frankenstein, The Scottsboro Boys, Liza Minnelli Live from Radio City Music Hall, A Sondheim Celebration*, and *An Evening with the Boston Pops: A Tribute to Leonard Bernstein*. Additional highlights include *A Little Night Music, 110 in the Shade*, and *Don Giovanni* for New York City Opera, and *Double Feature* and *Blossom Got Kissed* for New York City Ballet, and for film, *Center Stage* and *The Producers: The Movie Musical*.

CRAMER: Susan, I understand your father was quite a pianist and in your childhood you danced with abandon in the living room of your Delaware home while your father played. He was a huge influence in your life.

STROMAN: Yes, that's all true.

CRAMER: You began formal dance training at 5. Tell us what you studied when you started.

STROMAN: When I studied, I started with ballet, of course. And then I got very interested in everything else as I got a little older: tap, jazz, baton, ballroom dancing, everything. I loved anything that kept me moving. My childhood was filled with piano, guitar, and vocal lessons, art, theatre, and wonderful old movies. I just loved the whole idea of singing and dancing. Ever since I was a little girl, I have had this passion, this obsession. When I hear music, I see visions of people dancing. It's always been that way, so I can't listen to music if I want to relax. I dream of people moving, dancing, and acting. I visualize music. If I had not had a choreographic outlet, I probably would have gone crazy.

CRAMER: After working in community theatre while finishing your English Literature degree at the University of Delaware, you made your way to New York City in 1976. You performed in *Whoopee!* and *Musical Chairs* on Broadway where you met fellow performer and future associate Scott Ellis. You were the assistant director and choreographer as well as dance captain on *Musical Chairs*.

STROMAN: Yes, the show only lasted about two weeks. Scott wanted to be a director and we both wanted to be on the other side of the table.

CRAMER: Meaning you wanted to direct and choreograph and create the work rather than being a performer. You knew that very quickly, right?

STROMAN: Yes, absolutely. For me, it was always about creating theatre, creating dance, and Scott shared my dream. The writing team of John Kander and Fred Ebb already knew Scott because he performed in another of their Broadway shows, *The Rink*. I knew Kander and Ebb a little bit because I had done the national tour of *Chicago*. We decided that we were going to approach them and ask if we could do an off-Broadway version of *Flora, the Red Menace*, one of their shows that had a very short run on Broadway. We had an idea of how to redo it for a very small space, in the vein of a WPA Theater. And we both thought, "What's the worst that could happen? They'll say no, and that's fine, or they'll say yes, and we'll be in business." This scenario serves as *very* good advice for young people. So these two kids went up to Kander and Ebb and said, "We have an idea of how to do *Flora, the Red Menace*." And they said yes.

CRAMER: Your career resembles a wave, there's an ebb and flow between being asked to helm a project and instigating a project yourself.

STROMAN: I think you can't wait to be hired. If you really believe in your talent, and in your art, and believe that you have a voice in the theatre, then you can't wait for someone to hire you; you have to go out and create it. I think for Scott Ellis and me that was our first time to take a chance like that. And again, you have to ask the question: "What's the worst that could happen?" Kander and Ebb said yes and I think we made about $400 for the whole summer. We took the show down to the Vineyard Theater, which is off-Broadway. It only had about a 100 seats, maybe even less. It ran during the summertime and had a big cult following because of Kander and Ebb. Producer Hal Prince came to see it and from there Hal chose me to choreograph the New York City opera *Don Giovanni*. When that closed, we did the Broadway revival of *Show Boat* together. Liza Minnelli came to see it so Liza asked me to choreograph her big show at Radio City Music Hall. This business is all about building relationships.

CRAMER: You received an Emmy nomination for Liza's show. Is that correct?

STROMAN: That is correct. We shot that for HBO. It was my first foray into film.

CRAMER: Your career has run the gamut from stage to screen, classical ballet concerts to musical concerts. You've been at the Tony podium *five* times! Three times for Best Choreography for *Show Boat, Crazy for You*, and *Contact* and twice for *The Producers* as Best Director and Best Choreographer.

STROMAN: That was a thrilling night. I think that all of us who were involved in *The Producers* will never forget that time.

CRAMER: What do you think made *The Producers* such a hit in *that* moment in time, earning it 12 nominations?

STROMAN: Well, it's interesting because I do think musicals have a moment in time. What's happening in society at the time really can tip a musical one way or the other. And, at that point, we hadn't had many real, true musical comedies. They just hadn't been around. In fact, this was more than a musical comedy; this was a comedy musical. I think people just couldn't believe it and realized what they had been missing. *The Producers* paved the way for other musicals like *Spamalot* and *Hairspray*. This started a whole influx of *real* comedy musicals.

CRAMER: *The Producers* followed countless heavy dramas and numerous shows that moved from London to New York City.

STROMAN: Yes, it did. I think audiences were ready for a change. At *The Producers* preview I still didn't know what we had. That first night hearing the audience—the roof blew off the theatre. It was amazing. I thought we would have a little following because of Mel Brooks (the writer and creator of *The Producers*), but I didn't realize what we had. And it was glorious; it was a wonderful time for all of us.

CRAMER: I'd like to turn now to another arena of your diverse career. You have been an integral part of the New York City Ballet. You're the first woman, I understand, to choreograph a full-length ballet. That's a complete surprise to me. Peter Martins, artistic director of New York City Ballet, hired you, correct?

STROMAN: Yes, I got the phone call from Peter and he invited me to his office. I had done a small piece for his company's gala called *Blossom Got Kissed*, which was a little short story. He said, "I want you to do a full-length ballet," but he didn't let me know what he wanted or if he wanted me to come up with my own idea, so I walked out of there thinking, "Oh, my goodness, can I do this, a full-length ballet, a classical ballet?" On my walk home I thought, "I have to do this because I have been asked. It's a responsibility to do this." So I put my thinking cap on and tried to figure out what I could possibly do for a full-length ballet. Because I'm

from the theatre, I'm a storyteller, so that's what it's all about for
me. The closest thing to silent film is ballet. So I had the idea to
do an evening with a nod to silent film. The whole Ballet's called
Double Feature. The first act is a melodrama and the second act
is a comedy. It's all done with beautiful shades of black and white,
with other colors mixed in, purples and lovely light hues. It turned
out to be a wonderful experience and great for the New York City
Ballet because it actually brought theatre to them. I think the ballet
dancers loved playing characters.

CRAMER: You've also worked with the Martha Graham
Company and Pacific Northwest Ballet. It must keep your work
and your approach fresh to choreograph for dancers in different
genres.

STROMAN: Yes, each one is a unique challenge.

CRAMER: Was there a turning point for you professionally and
personally in your career; perhaps a show that changed the tide?

STROMAN: I've been lucky to have several. Of course, *Crazy
for You* on Broadway was a very important time for me. I'm very
familiar with and love all of the traditional American composers
like Ira and George Gershwin, Irving Berlin and Jerome Kern.
When I was approached about doing *Crazy for You* and allowed to
develop Gershwin's music for my choreography, I thought, "This is
a great match because I know that music so well." It was a perfect
opportunity for me. Again I'd like to point out that *Crazy for You*
happened at a time when there was a British invasion of musicals
that didn't have any dance. So *Crazy for You* hit at a time when no
one had seen dance for almost a decade. Shows like *Les Miserable*
and *Chess* were dominating Broadway. *Crazy for You* had dance
from beginning to end and that was my first Tony Award, so that
was a very, very special time for me. Actually I met my future husband at that point, Mike Ockrent, the director of *Crazy for You*.
And so, of course, that was a big life-changing experience—that
first big Broadway show.

CRAMER: Any critic would argue that you are a magnificent storyteller, but audiences are so fascinated by your ingenious use of
props. In "I've Got Rhythm" from *Crazy for You*, the lead character Bobby Child teaches the folks out West all about rhythm using
their mining tools: pix axes, tin pans, hammers, corrugated tin,

even rope. In the number "Slap That Bass" from the same show, you made the female dancers actual upright basses. In *Steel Pier* you placed the female dancers on the wings of a plane. In *The Producers*, little old ladies do an infectious rhythmic number with their walkers. In *Contact,* the kinetic antics on the swing in the first piece are ridiculously clever and a bit death defying. No one working today uses props quite like you. I know you are motivated by story, but how in the world, Susan, do you come *up* with these ideas? Where does your head go?

STROMAN: That has to do with the collaboration of the set designer, the costume designer, and being true to a period. For example, in *Crazy for You*, there was a mining store on stage filled with mining equipment and tools designed by Robin Wagner. So in my head I would think, "What can we have here?" Well, we had a big spool of rope and Bobby Child is teaching them how to dance, so he thought he would have fun with them, and his girls would show them how to play the bass by actually letting the girls *be* the bass instruments. What man wouldn't love that? Most of the time, the ideas are right in front of you. You just have to be imaginative.

CRAMER: The next big Broadway show for you was *Steel Pier*, also a Kander and Ebb musical. That show actually opened the door for your next project, *Contact*. Tell us about that.

STROMAN: We had a good off-Broadway track record with Kander and Ebb since doing *Flora, The Red Menace,* and The *World Goes Round*. We had become such good friends and collaborators that they wanted to team up again to create *Steel Pier*. Although the show didn't last very long, it was highly respected. Andre Bishop from Lincoln Center Theater saw it and asked me to come up to his office. He really enjoyed the choreography of *Steel Pier* and he said to me, "If you have an idea, we will help you develop it." That was like hearing, "Gold!" My head is spinning with ideas and again I thanked him and I walked away thinking, "Okay, I gotta think of something." I did have one idea because about two weeks before that, I had visited a swing club downtown in the meat-packing district. It was about one in the morning in a dark club where all New Yorkers wore black except one girl. She wore a yellow dress. She would step forward when she wanted to dance, and she'd retreat when she didn't. I watched her and I thought to myself, "That girl's going to change some man's life tonight." That image of the girl in the yellow dress was in my head, and so when André Bishop said, "Do you have an idea? I will help you develop it," I had this idea of the girl in the yellow dress. I called my dear friend, John Weidman, and we started to collaborate and to flesh out a short story about what that could be. André Bishop and Bernie Gersten at Lincoln Center allowed me to choose 18 dancers to begin work. Lincoln Center has these beautiful studios in the basement and we went down there and started this short story. Andre and Bernie left me down there for about four weeks and never popped their heads in. When they finally did, they loved it so much they said, "Oh, we have to produce this. Do you have any other short stories?" And I said, "Yes, I am just filled with short stories." So John and I started to work on two other stories that could go with that story of the girl in the yellow dress.

CRAMER: *Contact* was presented in three acts. Act Three involved the girl in the yellow dress. The first act encompassed a trio of dancers that performed primarily on a big swing and the second act took place in a restaurant with dynamics between a wife, her husband, a bartender, and restaurant patrons. Which idea came first, the swing or the restaurant?

STROMAN: They were a bit simultaneous. It was very important for us to make the entire piece gel. The first piece, "The Swing," is based on a Fragonard painting that John and I both knew. It's about three people who have no problem making contact *whatsoever.* The second piece is called "Did You Move?" It's about a woman who is in a relationship but it's abusive. She is married but can't make contact with her husband. And then the third short story about the girl in the yellow dress concerns a man who, if he doesn't make contact, will die that night. So it all started to fall into place. After André and Bernie gave me a few more weeks to work out the other two, we had *Contact*. It ran over three years, the longest-running show at Lincoln Center.

CRAMER: It's my understanding that you were in a smaller theatre at Lincoln Center and then you moved to the Vivian Beaumont, upstairs, and you had more space.

STROMAN: Yes, so we got to adjust the choreography. It was a luxury.

CRAMER: For *Contact,* you received a generous amount of time to develop your project. That does not happen often. With the financial difficulties of producing big musicals today, you really have to work efficiently whether you're directing or choreographing. Do you normally feel pressured to work fast? Is the time frame different whether choreographing, directing, or both?

STROMAN: Well, it's different with each endeavor. When I'm creating a project, people don't know that it's taken two years or more to develop. For example, *The Scottsboro Boys,* once we really dug in there and started working on it, was a good two-year process. When rehearsals started, we only had four weeks. But before I go into rehearsal I do my own preproduction. So I work everything out in my head and the way I think it might go, and then I go into rehearsal. Now I don't always share that with the actors. I want to feel it's almost like a safety net for them. We start to create together and I can guide them a certain way. But with their input and collaboration, my preproduction work absolutely develops and takes another turn. The actors always inspire me. I find that my preparation establishes a safety net for everyone—designers, actors, and stage management—because I've thought it through at least one way. But it is always enriched when the actors join in. I want it to look like that's the only way they could've said it, danced it, or done it, as if they'd made it up themselves.

CRAMER: Do you feel that you approach actors and dancers differently?

STROMAN: No. I approach them the same way. All work is character driven. We are all telling the same story.

CRAMER: Using *Steel Pier* or *Contact* as an example, tell me how much latitude you give your dancers, if any. *Steel Pier* is set against a dance marathon. There is nonstop dancing, or so it appears. *Contact* is nothing but dance. Are you managing every step and style on every dancer, or are dancers making any corresponding contributions?

STROMAN: I remember the audition for *Steel Pier,* I gave a combination, but then I asked them to dance the combination in a flirtatious way, dance it as if they were drunk and dance it in an aggressive way. I watch them take that choreography and make it their own within a certain character. That's very important to me.

Once they make it their own, it inspires me to change it in another way.

CRAMER: So you are always looking for an actor-driven movement, especially in an audition.

STROMAN: It's all about the character. Even when I choreograph, I have to have the character in mind. I have to choreograph and move as Max Bialystock (lead character in *The Producers*). Then I have to choreograph and move like Leo Bloom (Max's cohort), which are two different ways to move. So I always have the character in mind when I'm choreographing. When you are working in the theatre you must speak to actors, dancers, and singers from the standpoint of their character. It is somewhat different in classical ballet and abstract dance forms, but theatrically your character informs how and why you move.

CRAMER: Let's speak specifically about *Contact* and Boyd Gaines who played the lead in the third piece. He was the man who was suicidal until he met the woman in the yellow dress. He is an actor, a kinetic being, certainly, but an actor nonetheless. He is surrounded by technically proficient dancers. The approach has to be different, how do you do it?

STROMAN: The thing is Boyd, like that particular character, was walking into a room of thoroughbred dancers. The character had to be brave enough to ask that girl in the yellow dress to dance. That act symbolized him having courage to go on with his life and overcome even the biggest obstacles. And in the character's case, the metaphor was reaching out to ask that girl in the yellow dress to dance. Now Boyd doesn't dance at all. As a matter of fact, when I called him for the workshop, he said, "And I would be doing?" I said, "You'll be dancing." But it worked out great because Boyd can't look like someone who moves easily. It had to look like a struggle and that he was brave to ask that girl to dance.

CRAMER: Do you have a softer touch with people like that than you do with professional dancers?

STROMAN: Of course. On the first or second day of rehearsal, you have to figure out who is quick, who is not, and you have to respect that. You have to deal with your process according to how fast someone learns. I've been in shows where I've had the quickest person and then the slowest person in the same process and somehow you have to manipulate your rehearsals so everybody is not aware of that. You give time to those particular performers appropriately. When you give direction, many people just want to know exactly where to go and when and they won't question you. Then you have to recognize quickly who is going to question you, so you have to back that up: "You have to go over there because your character would *never* go the other way." So you do treat people differently according to their process.

CRAMER: You don't find yourself approaching musical staging differently than choreography?

STROMAN: No. It is the same.

CRAMER: Was there a specific time when you thought, "I have to direct. I can't simply choreograph any longer. I need to be a director."

STROMAN: You know what? Everything about it was natural. The real success of a show is its collaboration and the director allowing all ideas onto the table. Considering who that includes scenic, lighting, costume design, writers, composers, and management, it is a miracle a musical gets up. It's a miracle because of the input of all those people, but it's very natural that everybody is on the same page. So, for me, it was a natural stepping stone. The first show where I wore both hats was *The Music Man* revival on Broadway. It was the perfect show for me to do because a lot of it is about a man coming into town and changing it because of music and rhythm. A town that, when you first see it, is very still and stoic and motionless; but by the end, everybody's doing the "Shipoopi" (a dance number from the show, famous for its exuberant movement). It's a journey in movement, choreography, and love, so it was a very appropriate show for me to wear both hats.

CRAMER: Based on our conversation thus far, I believe our readers would agree that you do a significant amount of research. I was fascinated to read about your research on two such pieces: *Oklahoma!* and *Show Boat*. Can you discuss your research on the Old West as well as the period depicted in *Show Boat*?

STROMAN: I think when you are a choreographer or director in the theatre, you do immerse yourself in a specific geographical area, decade, and societal norms of that particular time period. Most musicals are set in a specific time period. There are not *that* many musicals that are in the present day or current. And what is current? "Now" is different for everyone. First I look at when the musical takes place, and make sure I understand what was going on in that place at that time. In *Show Boat*, the North danced very differently than the South, and that needed to be different. Even their carriage, the way they walked in Chicago and the way they walked down on the levee in the South had dramatic differences. These are all things you need to take into consideration. Now *Oklahoma!* takes place when people were fighting for territory, just fighting, so there's a lot of fight choreography and a confrontational style in the show, that game of "Can you top this?" that plays in numbers like "Kansas City." The characters go against each other, trying to outdo one other, which speaks to the period's history. The farmers and the cattleman were constantly at odds since their interests were so diverse. In "Farmer and the Cowman" which opens Act Two, the character of Aunt Eller is desperately trying to keep the peace between the two factions and that informed my choreography completely.

CRAMER: In the original production, and most subsequent productions, of *Oklahoma!,* Laurie, Curley, and Judd do not perform in the Dream Ballet. Their characters are temporarily replaced by dancing characters. A dream Laurey, a dream Curley, and a dream Judd suddenly appear as if out of the mist. Why did you choose a different path in your revival?

STROMAN: The audience today is very different from the audience of 50 years ago, 40 years ago, even 30 years ago. I'd say now an audience sees theatre with a more cinematic eye, where the story has to be told all the time, all the way through, even in set transitions. In the case of *Oklahoma!*, the older audience accepted that all of a sudden a Curly and a Laurey that you'd never seen before came out and danced. I didn't feel a contemporary audience would accept that. If we've spent all night with this Curly and this Laurey, you want to see them dream about each other. And so we found our Curly, Hugh Jackman, and a wonderful Laurey. They were both dancers. So along with Judd, they did the *Dream Ballet.*

CRAMER: Do you read music and still play piano?

STROMAN: Yes, I do. I wish I still played piano.

CRAMER: How much does being able to read a score help you in this business?

STROMAN: Any bit of knowledge is helpful. And I think that as I go along, the more I know about every single department, the better my work. I could do the greatest dance step, but if the lighting is not right, it won't matter. The more you know about lighting, the more you know about the set, the more you know about costumes, same thing. You could do the greatest dance step, but if the costume is not right, it too won't matter.

CRAMER: Aspiring choreographers and directors think about the path they are going to take, and so logically the path could be as a swing (dancers who cover several roles or tracks), dance captain (dancers who maintain choreography throughout the run of a show), assistant choreographer, associate choreographer, and so forth. They think in terms of a progression. You were a dance captain, an assistant choreographer, and an assistant director as well so you know their value firsthand. Please explain your use of assistants, how many you have and how you use them.

STROMAN: Dance captains are very important to me. They are vital to a production. Swings are the smartest people in the room. I have such great respect for swings. Now I use my assistants when I do my preproduction. I work out a great deal of choreography for a cast of 30 or 40 with just 2 people and sort it all out. So I really use them. I want my assistants to be people who can collaborate and also have the right personality to deal with anything that could go wrong. They must also be diplomats and deal with the eccentricities of actors and designers.

CRAMER: Do you feel that you can leave them with something, enabling you to focus elsewhere?

STROMAN: Yes, absolutely.

CRAMER: Have these assistants worked for you as dancers or actors in some capacity previously?

STROMAN: Not necessarily. Every show isn't right for each assistant. The assistants I had on *The Producers*, for example, were going to be dealing with some big, eccentric personalities, so I knew I had to choose those people who were not only talented but could deal with some of these wild personalities. For something like

Contact, I needed assistants who understood partnering because every dancer does not understand how to partner. You can be the greatest dancer in the world; the minute you get a man in front of you or a woman in front of you, you can't dance. So I had to have an assistant that understood that. For something like *Oklahoma!,* I had a big ballet at the end of Act One, so I had an assistant who was more balletically trained. *The Scottsboro Boys* had a lot of tap dance in it, thus my assistant was a tap dancer. Not every assistant is right for every project. I also want someone who the actors are going to feel comfortable with.

CRAMER: I would like to turn our focus to your recent project, *The Scottsboro Boys*. The theme is dark but you are not new to serious subject matter. *Contact* had disturbing themes about suicide. Your next Broadway show, *Thou Shalt Not*, told the story of a woman who killed her husband and the piece focused on the ideas of guilt and death. *Scottsboro Boys* deals with the true story of a group of young boys, wrongfully accused, and their ultimate fate. Even in the darkest moments, your unique creativity is present. A remarkable sequence includes a tap trio conveying the horror of the electric chair. The inventive way you combined tap dance and the eye-popping visual electric currents was unique, because it came from your imagination.

STROMAN: These nine innocent boys between the ages of 12 and 19 were thrown into jail and accused of a horrific crime. The guards, all white, would have fun with these nine black boys by putting them next to the electric chair. They would turn the chair on at night and fry something, anything they could find. Even when they would officially electrocute somebody, the guards would make sure the boys heard it and then make the boys remove the dead body and carry it out. What a horrible thing to happen to these nine kids. And reading this, it was Kander and Ebb who said they wanted to write a song about the guards teasing the boys with the electric chair. The idea of the tap dance comes out of that time period. Reading the boys' true stories, they would have nightmares about the electric chair. So we created a nightmare for these dancers to tap.

CRAMER: Have you ever had to scrap an entire idea and then start over or do you do so much preproduction work that those kinds of things don't *necessarily* happen?

STROMAN: Well, I don't think we've ever had to scrap a big number, but I have to say when we were working on *Crazy for You*, we did "start over." We had our last run-through and all the designers and stage crew were already down in Washington, DC, where we were going to open out of town. The writers and the director, Mike Ockrent, decided that we needed to totally rewrite the second act. So we all got on the Amtrak train and we rewrote the second act of *Crazy for You* in the three hours it took to get to Washington, DC. By the time we got there, we had a whole second act for stage management to tech, and within that, we did lose a big number. It was called "By Strauss," a big Gershwin number, and William Ivey Long had created these beautiful costumes. But that had to do with storytelling more than a particular idea. That number no longer worked with the new story. Until you get a whole piece up on its feet, you don't really know. I have to say that this is why previews are so helpful, because the last element that you add to your work is the audience; then you're going to know if it's right. Sometimes you think something is really funny in your living room and then, of course, you get it in front of the audience and there's silence, crickets. A good example of that is "What Causes That?" in *Crazy for You*. It's Zangler and Bobby Child, drunk, both dressed like Zangler, doing a number together. Bobby is supposed to be like Ziegfeld, so I thought it would be funny if he flipped the chair up and put it on his head like a Ziegfeld headdress and start to strut. I thought that was hysterical. And, of course, when the number opened in Washington, it was not. You could hear nothing in the audience. No one thought it was charming or even moderately amusing. I couldn't figure out why no one thought that was funny. And my director, Mike Ockrent, said, "Well, the minute he puts that chair his head and you change that spotlight to pink, the audience will know there's something they're supposed to think and it will help them." So that night, the minute the chair went up, the gel went to pink, and we got a laugh. So the audience is the last piece of the puzzle, the last part of the process. And again the result of the laugh was an effort of total collaboration.

CRAMER: What do you find is the key difference between your approach to new musicals versus revivals?

STROMAN: I've been quite lucky. The revivals I've done, *Show Boat*, *Oklahoma!* and *The Music Man*, are, in my opinion, the three greatest American musicals written. But when we did those, everyone approached each one as if it was new material. We thought of it as fresh. Part of my choreography is developing the music so that when you see the choreography, the music matches it perfectly. For *Oklahoma!*, the Rogers & Hammerstein estate allowed me to develop the music according to my choreography. It supports all the dance numbers. The Kern estate allowed me to do that with *Show Boat*, and *The Music Man* estate allowed me to change the dance arrangements, so it all matched.

CRAMER: So you work with an arranger once your choreography is in place?

STROMAN: I work with an arranger and the orchestrator in the room. So I say, "I need to have a harp gliss on this," or, "I need this to modulate." So the dance is supported by the arrangement and the orchestration. I might mention that the Ballet I recently choreographed for New York City Ballet, *Frankie, Johnny & Rose*, is set to Duke Ellington music. I worked with the orchestrator, Doug Besterman, and I'd say, "I need this to modulate when she does her fouette turn so it's more exciting. I sit with these music people and figure it all out time and time again. It truly enriches the choreography, the symbiosis of music and movement."

CRAMER: And that goes back to dancing in the living room at 5 years of age with your father at the piano.

STROMAN: It sure does.

CRAMER: Now that your reputation and your track record precede you, people feel confident in your ability to open a hit. Do you still do workshops, out-of-town tryouts, or even readings of new pieces?

STROMAN: Again, it depends on the project. I think readings are really, really helpful. When I work on a piece, it's usually me and the composer, the lyricist and the writer, and we work and we work, but we're reading it with each other. You need actors to read it, period. It really is quite helpful for making all necessary changes. We did two readings for *Scottsboro Boys* and those readings were invaluable. We didn't do a workshop; we just went right into production.

CRAMER: You opened off-Broadway?

STROMAN: Yes. It was a big hit off-Broadway and then we moved to the Guthrie Theatre where, once again, it was a huge hit. We moved to Broadway and we had trouble selling tickets. I think we opened around Christmas. Not the jolliest of musicals.

CRAMER: *Young Frankenstein* had readings, did it not?

STROMAN: Yes, it had two readings also.

CRAMER: What does a reading entail?

STROMAN: We usually have the actors learn all the music. Then the day of the reading, actors sit in a semicircle with the material on music stands and they sing the score.

CRAMER: Do you have people in mind for roles and discover in readings that perhaps you have not made a good choice?

STROMAN: Oh, of course.

CRAMER: And does it work in reverse?

STROMAN: Absolutely. You know, when you cast readings, you try to get as close to whom you would ultimately want, but you can't always with a reading.

CRAMER: A dancer comes into an audition room. What's the first thing that you want to see when that dancer walks in the door?

STROMAN: Confidence, first and foremost. Dancers also need to find out all they can about the show for which they are auditioning, not necessarily dress like the period of the show, but more like avoiding inappropriate dress. You never want to sabotage your audition by dressing in a way that draws attention to the fact that you know nothing about the show. Sometimes it's not only you (the director) who's making the decision. You have producers and a whole table full of people who make casting decisions. Someone at the table might not have the right imagination. So if you're auditioning for *Oklahoma!,* you need to come in looking corn-fed and well-scrubbed. But if you're auditioning for *Contact*, you need to come in looking like a sexual being.

CRAMER: Let's talk about the girl in the yellow dress: Deborah Yates. What struck you when she walked in the door for the audition?

STROMAN: When she came in, she had a mystery about her. She was very confident. But when she walked in, I had a roomful of beauties. They were all beautiful and all wonderful dancers, but there was a mystery about Deborah. She had a confidence and an aloof quality that was appropriate for that particular character. I could recognize it right away. It was like her beauty was untouchable.

CRAMER: Did dancers auditioning have accessibility to the story? Did they know what it was about, what to expect?

STROMAN: They knew coming in what the story was. They also knew there would be partnering in a club and that it was sexual. So everyone had to possess a steamy, sexual personality. What you're looking for is absolutely different with every show. The end of a day of auditioning is the hardest day for me because there are so many talented people. You have two dancers, and one just didn't make it because the person next to them was a better choice. They are both equally talented but one was more correct for the style or the look of the show. So it's horrible to reject people who are so talented and that happens because there's so much competition.

CRAMER: Did you have an assistant that's gone on to their own successful career?

STROMAN: Yes, I have. Warren Carlyle, who assisted me on *The Producers* and *Oklahoma,* also assisted me on the movie *Center Stage* that I did with Nick Hytner. He's gone on now to be his own director-choreographer. He did a wonderful revival of *Finian's Rainbow, Follies,* and he directed and choreographed Hugh Jackman's recent return to Broadway. He's got a couple of irons in the fire now, too. He's doing very, very well, and deservedly so.

CRAMER: Well, you brought up Nicholas Hytner, so I'm very excited to ask you about the film *Center Stage.* Tell me how you were approached to choreograph that movie.

STROMAN: Nick was directing and one of the characters in the movie was a rebellious choreographer played by Ethan Stiefel, a principal dancer at American Ballet Theatre. There was also a choreographer who set all the classics perfectly, you know, all the right way. Nick wanted me to choreograph what the rebellious character might do. So I was brought in to dance to Michael Jackson and the Red Hot Chili Peppers, all this great pop music and to "be" that character's thoughts and talent. It was so exciting. At one point, I had the character on a motorcycle zooming across the stage. I had an extraordinary time. It was such a wonderful experience and I got to meet many of the dancers at New York City Ballet and American Ballet Theatre since they were in practically every frame.

CRAMER: Several years before *Center Stage*, you shot *Liza Steppin' Out at Radio City Music Hall* for HBO. We mentioned this earlier. These two projects filmed in a significantly different way. The two projects must have really helped your learning curve when shooting *The Producers*.

STROMAN: For Liza's show, we actually didn't reconfigure the numbers at all. We shot a core performance from multiple camera angles. *Center Stage* was closer to a true filmmaking experience. They both informed my work on *The Producers*. I learned so much on those films.

CRAMER: Years ago *The Producers* began as a Mel Brooks feature film. With that in mind, what was the biggest challenge for you filming the stage version of the Broadway musical?

STROMAN: Well, of course, budget was the biggest challenge. When we did *The Producers: The Movie Musical,* Mel really wanted it to be *the* musical. He wanted the musical on screen. So when we started it was like shooting this giant stage. We had a huge sound stage at Steiner Studios, complete with the set of Times Square and Shubert Alley. It was really, really thrilling. We all wanted it to be more like the *Guys and Dolls* movie, a real old-fashioned musical. And I think we accomplished that. I know the crew had the best time because they don't get to shoot musicals much. All the camera guys loved Nathan Lane and Matthew Broderick (Max and Leo) and they loved having all the beautiful showgirls around, as you can imagine. It was a joyous time for everybody.

CRAMER: What is the biggest obstacle or challenge for a director-choreographer in theatre today?

STROMAN: Today it's all about money. It's financial. I think that's why you see so many revivals now because investors are afraid to take a chance on new material. Even though I have a track record, it is difficult now for someone who only wants to do new works to get them financed. Investors want to bank on what has come before, a sure thing, before they'll take a chance with their money. But I feel that that will change. It's all cyclical. As I said before, young directors and choreographers have to make their own work; and trying to make your own work without the financial support is quite difficult.

CRAMER: Do you think that's why so many movies are being made into Broadway shows such as *Legally Blonde, Hairspray, Catch Me If You Can,* and *The Full Monty*; because for investors it's still a bit of a sure sale?

STROMAN: Yes, absolutely. And I think *The Producers* might have a hand in it too.

CRAMER: How right you are to add that one to the list and it's your biggest hit to date, both critically and financially. It is my understanding that you had to have your arm twisted a bit to do *The Producers*? When you were first approached, it was you and your late husband; you were approached together as a team. Mel had to talk you into going solo.

STROMAN: Yes, he did. He sang the song "You Can Do It." Mel convinced me. At that particular time in my life, I had lost my husband and I didn't know that I could throw myself into a giant musical. Mel knocked on my door every day for a good month and convinced me. He was great. He was wonderful. He's an extraordinary creature, you know. He is funny all the time and he's gracious and good and has a spontaneous mind that is a treat to be around.

CRAMER: Was this the first time that you had worked with *The Producer*'s book writer Thomas Meehan?

STROMAN: Yes, my first time with Tom.

CRAMER: You wrote the script together, so you were a big part of it from the very beginning. I think that's an important role for a director when you're creating something new.

STROMAN: Agreed. That's why these shows take two years. This is the thing an audience doesn't know, that you've been eating bagels for two years with everybody trying to get it to work.

CRAMER: You must have relationships, friendships, and camaraderie with particular people who are successful with your work every time. You must come back to people that you've used before time and again. Networking must be critical in this business. Just how important is your reputation when it comes to getting the job?

STROMAN: Reputation is very important, I have to say. If you get down to two pictures and you don't personally know either person, you haven't worked together before, and these people are equally talented, you are going to flip that picture over and call somebody listed on the back of it that you know and trust. You're going to find out whether or not this person was great to work with. And even if there's the slightest hesitation, that person's out. Your reputation is everything. It's hard enough to put up a musical, so to have someone who's known to be trouble is not worth it when there are so many other talented people who aren't. It's very important to work in a mutually respectful atmosphere. In the end, I think that's all anybody really wants—to have the respect of each other's talents and collaboration.

CRAMER: If I danced for you in three shows and I came in to audition and I was the right person, would you feel good about hiring me again because I have worked with you three times before and delivered?

STROMAN: Yes, of course, absolutely.

CRAMER: I think it's really important for our readers to hear that because their very first show needs to be the experience that solidifies them as a team player.

STROMAN: Absolutely. I do check on people. I don't think actors really think you do, but if I don't know somebody, I call, I ask. Do they play well with others?

CRAMER: Susan, this was delightful. I cannot thank you enough.

STROMAN: Absolutely.

CRAMER: I appreciate you taking the time out of your busy schedule.

STROMAN: You are most welcome.

CHAPTER ELEVEN

Sergio Trujillo

Sergio Trujillo was born in Columbia to parents with a strong work ethic who longed for their son to have real opportunities in life. The family moved to Toronto where Sergio became a biochemistry major, earning a Bachelor of Science degree from the University of Toronto. Family expectations led Sergio to chiropractic school, but dance beckoned.

During his second year at the university, Sergio tried to balance his studies at school with his study of dance. His passion for dance forced him to take a sabbatical from school to focus completely on his dance training. Classes in Los Angeles, encouragement from a mentor, and a national dance competition win put him on a career track as a performer and his future on the Broadway stage.

Sergio made his Broadway debut in *Jerome Robbins Broadway,* and also danced in the 1992 revival of *Guys and Dolls* and *Fosse.* He has danced in film, on television, and in national tours. His first job as a Broadway choreographer came when he was hired to retool several dance numbers in *All Shook Up.* His work on that production was closely followed by choreographing one of the longest running shows on Broadway—*Jersey Boys.* Choreography for *Guys and Dolls, Next to Normal, Memphis,* and *The Addams Family* all followed.

He is one of the most prolific choreographers working on the Broadway stage today. At the time of this interview, he was in rehearsal for his first effort as both director and choreographer for the Chicago premier of *White Noise.* He has received a Drama Desk and Lucille Lortel nomination for his work on *Jersey Boys* and *Saved,* respectively.

Sergio has choreographed off-Broadway, for film, television, for Playwrights Horizons, City Center Encores, in Vegas, London's West End, at the La Jolla Playhouse in San Diego, in Amsterdam, for Ballet Hispanico, and for several national tours. He has also choreographed two operas for the Los Angeles and New York City Opera.

CRAMER: It's just tremendous to have you with us. Thank you so much for doing this, and taking time out of your busy schedule to speak with me.

TRUJILLO: Thanks. I'm happy to be here.

CRAMER: Not since Susan Stroman, in 2001, has any choreographer had four shows running on Broadway. You have *Memphis*, *Next to Normal, Jersey Boys*, and the *Addams Family*—all enjoying long runs. Each show has also produced a tour or out-of-town production, correct?

TRUJILLO: Correct.

CRAMER: You were born in Columbia and lived there until age 12. Why did your family then move to Toronto?

TRUJILLO: My father believed it was the land of better opportunities. Many of my uncles and aunts had moved to Toronto already, so it was just a matter of time before we did. My brothers and my sisters actually moved before my parents and I did. My mom wanted to be closer to her other children, and I was young enough to be uprooted without too much problem, so we moved.

CRAMER: Even though you didn't have formal dance training until you were much older, you had music, dance, and rhythm all around you throughout your childhood.

TRUJILLO: Being Latin and Columbian, there's always been music and dance in my life. It's in everyday life. It's part of our heritage. It's part of our blood. Whenever there is a family gathering, there's bound to be a dance-off. You know, I'm sort of intimidated when I go visit my family because at one point or another, there is some couple on the dance floor that's trying to outdance other couples. They're so full of life. They just love constantly showing off.

CRAMER: You must have been quite an intelligent student, because you decided to major in science in college. You were biochemistry major and ended up in chiropractic school. Do you have your license?

TRUJILLO: No, I left chiropractic school in my second year because I fell in love with dance.

CRAMER: That was a pivotal moment, I understand. It is a theme park story. Would you share that?

TRUJILLO: Yes. Being an immigrant and moving to Canada for more opportunities placed upon me a sense of duty to my family. I felt I should become a doctor or at least graduate with a degree that enabled me to select a higher quality profession, earn more money, and help my family, because that's what a good Latin boy does. So, I went to university and, in a way, tried to please my parents. But what was really at the core of who I was and what I wanted to do was dance. I remember going to see the show *The Best of Broadway* at a theme park called Canada's Wonderland. I fell in love with it. I was 18 or 19. I remember seeing the show and thinking, "Oh, my God! That is exactly what I want to do." I thought, "I want to learn how to dance like that. Where can I go?" I did the research, found a dance school downtown, and took classes. At the same time, I had enrolled myself at the University of Toronto in biochemistry. So, I did that for three years. I balanced my curriculum between studying sciences and dance. I would go every Saturday and take dance for 8 hours then perhaps go to the library and study. This love of dance just kept eating at me. I knew it's what I really wanted. When I started chiropractic school, I didn't dance at all. It really broke my heart. There was no dance whatsoever. I felt this emptiness and knew something was missing. So, during my second year of chiropractic school, I returned to class. While I was taking class, I found out that they were auditioning for *Star Search*.

CRAMER: It was the precursor to most of our television talent competitions today.

TRUJILLO: Right. *Star Search* was auditioning in the same studio, and I asked one of the girls in my class, "Do you want to audition for *Star Search?*" She looked at me like I was crazy and said, "Well, what are we going to do"? And I said, "I don't care. Let's do the combination we learned in class." So, sure enough, we went in there and auditioned for the show. I got *Star Search*, went to Los Angeles, and performed on television. While I was in Los Angeles taking class, I met Michael Peters.

CRAMER: Michael Peters was a huge influence in your life.

TRUJILLO: He absolutely was. Michael traveled to Toronto after teaching in Los Angeles to audition dancers. He was the choreographer of a television show called *The Hot Shoe Show*. I had taken his class out in Los Angeles and he remembered me. I was also really hungry to get the job, and really hungry to impress him. I was hired. Remember, I was in the middle of my second year of chiropractic school, which is actually harder than any of the other years. He pulled me aside one day after rehearsal and he said, "Kid, you have something really special. You have a God-given talent. Don't waste that talent." I really listened to that. That resonated with me. I was already halfway through my second year, but I really thought about it. I talked to my deans, teachers, and other friends, and decided to take a sabbatical.

CRAMER: For our readers, a sabbatical is a period of leave from work for research, study, or travel. You used it for performance and dance study. Now, you were in and out of Los Angeles a great deal at that time. You were cast in *Jerome Robbins Broadway* via Los Angeles in an odd way, right?

TRUJILLO: I did. My sabbatical time was running out. So, I came to study in New York first, and then I went out to Los Angeles to study as well, because I wanted to learn about music videos. I wanted to audition for Paula Abdul, Michael Jackson, Debbie Allen, and all of those stars. I was taking class one day with a woman by the name of Jackie Sleight, and she said, "They're having auditions for this Broadway show called *Jerome Robbins Broadway*." Unfortunately, I didn't know who Jerome Robbins was at the time. So, I went to the audition not knowing anything. I remember it vividly. I was kept all the way until the end. It was an amazing day. I didn't hear anything from them for about two months, and then in June of 1989 they called me and said, "Are you interested in replacing someone in the Broadway company?" And that was it. I never went back to school. On July 17, 1989, I made my Broadway debut.

CRAMER: You know the date exactly.

TRUJILLO: Yes, of course. There's an appreciation that comes when you're older. You're so hungry for opportunities. I think it makes such a huge difference.

CRAMER: You performed in a limited number of shows on Broadway before you changed your path and became a choreographer. However, those were iconic shows. We already mentioned *Jerome Robbins' Broadway*. You did Christopher Chapman's choreography for *Guys and Dolls* as an ensemble member in 1992, and came full circle 17 years later to choreograph the Broadway revival in 2009. You also danced in *Fosse*. Though not on Broadway, you danced in *Promises, Promises* for Rob Marshall at Encores!, as well as *Kiss of the Spider Woman* and *Victor/Victoria*. Did you have any idea, as you began, that you were part of something so exceptional, dancing in those iconic shows?

TRUJILLO: You know, I don't think I knew it at all. I always say go with your instincts—go with your gut and your heart. All of these things that I've experienced, all the choices I have made, even as a choreographer, are always instinctive and right from my gut and my heart. I knew that I was a dancer. I wasn't a singer. And I knew that I if I was ever going to audition for a Broadway show, it was going to be a show that had dance in it, because I knew that was the thing that I loved the most. I wasn't trying to be a singer. So, when I auditioned, I only came to calls for dance shows. I had a very specific agenda. When I look back it's a bit unbelievable to realize that my first show was *Jerome Robbins' Broadway*, and my last show was *Fosse*.

CRAMER: You've worked in every medium. You danced in the film *Chicago* for Rob Marshall; *Death Becomes Her* with Meryl Streep and Goldie Hawn, and *Cinderella*, with Brandy. You've choreographed two operas and choreographed two shows: *Kismet* and *A Tree Grows in Brooklyn* for Encores! Extensive work off-Broadway has earned you awards and award nominations. You've worked for Playwrights Horizons. You got a Lucille Lortel nomination for Outstanding Choreographer for *Saved*, which is based on the MGM movie. You've choreographed television shorts and video documentaries, worked in regional theatres around the country, like the La Jolla Playhouse in San Diego, and staged the national tour, West End, and Vegas productions of most of your Broadway Shows. How do you select your projects?

TRUJILLO: I always felt I was a late bloomer. I started dancing and choreographing late, so I always feel like I'm catching up. So, my interest and the way I think about things or figure out what my next project might be are quite basic. I think about the following: what I will gain from the experience, what will help me grow and evolve. When I started, I felt that it was important for me to pick material that was challenging and interesting, and that would allow me to improve as a choreographer. After I did *Jersey Boys*, I became very selective about what projects I did.

CRAMER: There must have been many, many offers made after *Jersey Boys,* which was such a hit. You had some serious decisions to make.

TRUJILLO: I was lucky. But, you know, I wanted to work with directors that could teach me something. I wanted to work with creative teams I felt could inspire me. The material needed to challenge me and allow me to grow. Another big mentor of mine is Des McAnuff, because I think he is brilliant and has taught me so much. He offered me many of his projects, which were wonderfully creative and smart pieces of theatre. With *Next to Normal*, I always wanted to work with Michael Greif. It was easy to select that project, even though it was musical staging and not specifically choreography or "dance steps." Chris Ashley is somebody who I worked with before I did *Jersey Boys*. I did a show called *All Shook Up*. I was called in to doctor that show. They asked me to do two numbers, but I ended up retooling the whole show.

CRAMER: Is it true that when you were doing *All Shook Up* with Chris Ashley that *Memphis* came up and you were in discussions for that show even before *Jersey Boys* materialized?

TRUJILLO: Not exactly. While working with Joe Di Pietro and Chris Ashely on *All Shook Up*, Joe said, "I have a show that I want you to do called *Memphis*, but we're not quite ready for you yet." And I said, "Okay, just let me know when you're ready." It was that simple.

CRAMER: Directors and choreographers have to have so many irons in the fire at any given moment.

TRUJILLO: Oh, yes, always. I can't think about next year alone. I have to think about the next 15 years of my life. I've always thought about choreography. Even when I was dancing, I knew I was going to choreograph. When I was doing *Guys and Dolls* in 1992, I started to think like a choreographer, but I didn't start professionally until 1998. I was thinking six years ahead. Simply because I have four shows on Broadway doesn't mean that I'm going to sit back and relax. I'm just restless, and this is my time. I know it won't always be my time. It's all relative. I'm going to keep myself invested in as many things as I can, projects that I feel passionate about and that are important to me.

CRAMER: You've come up through the ranks as an assistant, correct?

TRUJILLO: Yes. I assisted many people including Jerry Mitchell, Debbie Allen, Vince Patterson, and Rob Marshall. It's not like all of a sudden I decided I was going to be a choreographer. It didn't happen overnight. There's no school for musical theatre choreography, at least that I know of. There's nothing like learning by being in the trenches with those you admire and who can really teach you the ropes.

CRAMER: Were you a dance captain before you became an assistant?

TRUJILLO: I was a dance captain only once, and was terrible at it. That particular skill is not in my frame of reference. I have to look at the whole picture. I need more to do more on my plate. Even though I was a dancer, I was restless. I'm restless as a choreographer. Can I do something else? Can I be more invested in the process? Of course I can, so now I am directing.

CRAMER: How do you find assistants that can service your vision, and how do you use them?

TRUJILLO: I'm attracted to people that have a sense of who they are and a specific sense of their individuality. I like them strong-minded. I'm attracted to great dancers. I'm attracted to talented, intelligent assistants. I think I've been very lucky about who I've hired and who I have in my family, taking care of my shows.

CRAMER: And you have different assistants for different projects?

TRUJILLO: I do, yes. My associate for *Jersey Boys*, I've known since 1983. He's one of the first people I met when I was dancing, and he takes care of the shows just like I would. Your former student, Dontee Kiehn, takes care of *The Addams Family* and *Next to Normal* for me. I found her when she was auditioning for me for a show called *Mambo Kings*. I saw this young girl with all this fire, with this quality that I couldn't put a finger on. When I ask someone to come onboard my team, it's because they offer something different. They all have a very unique, rare quality about them, but I can't pinpoint what it is. For me the selection is instinctive.

CRAMER: At what point do your assistants join you on preproduction?

TRUJILLO: I do a lot of my work on my own, in my head. I spend a great deal of time with the script and am a bit tormented by it. The real work starts for me when I get in the room with my associate or my assistant. I'm not the kind of guy who goes into a room and dances by himself. I've tried that. I've videotaped myself. I look like a crazy madman and don't enjoy that. I like the relationship and the conversation with my associates. I'm a physical individual. I need to be stimulated. I need to have ideas and movement around me. All of the preparation happens in preproduction. It's where I take all of my tools and start carving and creating a blueprint for whatever show I'm doing with my associates. Most of the time, when I walk out of preproduction, all the vocabulary is done and all the numbers are done, so when I walk into rehearsal, I can play.

CRAMER: You can make any changes you want because you're completely prepared.

TRUJILLO: Yes. Sometimes my assistants get crazy because, all of a sudden, the plan changes. I'm working with the actors, I'm working with the dancers, and they all have creative input. I try to stay pretty close to what it is that we did in preproduction but it doesn't always work out that way. In terms of working in the room, finding the language or the vocabulary is probably the trickiest thing for me. But once I have that, then it goes quickly. And I'm not the kind of guy who uses the same vocabulary for every show. *Memphis* is different from *Addams Family,* from *Jersey Boys,* from *Tarzan,* from *Next to Normal*—they're all very different. I am not interested in having the Trujillo trademark or the Sergio Trujillo style.

CRAMER: You don't want to hear someone say, "That's a Sergio show."

TRUJILLO: No, I don't. I'm servicing the material. I challenge myself and push myself to create a language that is specific to a particular show.

CRAMER: I've heard you say that working with a dance arranger is the most important relationship you can have on a show. Do you read music, and do you feel it's a necessary skill to work with a dance arranger?

TRUJILLO: I think the dance arranger is the unsung hero of dance in terms of musical theatre. Choreographer and dance arranger is one of the most important relationships on a show. Since I don't read music, I approach communication differently. For example, when I started to choreograph *Guys and Dolls*, I read a great many of the Damon Runyon stories because I wanted to get into that world.

CRAMER: You and Des McAnuff set the show in the time of the Runyon stories, rather than the time periods of past productions, or the film version.

TRUJILLO: Right. We're talking about the 1930s, rather than the 1950s. So, I approach the ideas associated with dance arrangements by listening to the swing tunes of the Big Band Era like Benny Goodman's "Sing, Sing, Sing." That's where my dance arranger and I start to build the vocabulary. Since I don't read, I find a great source, something we can focus on right from the start. From there, we start to work on dance structure, dynamics, style, and the like.

CRAMER: How about a show like *Tarzan*? I should explain that you retooled the Disney *Tarzan* that ran here in New York, opened it in Amsterdam, and now it's running in Hamburg, Germany.

TRUJILLO: For *Tarzan,* I had to find the vocabulary first and the music second. I went for primal, African music, in terms of finding what the language was. But with the dance arranger on the show, it felt much more like composing because we made so many changes. I always like to find musical themes that can help us tell the story.

CRAMER: When you have a musical phrase or idea to communicate to the arranger, do you hum?

TRUJILLO: I sing it. Sometimes I'll just dance it with accents. It's really collaboration. I think some arrangers will go away and work on a piece of music, and then bring it back to the choreographer. That's not how I like to work. I like to create it with them while we are both in the room. That's the way it works for me. I have to be really hands-on.

CRAMER: You've choreographed many projects set in the 1950s and 1960s. Do you favor those eras?

TRUJILLO: Well, I've done so much research in those eras. I did a show in London called *Peggy Sue Got Married,* same time period.

I have the foundation vocabulary-wise, so you can give me shows in that era and it just comes out of me like a dam bursting.

CRAMER: Do you think your research enhances your own choreography or do you use it as a practical application?

TRUJILLO: I use it as an enhancement. I think research enriches the choreography and empowers the choreographer. You'll read about a particular period, look at pictures, study the style, clothing, hair, dance, music, and social values of the time, process all of it, and let the choreography come out of you naturally. In terms of *Jersey Boys*, I didn't want to copy *The Four Seasons*; I wanted the "flavor" of what they brought to the genre.

CRAMER: For our readers, *Jersey Boys* is based on the true story of the 1960s band, *The Four Seasons*. The real guys didn't dance as much as your *Jersey Boys* do in the show. You enhanced all of the movement from research and created it specifically for the show.

TRUJILLO: I wanted it to be sexy and wanted it to feel individual, so I came up with a formula that worked for them. It's different than the work I'm doing in *Memphis*.

CRAMER: *Memphis* hit the scene like no other show in years. It's true Broadway dance. It is also quite different from *Jersey Boys* and the staging you did for *Next to Normal*. We are mentioning the titles of three extremely different show styles. You must differentiate between musical staging and choreography. How do you approach those differently?

TRUJILLO: Working with a director and choreographer is so integrated; there are times when a song moves into movement and storytelling then moves into dance. That gray area between the song and the dance, I coin that musical staging. In terms of *Next to Normal*, there was no real dance in the show. There is choreography, but most of it is musical staging. How does Gabe move? He is a ghost after all. But I didn't want him to move like a ghost. I wanted to give him movement that feels natural and organic. It also must be athletic because he has to move through the house. Once again, you're servicing the actor. The emotion and the storytelling lead in a different way than traditional choreography does.

CRAMER: Do you feel you approach an actor significantly different than you approach a dancer?

TRUJILLO: Oh, yes, of course. It's a different set of rules. Dancers want to know when to go, on what count, where they travel, and where they land. You have to be very authoritative. They're used to it. That's the way dancers grow up. They're disciplined, and they've had tough dance teachers. With actors, you sort of have to stroke them or massage them a little bit. You have to gain their confidence and allow them to have input. They are the ones living in the character, so there is much more of a conversation.

CRAMER: What kind of a rehearsal environment do you try to create?

TRUJILLO: I'm old school. I like the rules. I like people to be there on time. When there's going to be a dress rehearsal, I like the cast to be warmed up and ready to go. What happens with all the shows is simple. I fall in love with them and with my dancers in a very paternal way. I'm their coach, so I become very protective of them, but I'm tough with them. So, it's tough love. It's also been very useful to my skills in the health industry. Studying to be a chiropractor has come in handy. If something happens to one of my dancers, I go into my health practitioner mode. I become incredibly careful and play caretaker for whoever gets injured.

CRAMER: Auditioning is an art form. I've heard you say that twice in interviews that I've watched. What do you mean by that?

TRUJILLO: I think you have to do your research. You have to understand for whom you're auditioning, what that choreographer is looking for, how you're going to dress for the audition, and how you're going to approach it. There are people that get the job in terms of how they present themselves to a choreographer. And you know what? There are times where I can be standing in the back of the room and can spot someone way on the opposite side, simply because there's that "thing" about them. It's instinctual. You just know that dancer has that special quality you're looking for. Whenever I was dancing in a show, I felt very constrained. I felt very much like I wasn't being true to who I really wanted to be, because I was dancing someone else's choreography. And so, what I try to do with my work is allow the dancers to have a point of view in the audition. Then it doesn't matter if I'm actually watching 10 dancers or 18. They are individuals, each with a character and a point of view. I also look for dancers with specific qualities. That dancer is fearless. That one is dynamic. That one is passionate. Even if they're working the choreography way in the corner, I can see their process right in the rehearsal room.

CRAMER: How is the audition process different for actors and singers that walk in the room? For example, does that special quality manifest itself differently?

TRUJILLO: With singers and actors, I've usually already seen them in their vocal and acting auditions, so I'm aware of their talent. Now, I have to treat the situation more mathematically. Can this person learn the choreography quickly? How focused are they? Do they have rhythm? Can they count? So, I can't really treat it the same way as a dance audition. I must use a different set of rules.

CRAMER: You have staged many international companies of your Broadway shows. As a choreographer, what's it like casting in different parts of the world, compared to the United States?

TRUJILLO: The talent level varies dramatically. Americans are hungry, so there's more competition here. That's not to say that there isn't phenomenal talent in Europe. The audition for *Tarzan* in Hamburg and Amsterdam produced unbelievable, extraordinary dancers. There are just smaller numbers. It really varies, and the dance world is changing. There are fewer jobs, so the business as a whole is more competitive.

CRAMER: What other changes have you seen over the years?

TRUJILLO: I've seen better dancers in America now than I've ever seen before, better male dancers, certainly. There's a lot more of them too, which is great for us. I think there are more exceptional dancers in America, but every country has unique dancers.

CRAMER: Do you have a preference between retooling an existing piece, such as *Guys and Dolls*, or working on something brand new?

TRUJILLO: Brand new. However, *Guys and Dolls* is a good example because it was a challenge for me. We made some pretty big changes to the show. It's tricky. Also, I danced in the 1992 revival. Everyone expects so much from that show because it's a classic; it's one of our treasures. I did enjoy retooling it, but I prefer to work on original material.

CRAMER: Have you ever had to produce an audition tape for a choreography job?

TRUJILLO: No. I think my auditions for the industry was my work in *All Shook Up* and *Mambo Kings*. Because of working on those shows, I got offered bigger productions.

CRAMER: Can you give us a little background on a show like *Mambo Kings,* and why it never made it to Broadway?

TRUJILLO: We rehearsed it in New York, and it was first produced in San Francisco. From San Francisco we were headed straight to Broadway. I would have had two shows running then—*Jersey Boys* and *Mambo Kings.* As to why it never made it? That's another interview.

CRAMER: You're very passionate when you talk about the style of *Mambo Kings* and *Memphis.* Can you speak to that?

TRUJILLO: I never had a better sense of who I was than when I was doing *Mambo Kings* and *Memphis.* There are shows where I'm constantly restless about the steps or the choreography. But with those shows, I felt like the steps were pouring out of me, like a part of me was actually being steered without conscious thought. It was so natural.

CRAMER: So, you felt that *Mambo Kings* was your audition for the theatrical community? They saw *All Shook Up,* they saw *Mambo Kings,* and your good work was perceptible and evident.

TRUJILLO: I understood what *Mambo Kings* represented in terms of the opportunity and the visibility that it could have, so I took that opportunity and I ran with it.

CRAMER: How do you work with your creative team? Let's start with a director.

TRUJILLO: You'll love this. The meeting for *Jersey Boys* lasted 20 minutes. I went to speak with Des McAnuff, the director, and we talked about what I had done, the way I saw the show, and the way he saw the show. It was a simple conversation.

CRAMER: What about your conversation with Chris Ashley on *Memphis?* Was that easy too?

TRUJILLO: He just turned me loose. I love him. He really has been supportive, and because we worked together on *All Shook*

Up, we have an unspoken respect for each other and great trust. He's very supportive of me as a choreographer. Like any choreographer, you want to please your director. But Chris is honest and straightforward and he would tell me, "You know, you're going in the wrong direction. You might want to rethink that." The lines of communication are always open. I believe it is that way with all directors I collaborate with. There is a fine line between the two jobs, and respect and trust are key.

CRAMER: What kind of dialogue do you have with lighting designers? What kind of influence do you have?

TRUJILLO: Well, my first experience with a lighting designer was with Jules Fisher and Peggy Eisenhauer. They're the royalty of all lighting designers. We worked together on *Mambo Kings*. I was very timid with them at first, until they lit one of my numbers and I felt like it wasn't really what I had imagined. I went up to them and said, "May we rework the number?" They were incredibly supportive and generous. So, after that, I am candid and open with Natasha Katz, Paul Binkley, Don Holder, Kevin Adams, and, of course, Peggy and Jules. I have a vision and I make sure that they hear it, because it helps them.

CRAMER: When you speak to your lighting designer, do you talk about specifics—using lighting terminology—or do you speak to them about an overall visual design?

TRUJILLO. I do both. I let them have their go at it, and then once they've made their first pass, I offer my input. If I see that they're going in the wrong direction, then I speak up.

CRAMER: What's your relationship like with costume designers? Do you understand fabrics and what you think might work or move better? Do you offer suggestions at any time before the first round of designs is presented?

TRUJILLO: I think it's the same approach as with lighting designers. I have to respect their vision. I have to respect their design. Then I can give an opinion. I don't really care about fabrics because I feel that every designer should know that. When you're designing for dance, you have to know what fabrics best suit movement. Costume designer Paul Tazewell and I worked closely together on *Memphis*. If I saw certain looks or dresses, I would say to Paul, "You know, I think these dresses might look better in this number."

Or, "These dresses will work better in this other number." I felt very comfortable with that.

CRAMER: When you danced in *Fosse,* did you tell yourself it was your last show? Did you know then that you must choose choreography as your path?

TRUJILLO: I knew before *Fosse* that it would be my last show. I knew two years before.

CRAMER: What was the turning point?

TRUJILLO: Well, I think it's a combination of everything. I was restless, as I've always been, and it was part of the journey in my evolution as a person and as an artist. It's not as if I go about my day without a care. No, I make a plan. I think it's important to have a plan. I think it's important to know where you're going before you get there, whether it's your work life or your daily life. I'm going to be 65 before I know it, or even 75. There's got to be a plan. Time is running out really fast. You've got to be ready. I knew that *Fosse* was going to be my last show two years before, as I said. Therefore, I had started to choreograph other smaller shows. So, not only was I assisting then, but I was also working on my choreographic career. As a matter of fact, when I was dancing and playing *Bojangles* in the show, the only way I could get into the character was seeing myself ten years down the road, always wanting and still trying to dance, but no longer being able to. So, I certainly brought that into my song's story. It was like I was dancing my way to a funeral every night. As sad as it sounds, it's an expression and an extension of who the character is anyway. So, in terms of people really going after something they want, they have to make a choice. I had to make a choice. I had to call myself a choreographer, and take the leap to commit to my goal.

CRAMER: Was there a definitive moment when you declared, "It's time to make a transition. It's time for me to direct. I need to be wearing both hats?"

TRUJILLO: I'm always going to choreograph. But whenever there is a project that I feel I can direct and choreograph, I will. As I said before, I am restless. I'm always looking for ways to grow, and directing is a natural extension of choreography. It's not a huge stretch if you've worked closely, as I have, with directors in true collaborations. It's a common progression.

CRAMER: So, now you are directing *White Noise*, the story of a white supremacist singing duo. It opens soon in Chicago?

TRUJILLO: Yes. Originally, my first directing project was supposed to be *Havana* with Frank Wildhorn and Rupert Holmes. It's just taking a little longer, as it is a more traditional piece. With *White Noise*, I am taking a real leap.

CRAMER: Let's tell our readers about *White Noise*. In the show, a volatile record producer, smelling a fortune to be made, plucks two sisters out of obscurity. He must get those girls to replace their hate-filled lyrics with coded words set to catchy tunes. You had experience with Chicago, out of town, because *The Addams Family* started there. It's a city that embraces you, I'm guessing.

TRUJILLO: I hope so. I think we're just going to see what happens. The show has had a volatile history itself.

CRAMER: Besides Michael Peters, who was the biggest influence on your career?

TRUJILLO: I've had great, smart, talented people along the way who have inspired me at different points in my life. Jerry Mitchell was instrumental in my career. I would have to say Des McAnuff has been, and continues to be, incredibly influential. He is a phenomenal director. Before I walked into rehearsals for *Jersey Boys*, I had come up with really show-off type choreography. He guided me to make sure that the choreography was character driven. We never wanted it to seem as though the actors were dancing. Instead, we wanted it to feel as if the *characters* were dancing, as if the movement was happening spontaneously. It doesn't always appear as if what's going on in the show is choreographed, but every single move is—all the way to the end.

CRAMER: Did you have a sense that he was really teaching you the ropes when you worked with him, or that he was inclusive with you? In other words, you were always present and were able to offer input.

TRUJILLO: Yes, of course. He is a big supporter of mine.

CRAMER: How do you give notes to your cast and crew?

TRUJILLO: Notes sessions. I sit with them to talk one on one. If there's something specific that may be embarrassing or something that I feel that would be disrespectful, I pull them aside. I think it's important to gain their respect. But, it's also important to be tough with dancers. They need it and are used to it. It's a different set of rules with actors and singers. I think it's always important to treat your dancers with the respect that they deserve. It's a very hard art form. It's a very enslaving art form, and one that is physically challenging. I think they deserve the respect that the art form doesn't get.

CRAMER: Once a show opens, how often do you go back?

TRUJILLO: Oh, I try to go as much as I can. It's tough for me right now because I have already moved on to another project.

CRAMER: When you go back, do you let people know?

TRUJILLO: No, I don't let them know until after I've already seen it.

CRAMER: I'd like to ask you to give advice to college students. You've been there. You've lived the college life. Now students can get degrees in musical theatre. They finish their education and move to the city, wherever they choose, be it Los Angeles, Chicago, or New York City. What would you say to a 21-year-old college graduate who is going to pursue a performing career?

TRUJILLO: I think that no matter what the challenges are, no matter what obstacles lie in front of you, if you really believe in it, what it is you set out to do, it's going to happen. I think you have to continue to work on your craft and stay committed and devoted to it. You have to have heart and passion to succeed. And, you know, when the time is right, when that opportunity presents itself, if you're prepared and able to deliver, big things will happen.

CRAMER: Thank you so much. I appreciate you taking the time.

TRUJILLO: It was my pleasure.

CHAPTER TWELVE

Anthony Van Laast

Anthony Van Laast grew up in London, interested in sports like any youngster, and steered clear of his mother's career as a dancer and dance teacher. He knew he would attend college and study medicine to become a doctor. When Anthony was 16, his mother took him to Covent Garden to see Nureyev dance and his entire world turned upside down. In ballet class the next week, he trained at the London School of Contemporary Dance. He joined the company as a dancer and ultimately was active as both an actor and a choreographer. He studied Graham technique with artistic director Robert Cohan and had several iconic teachers including Merce Cunningham and Anna Sokolov.

His career has been prolific and highly diversified. Oddly enough, it began in pop videos and quickly moved into commercials. He became a part of Andrew Lloyd Webber's Very Useful Group Ltd. and choreographed many book musicals. Beginning with *Song and Dance,* Van Laast has created the choreography for *Joseph and the Amazing Technicolor Dreamcoat, Mamma Mia!, Bombay Dreams, Jesus Christ Superstar,* and *Whistle Down the Wind.* Other West End productions include *Into the Woods, Sister Act,* and *A Little Night Music.* Shows such as *Joseph, Jesus Christ Superstar, Mamma Mia!, Bombay Dreams* and *Sister Act* made their Broadway debut with Van Laast's choreography.

He has recreated his choreography for European and US tours, Australian and Canadian productions, worldwide tours, and musical films including *Joseph, Jesus Christ Superstar,* and *Mamma Mia!*

Like many of the creative artists in this book, Anthony didn't stop with musical theatre productions. His career transcends genre, creating choreography for opera, operetta, the concert stage, and directing and staging productions in Las Vegas that include *Siegfried and Roy* at the Mirage and *EFX* at the MGM Grand.

Anthony has directed and choreographed television, world tour, and live events, such as *Burn the Floor* and *Batman Live,* and has an extensive film career that includes such movies as *Excalibur, Hope and Glory, Never Say Never Again,* and *Harry Potter and the Half Blood Prince.*

In 1999 Anthony was awarded the MBE (Most Excellent Order of the British Empire) for his services to dance and choreography. An MBE is an order of chivalry that was created by King George V in 1917. He has been nominated for Olivier Awards (London), Tony Awards (America), and Green Room Awards (Australia).

CRAMER: Welcome Anthony. I'm so delighted that you've taken time out of your hectic schedule. You are in the middle of rehearsals for the new Broadway show, *Sister Act*.

VAN LAAST: Absolutely.

CRAMER: A show that you have done in London.

VAN LAAST: I've done it in London and Hamburg. But this is a brand-new version. Douglas Carter Beane is writing a new script for us. The show is restructured for the American market.

CRAMER: Let's go back to your humble beginnings at the London School of Contemporary Dance. What age did you start and what forms of dance did you study?

VAN LAAST: Well, first, I thought I was going to be a doctor. My academic studies were leading me toward university to study medicine. My mum was a dancer and taught dance throughout most of my childhood and most of my early teens, so it was always present. Whenever there was dancing on television, my father would shout out, "Dancing on television, dancing on television!" and that was my cue to leave the room. Frankly, I was much more interested in soccer and tennis. I was more interested in a lot of things. Then my mum took me to Covent Garden when I was 16 years old and I saw Nureyev dance. It was like a calling. In the interval I said to my mother, "Do you know what, Mum? I don't know whether I'll ever be a dancer, but I want to be in the dance world." The next week I was in ballet class. At the end of the current term I left the school I had been attending and went to the London School of Contemporary Dance. I started dancing full-time. I was old—16 and a half. I did three years there studying Graham technique. Luckily at that time, there were very few men dancing, so the company needed any man they could get. I was very lucky. Our artistic director was a man named Robert Cohan, who had been one of Graham's partners, and the repertoire we did was Graham and Paul Taylor. Later, Merce Cunningham and Anna Sokolow came and taught us, so we worked with some of the greats. And, of course, the company members were encouraged to choreograph.

CRAMER: Dance is subsidized in England, isn't that correct?

VAN LAAST: Yes, the government subsidizes the arts, so we were on annual contracts. At the age of 21, I was nurtured and looked after and paid annually, with a holiday. So we're paid properly. I was very nervous about choreographing, even after being in the company for a few years because there were so many fine, young choreographers within the company. I'd find it very intimidating, but I did actually choreograph a couple of pieces in workshop. Robert Cohan helped us and taught us choreography. We had choreography classes. We would do workshops, though our work wouldn't be exposed too much. I choreographed one that was very successful and went into the company repertoire when I was in my mid-twenties. It was still intimidating, but I knew somewhere inside me I could choreograph. I knew I could do more. During dance class one day, we had a man watching. Being one of the foremost leading contemporary dance companies in Europe, we had a lot of observers. Well, I was a very good dancer. I danced principal roles. And the man watching came up to me at the end of class, and said, "How would you like to be in a pop video?" This was the mid-1970s. I said, "I'd love to be in a pop video. Why'd you ask me"? And he said (this is going to sound ironic), "Well, because you've got so much hair."

CRAMER: That's funny. Our readers should refer to your headshot at this point!

VAN LAAST: I used to have long, long black locks down to my shoulders. And I thought about it, you know, I'd been invited to be in a pop video because I had long hair, not because I danced well or anything like that. But anyway, it's strange just how little things in life work out. In the moments you least expect, your whole life changes. So, I did a couple of pop videos, and because the talent in the pop videos didn't realize we needed choreography, I started choreographing them as well. Then I worked with Kate Bush. She was a very big star in the 1970s, and is an icon really. So that was the beginning of my career. I'd actually found my "métier," my place, and it was actually more toward the commercial world than the contemporary dance world.

CRAMER: It's where you started but certainly not where your roots are.

VAN LAAST: Yes, and it's really interesting because that's where I started, but all my training, all my understanding of dance theatre came from contemporary dance. I didn't go into choreography with a musical theatre background.

CRAMER: Do projects find their way to you, do you seek them out, or is there a balance for you now at this point in your career?

VAN LAAST: That's a very interesting question. I create in lots of different areas. I work in musical theatre, I create shows, I work in opera, in film, and I also have my own production company that develops projects as well. And my idea was, if you keep moving around, no one catches up with you.

CRAMER: That's a great philosophy, very smart.

VAN LAAST: My production company is a very big part of my life at the moment, because my partner and I have just initiated a new project called *Batman Live*. This is not a musical, there's no dance in it whatsoever. I'm working with Warner Bros. and we're doing it in arenas. It's a play with huge special effects and I'm the creative director.

CRAMER: The inspiration came right out of your head, your imagination.

VAN LAAST: Yes. It goes back to all my theatrical sensibilities that I've learned through dance and through movement.

CRAMER: I imagine that because you work in so many different mediums, you swing back and forth between genres. There's no linear approach to your career whatsoever.

VAN LAAST: No. I mean, I think what's really exiting. Yes, I can choose the musicals I do. So when I get offered a musical, I look at it and say, "Is this the kind of thing that I can bring something to?" I think, as my career has gone on, that I'm extremely good at musical staging. That's one of my real strengths. I believe that I'm actually involved less now with step making, but actually much more with musical theatre staging. Also, another of my strengths is character development through musical theatre staging. So, when I look at a script, I think, "What can I develop within this project?" If it's something I don't think is for me, I'm very happy to pass on it.

CRAMER: The Lincoln Center Library did not record an archival copy of *Bombay Dreams*, one of your Tony-nominated shows. When we spoke by e-mail, you pointed me in the direction of YouTube, and I started watching every clip I could find. There's so much to see and it was very helpful to me. Even at that time, just several years back, you stated you served a very specific creative purpose. You had an assistant who was the key on-step creation and the style of the piece, and you had the overall vision to make it work. Are you finding that continues to be your role creatively today?

VAN LAAST: Yes, it's different than it used to be, say, in *Joseph* days or *Superstar* days. And that's just the way it's going. When Andrew Lloyd Webber came to me about doing *Bombay Dreams*, I realized if we're going to be really true to the style, we needed authenticity. I could watch hundreds of Bollywood films, and I could learn the steps, but it actually wouldn't be rooted in the true culture. So I worked with a woman called Farah Khan, who's one of the top Bollywood choreographers. I went over to Bombay, and I worked with her and her dancers to learn much more about it. And with Farah, we developed the language for *Bombay Dreams*. Farah had never choreographed for the stage, much less a 5-minute number. She had a lot of material, a lot of steps. So my job on *Bombay Dreams* was working with Farah, taking her material, adding my own as well, and crafting a number to have some kind of sense within the show. Unlike in Bollywood, where a number exists for the effect and the joy of it, in a musical, it has to have a dramaturgical purpose. You cannot put a number in a musical, I believe, which purely exists for the sake of dance. Maybe you can have a dance celebration, but the celebration would have to be part of the dramaturgical reason. If you just have a lot of dancing going on, or a lot of steps going on, that soon becomes very boring and doesn't help the play move forward. So working on *Bombay Dreams* included taking Farah's material, developing it, putting it into the play, and making sure it had a dramaturgical through line. It was simply fantastic, and a great opportunity to work.

CRAMER: Not to mention any visual effect that you added to enhance the number came out of your head.

VAN LAAST: Well, it comes out of my head, but I would say the art of musical theatre is collaboration, unlike choreographing a ballet or contemporary piece. It's the collaboration with your composer and then with your musical arranger to make sure that the music is, as you want it. It's the collaboration with your designer to make sure the costumes are as you want them and how the designer sees them. And it's also the collaboration with my assistant. You know, I have fantastic relationships with my assistants where we collaborate in the studios by ourselves, working and working.

CRAMER: How do you select your assistants, and how do you work with them in the studio during preproduction?

VAN LAAST: My assistant is really, really important, because I realize that I can't do Bollywood dance. I can learn Bollywood steps and I can see the style. There are some styles that I'm good at and some I'm not. I can imitate them, but actually it's not in my soul. So when I'm working on a job, I have different assistants that will fill in the holes where I know that I'm weak. I'm just talking about step style here. I normally work with women, because I also know that I have a very masculine way of moving, so I know that I can teach that way. But a female assistant is going to approach the work with a different way of moving and using arms. Let's use *Joseph* as an example. I have a wonderful assistant by the name of Nichola Treherne, and I've worked with her for maybe 30 years now. At this point, she can actually finish my choreographic thought. I knew that the choreography for *Joseph* had to be a specific style with the hands—I wanted it to be hieroglyphic. I wanted the hieroglyphics to become art deco. She could do these wonderful hands for me, and I knew I needed my assistant to help me in that way. I need someone I can bounce ideas off. When I work with my assistant on a show, I will spend weeks in the studio, preparing, thinking, working it all out, because after all these years with the two of us working in the studio, I can see the finished number in my head. I know what it's going to look like. I know what the whole number is and what will make it look right.

CRAMER: Now I'm certain at the same time you're working with your assistants, your dance arranger's in the room with you.

VAN LAAST: Yes.

CRAMER: Do you read music and do you feel it's a necessary skill for a choreographer?

VAN LAAST: I have played the piano. I do read music. Do I feel it's necessary? No. I think it's in your soul. I think if you're a choreographer, you just feel the music. I like to work with my dance arranger, because then he'll show me the music and say, "The accent's on five, the accent's on seven, but you're missing the one on five." And so, I work very, very closely with the music arranger.

CRAMER: And do you have an arranger that you've now worked with consistently, so you've developed a short hand?

VAN LAAST: The thing is, it's difficult. Let's say you're working with Andrew Lloyd Webber. He doesn't want his music "dance arranged." His music exists. I remember the first time I choreographed *Song & Dance* in 1981, and I'd worked extensively with my dance arranger, and reworked much of the dance score. It was sent to Andrew, came back, and it was exactly the same. And I just slowly and eventually got the message. Andrew thinks that is his music and that's how it stays.

CRAMER: Was *Song & Dance* your first collaboration with Mr. Webber?

VAN LAAST: Do you want a bit of history on that one?

CRAMER: I would love it, because you have a long collaboration with him.

VAN LAAST: My success with Kate Bush brought me to Andrew. I got a phone call one night, and I hear from the other end of the phone, "Andrew Lloyd Webber here." Of course, I started laughing because I didn't believe it. But once again he said, "No, this is Andrew Lloyd Webber here. Would you like to choreograph *Variations?*" That's what Act II was called. And I said, "Yes, we should meet, I'd love to." And so my first journey into musical theatre was 50 minutes nonstop dance.

CRAMER: I saw it here in the states with Bernadette Peters but you were not the choreographer, correct?

VAN LAAST: I didn't choreograph; but I choreographed the UK, Europe, and Australia productions. An American critic came over to watch the London production and didn't like it, so the producers changed the whole creative team for the states. Andrew was really great and quite fair about it all because it was tricky. We got on very well, but he was forced to change it because of the bad reviews. He apologized to me afterward, but I'm very happy I didn't do it. I was 29 years old in 1981, and even though it would have been a huge success here, I knew nothing about musical theatre. It was, after all, a 50-minute contemporary dance piece. The worst-case scenario—it was a big success, and then everyone would have asked me to choreograph his or her musical theatre project. So I was really lucky. I had a few opportunities to make big mistakes, out of the spotlight, in England, and figure it all out.

CRAMER: You've had this long history with Webber shows.

VAN LAAST: I did his stage production of *Joseph* with Donny Osmond as well as the film version and that was a huge, huge success. I did *Whistle Down the Wind*, *Superstar*, which was a big success in Europe. It didn't work so well on Broadway because we didn't do a good job. We still got a Tony nomination, but it wasn't as good as it should have been. *Whistle Down the Wind* was an average success. But *Bombay Dreams* was fantastic, absolutely fantastic.

CRAMER: The buzz on *Sister Act* is also fantastic. Talk to me about your rehearsal environment. What kind of room do you try to create for your actors and your dancers?

VAN LAAST: I always have a disciplined rehearsal room, but I don't believe people can actually work in a room where there is fear. I believe that I create a room that is fun, but hard working. I want to create a room where people can laugh and make suggestions and where actors want to come every day, because it's a room with a great atmosphere. I really do make that happen.

CRAMER: You have to recreate multiple productions of shows, whether it's a tour, or a show in the states, or Australia. In order to recreate something, how do you notate, or write each track?

VAN LAAST: I don't. Again, it's my associate Nichola Treherne. She was in *Song & Dance* for me, as well as other shows, then she became my assistant, and now she's my associate. She has done virtually every *Mamma Mia!* that's been produced. She writes it all and keeps track of everything. Our first show was London. Once you've got a show up on the stage, it's really hard to go in there and make big changes. It's very hard to find the time, unless the producers close a show down for a week or something. And so you wait for Toronto, which was our next one. Then I was able to make a lot of the changes I wanted to make. After that we did Australia, and I still had changes I wanted to make. She said to me, "No, leave it alone. Just leave it alone. Stop fiddling." I'm really good at creating an original show, but when it comes to reproducing, I'm really terrible at it. I forget everything. I forget what I did the day before, because it's just happening in the room. For example, "That was a great turn. Can you do that again, please? That's great. Now can you move over there?" I don't remember the details. I just paint the picture.

CRAMER: But that's why you have assistants.

VAN LAAST: So Miss Nichola and teams of others, who are really good at it, go all over the world and reproduce *Mamma Mia!* I give them a little bit of scope. There are some moments in it where they're allowed to play with the steps a little bit, so they have some creativity in the process, because I think it'd be really awful if all they did was say to performers, "Move to 3A, stand on 3A, turn your head left and your right arm is out." What fun would there be for them to reproduce the show all the time? It would be mechanical. But I only let people I really trust do that. And as Nichola was a part of the making of that show, she understands the soul of it.

CRAMER: It must have been fun to then make the movie since there was such a long stretch of time between the first production and the film.

VAN LAAST: Oh, the movie was a hoot. It was about eight years between the two.

CRAMER: What was the biggest difference choreographically?

VAN LAAST: What was really interesting was taking the material, which is made for a proscenium and is very flat-on choreography, and changing it so that it would work in the round or for a film with no fourth wall. It was an interesting process.

CRAMER: As a choreographer, do you approach staging and choreography differently?

VAN LAAST: What's interesting in musical theatre now, is that in nearly all the projects I am invited to do, I work with singers and actors who can move very well. Sometimes I work with dancers who are singers and actors, but very rarely now do I work with "just dancers." Working with actors who move very well is a challenge that I've enjoyed and now enjoy more and more. I know the limitations of singer's movement and how to choreograph for them. I have to understand the music and how they phrase their singing; because I have to make sure that all the moves I do work with the breath and the rhythms as they're singing. That's a huge part of the craft of choreographing and staging for musicals.

CRAMER: How long does it take you to size someone up to understand the way you're going to have to work with them kinetically?

VAN LAAST: Three minutes. I mean, that might be a slight exaggeration, but I can tell within seconds of working with somebody what their style is and how I'm going to have to approach them. Sometimes I work through improvisation, especially with actresses. I give them ideas and then I look at the material they're producing, and I'll take from them, because sometimes people are not perceptive to having steps thrust upon them. Sometimes it's much easier to let them improvise a little bit, see their movement style, take that style, and then work with them that way. I direct the improvisation.

CRAMER: When you are doing a book musical, do you have the entire project prepared in some fashion before you walk in on day one?

VAN LAAST: I have the big production numbers finished ahead. For example, if there's a big opening number, and in that big opening number, most of the company is involved, I will have enough material prepared to be able to go in on day one and start. Very often, I'll change a lot of what I've prepared, depending on the room, depending on the actors, but I would never go into a big, day one, opening production number without having the whole thing prepared in my mind.

CRAMER: Don't you find it's easier to make changes if you're prepared?

VAN LAAST: Oh, absolutely. I would never walk into a big production number unless I'm truly prepared, because then I've got enough material to make changes. I know where I'm going. I never want to get a horrible feeling when I have 20 people looking at me, and they're waiting for a step. Now sometimes, I'm absolutely contrary to that when I'm doing a small number, say with three. The day before yesterday, I was working with three boys in *Sister Act*. My assistant and I worked up what we wanted. I started to laugh as I saw within three steps that what I prepared was wrong, it was too "dancy." But I had enough material and I had enough idea of what the whole number was, what I wanted it to be. So I went step, step, step, knee bend, and it was great. And then I went step, step, step, knee bend, move the head. And suddenly we're laughing. I'm really good at comedy, and so I knew how to put comedy into a number. I prepared something, I changed what I prepared, but I had a map to go on, so I knew where I was going all the time. When the head turn went in, I saw this was going to be kind of a choreographic motif for the whole number. This head bit hadn't been in the preparation, it came out spontaneously in the moment, and I was able to then take it and develop it.

CRAMER: Do you storyboard, or draw, or anything like that, or is it all in your head?

VAN LAAST: Everything is in my head. But I'll go back even further. When I first get a piece of music for a number, I go to the gym and I will play that piece of music over and over and over again. I feel that my brain is like blank videotape. That's old fashioned, isn't it?

CRAMER: We still get it!

VAN LAAST: I have a very nice gym at home, so I keep myself in shape, not because of the choreography, but because I believe when you go for interviews, if you go in there and you don't look healthy, no one believes you're a choreographer. Anyway, I am at my home gym and I can see the whole number. I don't necessarily know what the steps are going to be, but I know what the number is going to be. I know what the style of the number is going to be and the dramaturgy of the number. I think that's a seriously important part of being a choreographer for musical theatre. You have to understand and create the story of that number. I'm a great believer that if you actually get the story right, and the music's right, the steps will just fall into place. I don't spend hours agonizing over a step. Because my choreographic teacher, Robert Cohan, said to me, "The worst way you can choreograph is sit on the floor and look in the mirror and think about the step." He said, "What you have to do is get up and move, then things will happen."

CRAMER: Tell me about your transition into Vegas. How did *Siegfried and Roy* come to you?

VAN LAAST: Siegfried and Roy had invited John Napier, the designer of *Cats, Starlight Express, Les Miserables*, and *Nicholas Nickleby*, to design their new show in Vegas. These shows were created by a team of artists that included John, directors John Caird and Trevor Nun, and me. John Napier had also worked with Michael Jackson. This was really the first show of the "new" Vegas. As you said earlier, there was no Cirque de Soliel anywhere on the strip. Up to that point, there were showgirls, topless showgirls, high heels, feathers, and comedians. So when we did *Siegfried and Roy* around 1988, the team and I wanted girls from 5'2" to 5'10". There was really no height restriction. And I wanted technical dancers since there was a full dance in this show. I wanted no high heels, or feathers, or topless showgirls, just great dancers. We were in the Mirage and we felt, at the time, we were doing something groundbreaking. We never realized that it was going to change the whole face of Vegas and grand-scale entertainment. When you're doing something like that at the time, you don't know where it's going to fit into history, you just do it. It was a fantastic experience to do something as challenging as that. To be given a football pitch (playing field) with 50 dancers and be told to make it look interesting, well, that was really huge. I mean, the stage was as big as a football pitch and the dancers jetéd like they had never jetéd before. That was the only way to cover the space. Oh, they hated it.

CRAMER: Did you also have a hand in staging the illusions?

VAN LAAST: Yes, and having to stage the illusions was a big artistic and choreographic challenge. I knew nothing about magic: nothing. It was like my foray into musical theatre. I knew nothing about musical theatre, and I suddenly found myself there. Pop videos and commercials, I knew nothing about them, and suddenly I'm choreographing them. So, this statement has defined my whole career: Suddenly I walk into a room and I know nothing about genre, and I have to learn on my feet.

CRAMER: There's a lesson to be had in there, Anthony.

VAN LAAST: I think there is. I think it is never say no. That's the lesson. Trust your roots. Mine are in contemporary dance. I learned about movement in theatre and I understood theatre. Working with Anna Sokolow, one of the great American choreographers, taught me so much about acting in dance. It was just phenomenal working with her. So I always took the gig and even if it's an unfamiliar media, if you're bright and you're quick, you can learn fast.

CRAMER: And *EFX* followed.

VAN LAAST: I did *Joseph* and *Hair* and then came back for *EFX*, which was a much less successful show, but again, the biggest show in Vegas.

CRAMER: The *EFX* productions that subsequently followed did so with different stars in different formats, so you started a whole trend at the MGM Grand.

VAN LAAST: That's right. And that show ran for years.

CRAMER: You're responsible for *The Mamma Mia!* production that ran in Vegas for seven years as well?

VAN LAAST: Yes, it's just closed now but it was the most successful book musical in Vegas. Most book musicals have come and gone like the wind, and *Mamma Mia!* just kept going and going. It's a phenomenon, it's really an absolute phenomenon. The Broadway run alone has lasted over 11 years.

CRAMER: What do you think is the most important trait a choreographer can possess to be successful?

VAN LAAST: I think as a choreographer you have to be really clear. You have to be precise, and know, absolutely, what you want. You aren't a choreographer without people. You need people who are then going to be your colors, your brushstrokes, your notes, and they will create whatever is in your mind. So you have to be able to communicate to them exactly what your intentions are, what your beats and brushstrokes are, and what your musical dynamic is. If you are very clear, then you can create the picture you need. Am I being too abstract?

CRAMER: No. After my students return from summer theatrical employment, I often ask them about the choreographer. If they liked the choreographer and enjoyed working with that person, then their response would always include the following: "They knew exactly what they wanted." I hear that phrase from students more than any other and that means they had a pleasant experience.

VAN LAAST: I think one of the biggest mistakes choreographers can make is choreographing to impress. You get people who make up these really difficult combinations, and all the dancers say, "Wow, it's so good," and the choreographers think it's going to be great for dancing, when actually, that's not what it's about. It's actually much more about making sure you're painting the right picture. It might involve some difficulty, but it's not about pleasing the performer with a load of steps for them. I think that's very important to understand if you want to be a choreographer. It's about being a team player. I think it's really important to collaborate with a director, but I think you have to respect that the director is the leader. Never challenge the director publicly. Confer in private. Whatever you think about the director, with whom you're working, never let it be known to anyone else if you have negative thoughts about them. Never undermine the director.

CRAMER: Have you witnessed that happening?

VAN LAAST: Yes and that's a primary thing. I've seen it go wrong. I've been brought into productions to help when the choreographer gets antsy, and I've seen tension between the choreographer and director in public, even with the show finished. You have to be able to sit around a table after a run through, and make improvements by compromise. That takes respect. We had a run through this morning of Act One of *Sister Act*. We put the first act up in 10 days, fast, because the producer wanted to see what it looked like, the writers wanted to see what it looked and sounded like. Now you have to be able to go into a meeting after that, and work collaboratively as a team player. That's crucial. It's absolutely about clarity and team playing.

CRAMER: Is there a specific way you approach working with a costume designer? Do you speak their language?

VAN LAAST: Yes. I'm working with Lez Brotherston now, who's designing the costumes for *Sister Act*. Lez is well known, because he designed Matthew Bourne's *Swan Lake*. Lez is a great friend of mine and we work together because I have a street dance company. So with *Sister Act*, there are specific needs. There is proper dance movement, and so Lez and I will discuss the costumes, and decide where we want, say, beads. He and I worked out exactly how the beads would affect the choreography and how it would look with the movement so as not to interfere with all the arm choreography. In the London version, I wanted a kind of showgirl look for the girls who had to double as nuns and showgirls, keeping in mind they might not have showgirl bodies. We had to believe that they were showgirls, so, therefore, we had to work on costumes that would suit their bodies, and arm choreography that would keep audience focus above the waist. It's always collaboration and I feel I have a great deal of input. Here again, I do know that I have a weakness. It's defiantly women's costumes, so that's why I love working with a woman like Nichola, or another female associate, because I know that they will cover all bases. Nichola is great with women's costumes.

CRAMER: Do you have enough lighting knowledge that you can propose a lighting idea with confidence?

VAN LAAST: Lighting is the one area where I feel I am quite strong. When I was a student, I had to earn enough money to pay for college, so I worked backstage in the theatre as an assistant to the lighting designer. I sat in on lighting meetings and soaked it all up. I worked on the old-fashion lighting boards and learned what colors and lighting areas could really do for a production.

CRAMER: That way when you're visualizing choreography, you can picture in your head if you wanted a "special" on a dancer or group of dancers.

VAN LAAST: Yes. I know what it's going to be. That's one part of the picture.

CRAMER: Now you have a big, new project, *Batman Live*. So let's talk a little bit about that.

VAN LAAST: It's an arena show. It will come to Madison Square Garden this year. We had the idea of doing *Batman*. We got the rights from DC Comics and from Warner Bros. and I've been working on it for two years now. How do you put a play into an arena? It's been a huge challenge. We have flying in the show. I knew if it was going to be in an arena, there had to be some sense of spectacle to it. It couldn't just be Batman and Robin walking around in the arena. I knew that for Batman aficionados, it was especially important. We decided to have Bruce Wayne come from a circus background. That enabled me to open the show with a circus. So, I'm working with top circus performers, and I'm staging a big circus opening. Then, of course, it's your aficionados who know Batman's back story. Wayne's parents get killed, and on the flying trapeze, you know it will be exciting. I've worked out this idea. We break the trapeze in the air, and in slow motion they will fall, spinning down to the ground. So, the whole show has this kind of choreographic eye to it. In our story, the Joker is the villain and decides to take over the circus. There's great theatricality to all this including the Batmobile, Catwoman flying in, and fights in the air. It's not nearly on the scale of the flying in *Spiderman* (currently running on Broadway), but it has a real theatrical quality to it.

CRAMER: You have a Vegas sensibility, so you know what's needed.

VAN LAAST: Right. If I hadn't done musical theatre and spectacle out in Vegas, I wouldn't have known where to start with this one. We have a fantastic writer, Allan Heinberg, who writes *Grey's Anatomy* and *Young Avengers* for Marvel Comics. This is a kind of departure for me, but it all goes back to what I've learned throughout my whole career.

CRAMER: The diversity is inspiring. How fulfilling, to never find yourself in a rut, because you're always doing something different. Let's talk about your film career because in some cases it is an extension of your musical theatre career. What was your first film?

VAN LAAST: I did a dreadful film in the late 1970s. It was a British version of *Saturday Night Fever*, and it was called *The Music Machine*. Believe me, it was truly appalling but I learned quite a lot on that film. It didn't even go to video, it was that bad. Then my next was *Never Say Never Again*, the James Bond film. I also danced with Kim Basinger in the film.

CRAMER: I can't wait to watch the film again and look for you.

VAN LAAST: Well then, you'll see me with my hair! So, I had to teach Sean Connery to tango. Now, this is a very interesting tip for anyone who wants to choreograph. I didn't know how to tango, but I went off the next day to one of the top ballroom specialists, and within three lessons, she taught me the rudiments of a tango. As a choreographer, I didn't want it to be a phenomenal tango, because Sean Connery's character is never going to know how to do a phenomenal tango. So I could learn the rudiments, add a bit of choreography to it—so it stayed in the correct style—and could teach Sean. I didn't have to be an expert tango dancer, but I needed to learn a little bit about it.

CRAMER: Then I have a correlated question. When you do research for a book musical or for something like this, a period piece or a style-specific dance, do you find that research is a practical application, or like you're just discussing, more of an enhancement?

VAN LAAST: I love research. It's always been a serious part of my process. Nowadays, if you want to see anything about a style, you can get on the computer, go to YouTube and bam, you've got it in front of you. It's absolutely phenomenal. When I first started choreographing, we didn't have access to that kind of material, so I used to look at pictures, watch movies, and read a great deal, to capture the style. I don't go and pinch (steal) a lot of steps, of course, but viewing the work really enhances my own creativity. I think it's fantastic to have that kind of visual information at your fingertips. I use it all the time.

CRAMER: What is the strangest choreography you ever had to do for a film?

VAN LAAST: I did a film called *Excalibur*, with director John Boorman, and I choreographed a lovely dance for his daughter. Normally on a film, you get called in to do one or two dances. You don't do the whole package. But he said he wanted me to choreograph a knight's disco. The idea of having all these knights in armor or half armor dancing seemed quite ridiculous to me. I thought how am I ever going to do that? So I managed to work out some material and we did it and it looked fine in rehearsal. Liam Neeson was in the film. Actually, a lot of great actors were in the film. I remember we had this big, big space and Cherie Lunghi, who was playing one of the leads, was about 20 yards from me. John Boorman turned back to me and said, "Whatever they're doing in the middle there is not working. Can you change it?" And I thought to myself, "I've got to walk 20 yards from here to Cherie and come up with an idea." I began walking toward her and I thought, "I've got 15 yards to come up with an idea." I was actually looking at myself walking from the outside. I got close, and I thought, "You've only got 10 yards now." There's a crew of about 50 people, 150 actors, and everybody's looking at me walking toward them. I've got five yards, and I thought, "This is one of the most surreal moments in my life. What am I going to do?" And I got there and Cherie said to me, "Shall I do this?"

CRAMER: Saved.

VAN LAAST: I said to Cherie, "That's a great idea." I asked John if he liked it and he was pleased. So you're quite right, saved.

CRAMER: What's up next for you?

VAN LAAST: I'm doing *Sister Act* in the UK when I get back. I'm going to do a new version that is made to tour. I have several book musicals in the works. But I take vacations, too.

CRAMER: I'm looking at your resume and I don't know if I believe you.

VAN LAAST: When we finish *Sister Act*, I'll take three or four months off.

CRAMER: So your life is balanced?

VAN LAAST: I try and keep it as balanced as possible.

CRAMER: What advice would you give to aspiring performers coming into the business today?

VAN LAAST: You must remember that this is a very difficult business, really tough. If you've started out as a performer, you've taken a big step anyway, because you've made the decision that this is the life you want. It's not necessarily going to provide you a lot of money. It's not going to provide you with any security whatsoever. It's incredible if it works, it's really exciting, and it's a privileged life. Even when you're knocked down, and this is such a cliché, you've got to keep going. Students, the time you have in college is more valuable than you'll ever realize. If you don't invest when you're in college, you're never going to make it because those are your roots. That's where it starts. The time you have in college is the most important time, because that's where you learn your technique. It's technique as a performer that will get you through. It's one of the most important tools you have.

CRAMER: Anthony, thank you so much for speaking to us. I'm sincerely appreciative. It's been a pleasure.

VAN LAAST: It's been an honor.

APPENDIX

Rob Ashford

Stage

Broadway: *Thoroughly Modern Millie* (Tony Award for Best Choreography 2002, Drama Desk and Outer Critics Circle nominations—Choreography), *The Boys from Syracuse, The Wedding Singer* (Tony and Drama Desk nominations—Choreography), *Curtains* (Tony and Outer Critics Circle nominations—Choreography), *Cry-Baby* (Astaire Award, Drama Desk, and Outer Critics Circle Award for Outstanding Choreography 2008, Tony nomination—Choreography), *Promises, Promises* (Tony and Outer Critics Circle nominations—Choreography), *How to Succeed in Business Without Really Trying* (Tony and Outer Critics Circle nominations—Choreography, Drama Desk nominations—Choreography, Direction, and Revival), *Evita* (Tony, Drama Desk, and Outer Critics Circle nominations—Choreography).

    Off-Broadway: *True History and Real Adventures, Tenderloin, Time and Again, A Connecticut Yankee, Bloomer Girl, The Thing About Men, Pardon My English.*

    Regional and Tours: *Up, Up, and Away—The Songs of Jimmy Webb, Pippin, Marty, Thoroughly Modern Millie, Doctor Doolittle, Curtains, Shrek the Musical, Leap of Faith.*

    West End: *Finding Neverland, Anna Kristie, A Streetcar Named Desire, Once in a Lifetime, Thoroughly Modern Millie* (Olivier nomination—Choreography), *A Funny Thing Happened on the Way to the Forum, Guys and Dolls* (Olivier nomination—Choreography), *Evita* (Olivier nomination—Choreography), *Parade* (Olivier nominations—Choreography and Direction), *Shrek the Musical.*

Opera

Candide.

Television/Special Events

Andrew Lloyd Webber—The Kennedy Center Honors, Barbra Streisand—The Kennedy Center Honors, The 81st Annual Academy Awards (Emmy Award for Outstanding Choreography).

Film

Love Walked In, Beyond the Sea.

Andy Blankenbuehler

Stage

Broadway: *The Apple Tree, In the Heights* (Tony Award for Best Choreography 2008, Drama Desk Award and Outer Critics Circle Award for Outstanding Choreography 2007, Outer Critics Circle nomination—Choreography), *9 to 5: The Musical* (Tony, Drama Desk, and Outer Critics Circle nominations—Choreography), *The People in the Picture, Bring It On, Annie.*

Off-Broadway: *Burleigh Grimes, The Wiz, The Apple Tree, In the Heights* (Lucille Lortel and Calloway Awards for Outstanding Choreography 2007).

Regional and Tours: *Quark Victory, A Wonderful Life, 9 to 5: The Musical, In the Heights, Waiting for the Moon* (Barrymore Award nomination—Choreography), *A Little Princess, Pippin.*

West End: *Desperately Seeking Susan.*

Television/Special Events

The Sopranos, MTV, Wendy's, Saturday Night Fever, The History Channel, So You Think You Can Dance, Concerts: Elton John, Bette Midler, Nights on Broadway at Caesars Palace.

Jeff Calhoun

Stage

Broadway: *The Will Rogers Follies* (Tony Award Best Choreography 1991—collaboration with Tommy Tune), *Tommy Tune Tonight!, The Best Little Whorehouse Goes Public, Grease!* (Tony and Drama Desk nomination—Choreography), *Annie Get Your Gun, Bells Are Ringing, Big River* (Tony Honor for Excellence in Theatre 2004, Drama Desk nomination—Direction), *Taboo, Brooklyn, Grey Gardens, Bonnie and Clyde, Newsies* (Tony nomination-Direction).

Off-Broadway: *Bouncers, Comic Potential, Holy Cross Sucks!, Strike Up the Band, It Came From Beyond, Grey Gardens.*

Regional and Tours: *Newsies, Bonnie and Clyde, 9 to 5: The Musical, The Civil War, White Christmas, Shenandoah, Himself and Nora, Brooklyn, Disney's High School Musical: On Stage, Disney's High School Musical 2: On Stage.*

West End: *Grey Gardens, Disney's High School Musical.*

Specialized Theatre: *Oliver!* (Ovation Award for Best Direction 2000), *Pippin, Big River* (Ovation and LA Drama Critics Circle Awards for Direction and Choreography 2003, Helen Hayes Award nomination—Direction, LA Weekly Theatre Award for Best Direction 2001), *Sleeping Beauty Wakes* (Ovation Award nomination—Direction, Ovation Award for World Premiere Musical).

Television/Special Events

Xena: Warrior Princess, Downtown, Happy Together, Weekend Warriors.

Warren Carlyle

Stage

Broadway: *The Producers, Oklahoma* (Associate to Susan Stroman), *A Tale of Two Cities, Finian's Rainbow* (Drama Desk nominations—Choreography and Direction), *Follies* (Drama Desk

nomination—Choreography), *Hugh Jackman: Back on Broadway,*
Chaplin—The Musical.

Off-Broadway: *Slut!, Working, You Again, The 24 Hour
Musicals, Stairway to Paradise, On The Town, Juno, Girl Crazy,
Cotton Club Paradise.*

Regional and Tours: *Pageant, The Baker's Wife, The Pirates
of Penzance, Mame, Dancing in the Dark, Lucky Guy, 101
Dalmations, Roundabout Gala 2006, A Tale of Two Cities,
Becoming Chaplin, Camelot, Buddy's Tavern, You Again, Harps
and Angels.*

UK Tours/West End/Europe: *Scrooge, Pageant, Moving On,
The Goodbye Girl, Me and My Girl.*

Television/Video

*An Evening with the Boston Pops, Great Performances, Elton
John: Made in England.*

Film

Deception, Hope and Faith, The Producers.

Christopher Gattelli

Stage

Broadway: *Chess, Martin Short: Fame Becomes Me, High
Fidelity, The Ritz, Sunday in the Park with George, 13, South
Pacific* (Tony and Outer Critics Circle nomination—Choreography), *Women on the Verge of a Nervous Breakdown, Godspell,
Newsies* (Tony Award for Best Choreography 2012, Drama Desk
Award for Outstanding Choreography 2012, Outer Critics Circle
nomination—Choreography).

Off-Broadway: *SILENCE! The Musical, Bat Boy* (Lucille Lortel
Award for Outstanding Choreography), *tick, tick . . . BOOM!,
Altar Boyz* (Barrymore Award for Excellence in Theatre for
Direction and Choreography, Lucille Lortel and Callaway Awards

for Outstanding Choreography, Drama Desk nomination—Choreography), *Tom Jones, I Love You Because, How To Save the World and find True Love in 90 Minutes, Adrift in Macao, 10 Million Miles, Sunday in the Park with George, Departure Lounge, Marrying Meg.*

Regional and Tours: *South Pacific, Little Miss Sunshine, O. Henry's Lovers, tick, tick . . . BOOM!, Tom Jones, The Baker's Wife, Altar Boyz, Radio Girl, Jim Henson's Emmet Otter's Jug-Band Christmas.*

West End: *SILENCE! The Musical, tick, tick . . . BOOM!*

Television/Benefit Concerts

Hair, Chess, Chance and Chemistry: A Centennial Celebration of Frank Loesser, The Rosie O'Donnell Show.

Kathleen Marshall

Stage

Broadway: *Kiss of the Spider Woman, She Loves Me, Damn Yankees,* and *Victor/Victoria* (Associate to Rob Marshall) *Swinging on a Star* (Drama Desk nomination—Choreography), *1776, Ring Round the Moon, Kiss Me Kate* (Tony, Drama Desk, and Outer Critics Circle nominations—Choreography), *Seussical, Follies* (Outer Critics Circle nomination—Choreography), *Little Shop of Horrors, Wonderful Town* (Tony Award for Best Choreography 2004, Drama Desk and Outer Critics Circle Award for Outstanding Choreography 2004, Tony, Drama Desk, and Outer Critics Circle nominations—Direction), *The Pajama Game* (Tony Award for Best Choreography 2006, Drama Desk and Outer Critics Circle Award for Outstanding Choreography 2006, Outer Critics Circle nomination—Direction), *Grease, Boeing Boeing, Anything Goes* (Tony Award for Best Choreography 2011, Drama Desk Award for Outstanding Choreography 2011, Drama Desk and Outer Critics Circle nominations—Direction and Choreography), *Nice Work If You Can Get It* (Tony and Drama Desk nominations—Direction and Choreography, Outer Critics Circle nomination—Choreography).

Off-Broadway: *Call Me Madam, Du Barry Was a Lady, Violet, The Boys from Syracuse, Li'l Abner, As Thousands Cheer, Babes in Arms, Saturday Night, Wonderful Town, Hair, Carnival!, House of Flowers, Two Gentlemen of Verona, 70, Girls, 70, Applause.*

Regional and Tours: *How the Grinch Stole Christmas, The Frogs, Little Shop of Horrors, Sunset Boulevard, Andrew Lloyd Webber's Music of the Night, As Thousands Cheer, Time and Again, Anything Goes, Diner.*

West End: *Kiss Me Kate.*

Television/Concerts

Grease: You're the One That I Want, Once Upon a Mattress, The Music Man (Emmy nomination), *Kristen Chenoweth at the Metropolitan Opera House and Disney Concert Hall, Broadway Bash Concert, Kennedy Center Honors Tributes Jason Robards, Angela Lansbury,* and *Steve Martin.*

Jerry Mitchell

Stage

Broadway: *Jerome Robbins Broadway* (Assistant to Mr. Robbins), *Grease* (Associate to Jeff Calhoun), *You're a Good Man Charlie Brown, The Rocky Horror Show* (Drama Desk nomination—Choreography), *The Full Monty* (Tony, Drama Desk, and Outer Critics Circle nominations—Choreography), *Hairspray* (Tony, Drama Desk, and Outer Critic Circle nominations—Choreography), *Imaginary Friends, Gypsy, Never Gonna Dance* (Tony, Drama Desk, and Outer Critic Circle nominations—Choreography), *Dirty Rotten Scoundrels* (Tony, Drama Desk, and Outer Critic Circle nominations—Choreography), *La Cage aux Folles* (Tony Award for Best Choreography 2005, Drama Desk Award for Outstanding Choreography 2005, Outer Critics Circle Award for Best Choreography 2005), *Legally Blonde* (Tony and Drama Desk nominations—Choreography, Tony nomination-Direction), *Catch Me If You Can, Kinky Boots.*

Off-Broadway: *One Two Three Four Five, Lips Together Teeth Apart* (Fight director), *You Could Be Home Now, The Years* (Fight director), *Jeffrey, Seconds Out, Hedwig and the Angry Inch, Corpus Christi, Captains Courageous.*

Regional and Tours: *Follies, The Full Monty, Hairspray, Dirty Rotten Scoundrels, Catch Me If You Can.*

West End: *The Full Monty, Hairspray* (Olivier nomination— Choreography), *Legally Blonde, Love Never Dies.*

Television/Las Vegas/Benefit Concerts

Step It Up and Dance, The Drew Carey Show (Emmy nomination), *Peep Show, Broadway Bares.*

Film

Camp, In and Out, Drop Dead Gorgeous, Scent of a Woman.

Casey Nicholaw

Stage

Broadway: *Spamalot* (Tony, Drama Desk, and Outer Critics Circle nominations—Choreography), *The Drowsy Chaperone* (Tony, Drama Desk, and Outer Critics Circle nominations—Choreography; Tony and Drama Desk nominations—Direction), *To Be or Not To Be, All About Me, Elf the Musical, The Book of Mormon* (Tony Award for Best Direction 2011, Drama Desk and Outer Critics Circle Award for Outstanding Direction 2011, Tony, Drama Desk, and Outer Critics Circle nominations—Choreography).

Off-Broadway: *Can-Can, Chef's Theatre: A Musical Feast, South Pacific, Follies, Bye Bye Birdie.*

Regional and Tours: *Lucky Ducky, The Drowsy Chaperone, Spamalot, Minsky's, Robin and the 7 Hoods, Aladdin.*

West End: *Spamalot, The Drowsy Chaperone.*

Concerts

Manhattan Rhythm Kings: A Tribute to Harry Warren, Candide, Sinatra: His Voice, His World, His Way.

Randy Skinner

Stage

Broadway: *White Christmas* (Tony and Drama Desk nomination—Choreography), *42nd Street* (Tony, Drama Desk, Outer Critics Circle nominations—Choreography), *State Fair* (Outer Critics Circle nomination—Choreography), *Ain't Broadway Grand* (Tony and Outer Critics Circle nominations—Choreography), *After the Night and the Music.*

Off-Broadway: *Do Re Mi, Abby's Song, Lone Star Love* (Lucille Lortel nomination—Choreography), *The Ballad of Bonnie and Clyde, Of Thee I Sing, After the Night and the Music, Gotta Dance, Face the Music, No No Nanette, Gentlemen Prefer Blondes.*

Regional and Tours: *Babes in Arms, Lucky in the Rain, Dames at Sea, Lone Star Love, White Christmas, 42nd Street, Happy Days, Stormy Weather, Puttin on the Ritz, George M!, Strike Up the Band, Pal Joey, Hello Dolly!, Swing: The Big Band Hit Parade, An American in Paris*

West End and Europe: *42nd Street, Lend Me a Tenor—The Musical, On the 5th.*

Television

2001 Tony Awards.

Susan Stroman

Stage

Broadway: *Musical Chairs, Crazy for You* (Tony Award for Best Choreography 1992, Drama Desk and Outer Critics Circle Awards for Outstanding Choreography 1992), *Picnic, Show Boat* (Tony Award for Best Choreograph 1995, Astaire Award, Outer Critics Circle nomination—Choreography), *Big* (Tony and Drama Desk nominations—Choreography), *Steel Pier* (Tony, Drama Desk, and Outer Critics Circle nominations—Choreography), *Contact* (Tony Award for Best Choreography 2000, Drama Desk Award for Outstanding Choreography 2000, Outer Critics Circle Awards for Best Direction and Best Choreography 2000, Lucille Lortel Award for Outstanding Direction 2000, Astaire Award, Tony nomination—Direction), *The Music Man* (Outer Critics Circle Award for Outstanding Direction and Choreography 2000, Astaire Award, Tony and Drama Desk nominations—Choreography), *The Producers* (Tony Award for Best Choreography 2001, Drama Desk Outer Critics Circle Awards for Outstanding Choreography 2001, Tony Award for Best Direction 2001, Drama Desk and Outer Critics Circle Awards for Outstanding Direction 2001, Astaire Award), *Thou Shalt Not, Oklahoma* (Drama Desk and Outer Critics Circle Award for Outstanding Choreography 2002, Tony nomination—Choreography), *The Frogs, Young Frankenstein* (Drama Desk and Outer Critics Circle nominations—Direction and Choreography), *The Scottsboro Boys* (Astaire Award, Tony, Drama Desk, Outer Critics Circle nominations—Direction and Choreography), *Big Fish*.

Off-Broadway: *Flora, The Red Menace, And the World Goes' Round* (Drama Desk nomination—Choreography), *A Christmas Carol* (Outer Critics Circle nomination—Choreography), *The Scottsboro Boys, Happiness* (Outer Critics Circle nominations—Direction and Choreography).

West End/London: *Contact, Oklahoma* (Olivier Award for Best Theatre Choreographer 2002), *Paradise Found, Crazy for You* (Olivier Award for Best Theatre Choreographer 1993).

Television

Liza Minnelli Live at Radio City Music Hall (Emmy nomination), *Sondheim: A Celebration at Carnegie Hal—PBS, An Evening with the Boston Pops: A Tribute to Leonard Bernstein—PBS, Great Performances—PBS, Oklahoma, Contact-Live at Lincoln Center* (Emmy Award 2003).

Film

Center Stage (American Choreography Award), *The Producers: The Movie Musical* (four Golden Globe nominations), *You've Got Mail.*

Ballet

Double Feature, Blossom Got Kissed, For the Love of Duke, Take Five . . . More or Less, But Not for Me.

Opera

Don Giovanni, A Little Night Music, 110 in the Shade.

Sergio Trujillo

Stage

Broadway: *All Shook Up, Jersey Boys* (Drama Desk and Outer Critics Circle nominations—Choreography), *Guys and Dolls, The Mambo Kinds, Next to Normal, Memphis* (Astaire Award 2010, Drama Desk and Outer Critics Circle nominations—Choreography), *The Addams Family, Leap of Faith* (Drama Desk nomination—Choreography), *Flashdance.*

Off-Broadway: *Bare: A Pop Opera, Kismet, Next to Normal, Romeo and Juliet, A Tree Grows in Brooklyn, The Great American Trailer Park Musical, Kismet, Saved* (Lucille Lortel Award for Outstanding Choreography 2008).

Regional and Tours: *Jersey Boys, Next to Normal, Zhivago, The Wiz, White Noise.*

West End and Europe: *Jersey Boys, Tarzan, Peggy Sue Got Married.*

Australia: *Jersey Boys.*

Television/Film

Memphis, Woo, The Washing Machine Man, Playboy: Wet and Wild IV.

Opera

The Marriage of Figaro, Salome.

Anthony Van Laast

Stage

Broadway: *Joseph and the Amazing Technicolor Dreamcoat, Jesus Christ Superstar, Mamma Mia!, Bombay Dreams* (Tony, Drama Desk, and Outer Critics Circle nominations—Choreography), *Sister Act* (Astaire Award nominee—Choreography).
   Regional and Tours: *Mamma Mia!*.
   West End and Europe: *Song and Dance, Budgie, A Little Night Music, Into the Woods, Mamma Mia!, Whistle Down the Wind, Hair* (Olivier nomination—Choreography), *The Begger's Opera* (Olivier nomination—Choreography), *Bombay Dreams, Annie Get Your Gun, The Royal Hunt of the Sun, Joseph and the Amazing Technicolor Dreamcoat* (Olivier nomination—choreography), *Candide,* (Olivier nomination—Choreography), *Sister Act.*

Television BBC/Film

So You Think You Can Dance, Absolutely Fabulous, Princess Caraboo, Michael Ball, Screen Two, The Return of the Antelope, The Tailor of Gloucester, Mamma Mia!, Harry Potter and the Deathly Hallow, Never Say Never Again, Who Dares Win, Excalibur, Outland, The Music Machine, Nutcracker, The Final Option, Bluebell, Joseph and the Amazing Technicolor Dreamcoat, Hope and Glory, Lionheart, Caught in the Act.

Concerts

Elaine Paige, Sarah Brightman, Wayne Sleep, Kate Bush, Cleo Lane, Berry Humphries, The Music of Andrew Lloyd Webber, Celebration: Andrew Lloyd Webber's 50th Birthday Concert.

World Tours/Las Vegas

Batman Live, Blaze, Extravaganza for Holiday on Ice, Burn the Floor, EFX, Siegfried and Roy at the Mirage.

Operetta

The Mikado.

ABOUT THE AUTHOR

A teacher, director, and choreographer for three decades, Lyn is an Endowed Professor of Musical Theatre Dance at the University of Oklahoma. Lyn's University Theatre production highlights include *On The Town*, *A Chorus Line*, *Anything Goes*, *Company*, *Baby*, *Sweet Charity*, *Cabaret*, *My One and Only*, *Rent*, *Nine*, *Urinetown the Musical* and *How to Succeed in Business Without Really Trying*. Lyn's regional theatre credits include a multitude of productions at theatres such as Lyric Theatre, the Pollard Theatre, and City Repertoire Theatre of Oklahoma, Music Theatre Wichita, Casa Manana, the Broadway Rose, and annual productions with the Oklahoma City Philharmonic Orchestra. She has released ten instructional tap videos and published *Jazz Jargon, a Pedagogy Guide for Teachers and Students* for Texas Association Teachers of Dance. She was named the 2005 Irene and Julian J. Rothbaum Presidential Professor of Excellence in the Arts by the Weitzenhoffer Family College of Fine Arts. In 2004, Lyn was honored with the Chicago National Association of Dance Masters Artistic Achievement Award. A 15-year member of the Stage Directors and Choreographers Society (SDC) and a 30-year member of Actors Equity Association (AEA), Lyn has served as a master teacher across the United States and has been both teacher and adjudicator of Musical Theatre Dance at the Hong Kong Academy for the Performing Arts.

INDEX